Study Guide

for

Brym and Lie's

Sociology
Your Compass for a New World

The Brief Edition

Study Guide

for

Brym and Lie's

Sociology
Your Compass for a New World

The Brief Edition

Judith Pintar
University of Illinois at Urbana-Champaign

THOMSON

WADSWORTH

Australia • Canada • Mexico • Singapore • Spain • United Kingdom • United States

Printed in the United States of America
1 2 3 4 5 6 7 09 08 07 06 05

Printer: Thomson West

ISBN 0-495-00071-X

For more information about our products, contact us at:
Thomson Learning Academic Resource Center
1-800-423-0563

For permission to use material from this text or product, submit a request online at
http://www.thomsonrights.com.
Any additional questions about permissions can be submitted by email to **thomsonrights@thomson.com.**

Thomson Higher Education
10 Davis Drive
Belmont, CA 94002-3098
USA

Asia (including India)
Thomson Learning
5 Shenton Way
#01-01 UIC Building
Singapore 068808

Australia/New Zealand
Thomson Learning Australia
102 Dodds Street
Southbank, Victoria 3006
Australia

Canada
Thomson Nelson
1120 Birchmount Road
Toronto, Ontario M1K 5G4
Canada

UK/Europe/Middle East/Africa
Thomson Learning
High Holborn House
50–51 Bedford Road
London WC1R 4LR
United Kingdom

Latin America
Thomson Learning
Seneca, 53
Colonia Polanco
11560 Mexico
D.F. Mexico

Spain (including Portugal)
Thomson Paraninfo
Calle Magallanes, 25
28015 Madrid, Spain

TABLE OF CONTENTS

PREFACE

Welcome to the Study Guide for the Essentials version of Robert Brym and John Lie's *Sociology: Your Compass for a New World, The Brief Edition*. The Study Guide is intended to guide you on your journey through your course in introductory sociology. The Study Guide chapters correspond to textbook chapters, and include the following components:

Components of the Study Guide

- Learning Objectives

- Key Terms

- Detailed Chapter Outline

- Study Activities

- Infotrac Exercises

- Internet Exercises

- Practice Fill-In-The-Blank Questions

- Practice Multiple-Choice Question

- Practice True-False Questions

- Practice Short-Answer Questions

- Practice Essay Questions

A SOCIOLOGICAL COMPASS

Student Learning Objectives

After reading Chapter 1, you should be able to:

1. Explain what is unique about sociology in comparison to the other seemingly similar humanities and social science disciplines like economics, political science, philosophy, drama, and psychology.

2. Explain the role of social forces in opening our opportunities and constraining our freedom.

3. Explain what C. Wright Mills referred to as the "sociological imagination,"—and its origins in relation to the three modern revolutions.

4. Discuss the contribution of Auguste Comte, Herbert Spencer, Karl Marx, Emile Durkheim, and Max Weber to the birth of sociology as a social science and a way of combating social ills.

5. Identify the major sociological theoretical traditions, their central features and key exemplars.

6. Contrast the perspectives of Emile Durkheim, Karl Marx and George Herbert Mead in the context of their respective contributions to functionalism, conflict theory, and symbolic interactionism.

7. Contrast Karl Marx's and Max Weber's perspectives on inequality and conflict.

8. Discuss the contribution of W.E.B. Du Bois to conflict theory and the study of race in the United States.

9. Discuss the contribution of Harriet Martineau, Jane Addams, and feminist theory to sociology, which was largely ignored by other pioneers of sociology.

10. Discuss the features of modern feminist theory.

11. Explain the notion of sociology as "a compass" to examine unresolved issues and dilemmas confronting the postindustrial era and the future.

12. Explain the usefulness of sociology as a practical source of advice to improve society—and as a perspective to enhance your understanding of how we, as individuals, fit in the larger social context of society.

13. Explain the role of objectivity and subjectivity in sociology.

14. Distinguish between scientific and nonscientific thinking.

15. Identify and describe the six steps of the research cycle.

16. Describe the main methods of collecting sociological data.

17. Explain the advantages and disadvantages of participant observation, experiments, surveys, and the analysis of existing documents in terms of the methodological issues.

18. Explain the issue of causality and association in sociological research.

Key Terms

(defined on the indicated pages of the textbook, and in glossary)

sociology (2)

social context (2)

social solidarity (3)

social structures (5)

microstructures (6)

macrostructures (6)

patriarchy (6)

global structures (6)

the Sociological Imagination (5)

the Scientific Revolution (6)

the Democratic Revolution (6)

the Industrial Revolution (8)

functionalist theories (9)

dysfunctional (10)

manifest functions (10)

latent functions (10)

conflict theory (11)

class conflict (11)

class consciousness (11)

the Protestant ethic (13)

symbolic interactionism (14)

social constructionism (14)

feminist theory (16)

the Postindustrial Revolution (29)

globalization (29)

participant observation (20)

field research (20)

exploratory research (21)

hypotheses (21)

variables (21)

operationalization (21)

reliability (21)

validity (22)

generalizability (22)

causality (22)

experiment (23)

randomization (23)

experimental group (23)

control group (23)

dependent variable (23)

independent variable (23)

surveys (24)

sample (24)

population (4524)

probability samples (25)

contingency tables (26)

association (27)

control variable (27)

Detailed Chapter Outline

I. INTRODUCTION

    A. Why Robert Brym Decided *Not* To Study Sociology
        1. Sociology: "Thin Soup with Uncertain Ingredients?"
        2. Is Sociology merely like economics, political science, philosophy, drama, and abnormal psychology?

    B. A Change of Mind
        1. Sociology "an altogether new way" to think.
        2. The dilemma of all thinking people ("Life is finite")—study, reflection and the selection of values and goals.
        3. Sociology's Unique Way of Explaining Social Life
            a. **Sociology** is the systematic study of human behavior in social context.
            b. *Social* causes or social forces are distinct from physical and emotional causes.
            c. The **social context** or the organization of the social world opens up some opportunities, but also constrains our freedom.
            d. Understanding the power of *social forces* can help us to know our capabilities and limitations.

    C. The Power of Sociology

II. THE SOCIOLOGICAL PERSPECTIVE

    A. The Sociological Explanation of Suicide
        1. Suicide: a seemingly antisocial, nonsocial, and private act.
        2. Based on his analysis of European government statistics and hospital records, **Emile Durkheim** demonstrated that suicide is more than just an individual act of desperation resulting from psychological disorder, as commonly believed at the end of the 19th century. Durkheim argued that suicide rates vary due to differences in **social solidarity,** which is the degree to which group members share beliefs, and the intensity and frequency of their interaction.
        3. Durkheim's research findings in the late 1800s France:
            a. Married adults are half as likely as unmarried adults to commit suicide due to their social ties.
            b. Women are less likely to commit suicide than men due to their greater involvement in intimate social relations of family life.
            c. Jews are less likely to commit suicide than Christians due to being more socially tight knit in defensive response to centuries of persecution.
            d. The elderly are more prone than the young and middle-aged to commit suicide, because they are more likely to live alone, have lost a spouse, lack a job, and lack a wide network of friends.
        4. The relevance of Durkheim's theory and research to here and now:
            a. Elderly are most likely to commit suicide, especially among the divorced and widowed elderly.
            b. Men are four times more likely than women to commit suicide.

     c. In some parts of the United States, high rates of church membership have low suicide rates, while areas with high divorce rates have high suicide rates.

     d. However, suicide among young people has become more common over the past half century. Why, sociologically?

B. From Personal Troubles to Social Structures

    1. **Social structures** are stable patterns of social relations, that affect your innermost thoughts and feelings, influence your actions, and thus help shape who you are. *Three levels of social structure* that surround and permeate us:

        a. **Microstructures** are patterns of intimate social relations.

        b. **Macrostructures** are patterns of social relations that lie outside and above your circle of intimates and acquaintances.

           i. **Patriarchy**, the traditional system of economic and political inequality between women and men in most societies, is an important macrostructure.

        c. **Global structures** are patterns of social relations that lie outside and above the national level, including international organizations, patterns of worldwide travel and communication, and the economic relations between countries.

    2. One of the sociologist's main tasks is to identify and explain the connection between people's personal troubles and the social structures in which they are embedded. Personal problems are connected to social structures at the micro, macro, and global levels.

C. The Sociological Imagination

    1. The **"sociological imagination,"** coined by C. Wright Mills, refers to the ability to see the connection between personal troubles and social structures.

    2. The sociological imagination as a recent addition to the human repertoire, was born in the context of **three modern revolutions** that pushed people to think about society in new ways:

D. Origins of the Sociological Imagination

    1. The **Scientific Revolution** which began in Europe around 1550, encouraged the view that sound conclusions about the workings of society must be based on solid evidence, not just speculation.

    2. The **Democratic Revolution,** which began about 1750, involved the citizens of the United States, France and other countries broadening their participation in government, and suggested that people organize society, and that human intervention can therefore resolve social problems.

    3. The **Industrial Revolution,** which began in Britain in the 1780s, refers to the rapid economic transformation that involved the large-scale application of science and technology to industrial processes, the creation of factories, and the formation of a working class.

III. AUGUSTE COMTE AND TENSION BETWEEN SCIENCE AND VALUES

A. French social thinker **Auguste Comte** (1798-1857) who coined the term *sociology* in 1838 was eager to adopt the scientific method in his study of society, yet was a conservative thinker, motivated by strong opposition to rapid change in French society – namely the French Revolution, early industrialization, and the rapid growth of cities.

B. Tension between the importance of science and a vision of the ideal society are seen in the work of **Karl Marx** (1818-83), **Emile Durkheim** (1858-1917), and **Max Weber** (1864-1920). They wanted to explain the great transformations of Europe (i.e. transition to industrial capitalism) and suggested ways of improving people's lives and combating social ills. They were also committed to the scientific method of research.

IV. SOCIOLOGICAL THEORY AND THEORISTS

    A. Functionalism:
        1. Durkheim
            a. **Functionalist theories** incorporate four features:
                i. Human behavior is governed by stable patterns of social relations, or social structures, usually macro structures.
                ii. Social structures maintain or undermine *social stability*.
                iii. Social structures are based mainly on *shared values*.
                iv. Reestablishment of *equilibrium* can best solve most social problems.
        2. Parsons and Merton
            a. **Talcott Parsons** was the foremost American proponent of functionalism who identified how various institutions work to ensure the smooth operation of society as a whole.
            b. **Robert Merton** proposed that social structures may have different consequences for different groups of people such as disruptive consequences referred to as **dysfunctional.** Merton also noted that some functions are **manifest** (intended and easily observed), while others are **latent** (unintended and less obvious).

    B. Conflict Theory:
        1. **Conflict theory** emphasizes the centrality of conflict in social life and incorporates the following features:
            a. Focus on large, macro-level structures, such as relations between classes.
            b. Shows how major patterns of inequality in society produce social stability in some circumstances and social change in others.
            c. Stresses how members of privileged groups try to maintain their advantages while subordinate groups struggle to increase theirs. Thus social conditions at a given time are the expression of an ongoing power struggle between privileged and subordinate groups.
            d. Suggests that eliminating privilege will lower the level of conflict and increase total human welfare.
        2. Marx
            a. A generation before and radically different from Durkheim, **Karl Marx** originated conflict theory in his observation of the destitution and discontent produced by the Industrial Revolution.
            b. **Class conflict**, the struggle between classes lies at the center of Marx's ideas.
            c. Marx argued that owners or capitalists, in their attempt to improve the efficiency of work and earn higher profits, concentrate workers in larger establishments, keep wages low, and invest little in improving working conditions.

      d. Marx felt that workers would become aware of their exploited class, referred to as **class consciousness,** encourage trade union and labor party organization, and eventually replace private ownership of property with an economic system based on shared property ownership—that is a "communist" society.

  3. Weber

      a. A generation after Marx, **Max Weber** pointed out major flaws in Marx's argument.

      b. Weber noted that growth of the "service" sector with its many non-manual workers and professionals.

      c. Weber showed that class conflict is not the only driving force of history, but rather politics and religion are also important sources of historical change.

  4. Du Bois and Mills

      a. As the first African American to receive a Ph.D. from Harvard who wrote at the end of the 19th century, **W.E.B. Du Bois** (1868-1963) was an early advocate of conflict theory, and conducted pioneering studies of race in the United States.

      b. He was a founder of the National Association for the Advancement of Colored People (NAACP) and the country's second Department of Sociology at Atlanta University in 1897.

      c. In his best-known work, *The Philadelphia Negro,* Du bois illustrates that poverty and other social problems faced by African Americans were not due to some "natural" inferiority, but to white prejudice.

      d. C. Wright Mills did much to lay the foundations of modern conflict theory in the United States in the 1950s.

      e. In one of his most important books, *The Power Elite,* Mills argued that power is highly concentrated in American society, which is thus less of a democracy than we are led to believe.

C. Symbolic Interactionism

  1. Weber, Mead, and Goffman

      a. In addition to his contribution to conflict theory, Weber also contributed the idea of subjective meanings and motives to sociological theory, which is central to symbolic interactionism. For instance, Weber concluded that capitalism did not develop in the context of economic forces alone, but rather depended on the religious meaning people attached to their work such as the **Protestant ethic** (the belief that religious doubts can be reduced, and a state of grace assured, if people work diligently and live ascetically).

      b. Weber referred to his research emphasis on the importance of understanding people's motives and the meanings they attach to things, as the method of *Verstehen* ("understanding" in German).

      c. Emphasis on subjective meanings found rich soil in the 19th and 20th century United States, therefore much of early American sociology focused on the connection between the individual and the larger society.

      d. The work of **George Herbert Mead** (1863-1931) and his colleagues gave birth to symbolic interactionism.

      e. **Symbolic interactionism**, coined by Mead's student at the University of Chicago Herbert Blumer (1900-1986), incorporates the following features:

i.   Focuses on face-to-face interaction.

ii. Emphasizes the subjective meanings people attach to their social circumstances as the basis of social behavior.

iii. Stresses that people help to create their social circumstances, and do not merely react to them. For instance, **Erving Goffman** (1922-1982) analyzed the many ways people present themselves to others in everyday life to appear in the best possible light, and compared social interaction to a carefully staged play, with a front stage, backstage, defined roles, and props.

iv. Validates unpopular and nonofficial viewpoints, which increases our understanding and tolerance of people different from us.

2. Social Constructionism

    a. As a variant of symbolic interactionism, **social constructionism** argues that when people interact, they assume things are naturally what they seem to be.

    b. Yet, natural features of life are often sustained by *social* processes that vary historically and culturally.

    c. The study of the subjective side of social life deepens our understanding of how society works, and supplementing the insights of macro-level analysis.

D. Feminist Theory

1. Although few women figured prominently in the early history of sociology due to the lack of opportunity for women in the larger society in the 19th century, there were a few exceptional women who introduced *gender issues* that were largely ignored by Marx, Durkheim, Weber, Mead, and other early sociologists.

2. Martineau and Addams

    a. **Harriet Martineau** (1802-76), often called "the first woman sociologist," and one of the first feminists, translated Comte into English, wrote one of the first books on research methods, undertook critical studies of slavery and factory laws and gender inequality, and advocated voting rights and higher education for women, and gender equality in the family.

    b. **Jane Addams** (1860-1935), a recipient of the Nobel Prize in 1931, co-founded Hull House (a shelter for the destitute in Chicago's slums) and spent a lifetime focusing on social reform.

       i. Through Hull House, Addams provided a research platform for sociologists at the University of Chicago.

3. Modern Feminism

    a. Since the mid-1960s, feminist theory has had a big influence on sociology. The various strands of **feminist theory** share the following characteristics:

       i.   Focuses on various aspects of *patriarchy,* the system of male domination in society, which is at least as important as class inequality in determining a person's opportunities.

       ii. Holds that male domination and female subordination are determined by structures of power and social convention, not biological necessity.

       iii. Examines the operation of patriarchy in both micro and macro settings.

       iv. Contends that existing patterns of gender inequality can and should be changed for the benefit of all members of society.

V. A SOCIOLOGICAL COMPASS

  A. Sociological founders attempted to solve the great sociological puzzles of their time, the causes and consequences of the Industrial Revolution.
    1. What are the great sociological puzzles of *our* time?
    2. How are today's sociologists responding to the challenges presented by the social settings in which *we* live?

  B. Today, sociology is a heterogeneous enterprise made up of hundreds of theoretical debates.

  C. The Postindustrial Revolution and globalization are perhaps the greatest sociological puzzles of our time.
    1. The **Postindustrial Revolution** is the technology-driven shift from manufacturing to services industries – the shift from employment in factories to employment in offices – and the consequences of that shift for nearly all human activities.
    2. **Globalization** is the process by which formerly separate economies, states, and cultures are becoming tied together and people are becoming increasingly aware of their growing interdependence.

  D. Equality versus Inequality of Opportunity
    1. Optimists suggest that post-industrialism will provide more "equality of opportunity," that is better chances for all people to get a good education, influence government policy, and find good jobs.
    2. The "dark underside" of post-industrialism involves growing inequalities between wealthy and poor Americans, wealthy and poor nations, women and men, and regarding racism and discrimination.

  E. Individual Freedom versus Individual Constraint
    1. Many people are now freer to choose who they want to be with respect to their identities and social relationships.
    2. Increased freedom is experienced only within certain limits; social diversity is limited by pressures of conformity.

  F. Where Do You Fit In?
    1. Rather than being apathetic, people are inclined to look for ways to improve their lives, and this historical period is full of opportunities to do so.
    2. It seems possible to erode some of the inequalities.

  G. Careers in Sociology
    1. Sociology offers some useful advice on how to achieve these goals, for sociology is not just an intellectual exercise, but also an applied science, with practical uses, especially in teaching and **public policy** (the creation of laws and regulations by organizations and governments).

VI. CONDUCTING RESEARCH

  A. The Research Cycle
    1. Six steps of the research cycle:
      a. Formulate a research question.

       b. Review existing literature.

       c. Select a research method.

       d. Collect data.

       e. Analyze the data.

       f. Report/publicize the results.

B. Ethical Considerations

   1. Researchers must be mindful of and have respect for their *subjects' rights*:

       a. Right to safety

       b. Right to privacy

       c. Right to confidentiality

       d. Right to informed consent

VII. THE MAIN METHODS OF SOCIOLOGY

A. Field Methods: From Detached Observation to "Going Native"

   1. *Eikoku New Digest* and dinner party rules − an example that by observing others casually, we can get things terribly wrong.

   2. Some sociologists undertake **field research,** or research based on the observation of people in their natural settings.

   3. *Detached observation* involves classifying and counting the behavior of interest according to a predetermined scheme.

   4. Two main problems of direct observation.

       a. *Reactivity* - the presence of the researcher may itself affect the behavior of the people being observed.

       b. The *meaning* of the observed behavior may remain obscure to the researcher.

   5. **Researchers** must learn about their entire culture, and develop an intimate understanding of their behavior.

       a. In rare cases, ethnographic researchers have "gone native," giving up their research role to become members of the group they are studying.

B. Participant Observation

   1. **Participant observation** research involves attempts by researchers to observe a social milieu objectively and take part in the activities of the people they are studying.

       a. **Exploratory research** is often the initial step in participant observation studies, - and involves attempts to describe, understand, and develop theory about a social phenomenon in the absence of much previous research on the subject. Researchers at first have a vague sense of what they are looking for.

       b. **Hypotheses** are unverified but testable statements about the phenomena in question.

       c. Observations constitute sociological data that allow researchers to reject, accept, or modify their initial hypotheses. Thus, researchers often choose their observations, which results in the creation of *grounded theory*, an explanation of a phenomenon based on controlled scrutiny of one's subjects.

C. Methodological Problems
   1. Measurement
      a. Researchers use mental constructs or concepts to think about the world. **Variables** are concepts that can have more than one value.
      b. **Operationalization** involves deciding which observations are to be linked to which variables.
   2. Reliability, Validity, Generalizability, and Causality
      a. Since participant-observers usually work alone and investigate one type of group, we must be convinced of three things to accept their findings:
         i. **Reliability** is the degree to which a measurement procedure yields consistent results. *Would another researcher interpret or measure things in the same way?*
         ii. **Validity** is the degree to which a measure actually measures what it is intended to measure. *Are the researcher's interpretations accurate?* Doubts may still exist if the criteria used by the participant observers to assess the validity of their measures are all *internal* to the settings under investigation. Our confidence in the validity of researchers' measures increases if *external* validation criteria are used.
         iii. **Generalizability** exists when research findings apply beyond the specific case examined. **Causality** is the analysis of causes and their effects. Information on how widely or narrowly a research finding applies can help us establish the causes of a social phenomenon. Participant observers tend not to think in mechanical, cause-and-effect terms, as they prefer to view their subjects as engaged in a fluid process of social interaction.
      b. In sum, participant observation is useful in exploratory research, constructing grounded theory, creating internally valid measures, and developing a sympathetic understanding of people's perceptions, - and is deficient in establishing reliability, generalizability, and causality.

D. Experiments
   1. An **experiment** is a carefully controlled artificial situation that allows researchers to isolate hypothesized causes and measure their effects precisely. Experiments involve **randomization** (assigning individuals to one of two groups by chance processes) to create two similar groups for comparison.
   2. Research steps of an experiment:
      a. Selection of subjects.
      b. Random assignment of subjects to the **experimental group** (the group exposed to the independent variable) and **control group** (the group that is not exposed to the independent variable).
      c. Randomization and repetition make the experimental and control groups similar, and eliminates bias by allowing a chance process to decide which group each subject is assigned to.
      d. Measurement of the **dependent variable** (the presumed effect in a cause-and-effect relationship) in experimental and control groups.

    e. Introduction of the **independent variable** (the presumed cause in the cause-and-effect relationship).

    f. Re-measurement of the dependent variable in experimental and control groups.

    g. Assessment of experimental effect.

3. Strengths of experiments:
    a. Precise and repeatable.
    b. High reliability and the ability to establish causality.

4. Weaknesses of experiments:
    a. Highly artificial situations.
    b. Validity problem.

5. Experiments on Television Violence
    a. *Hawthorne effect.*
    b. *Power Rangers.*

E. Surveys

1. Sampling
    a. **Surveys** ask people questions about their knowledge, attitudes, or behavior.
    b. Survey studies examine part of a group called a **sample** (the part of the population of research interest that is selected for analysis), in order to learn about the whole group, referred to as the **population** (the entire group which the researcher wishes to generalize).
    c. **Probability samples** choose respondents at random. The individual's chance of being chosen must be known and be greater than zero. This enhances generalizability and representative-ness within known margins of error.
    d. A *sampling frame*, which is a list of all the people in the population of interest, is needed to draw a probability sample.
    e. Once a sampling frame is chosen or created, individuals must be selected by a random-chance process.
    f. Large samples give more precise results than small samples.
    g. For most sociological purposes, a random sample of 1,500 people will give acceptably accurate results.

2. Survey Questions and Validity
    a. Three main ways to conduct a survey:
      i. *Self-administered questionnaire* (i.e. mail questionnaire) is a relatively inexpensive, but sometimes results in unacceptably *low response rates* (the number of people who answer the questionnaire divided by the number of people asked to do so).
      ii. *Face-to-face interviews* involve the presentation of questions and allowable responses to the respondent by the interviewer during a meeting. They are very expensive (i.e. training and paying interviewers).
      iii. *Telephone interviews* elicit relatively high response rates and are relatively cheap to administer.
    b. Two types of questions:
      i. A *closed-ended question* provides respondents with a list of permitted answers.
      ii. *Open-ended questions* allow respondents to answer questions in their own words.

        c. Threats to validity in survey research that researchers attempt to alleviate:
           i.   Undercounting
           ii. Non-response
           iii. Response bias
           iv. Wording effects

    3. Causality
        a. Although a survey is not ideal for conducting exploratory research, survey data are useful for discovering relationships among variables, including cause-and-effect relationships.

    4. Reading Tables
        a. **Contingency tables** (a cross-classification of cases by at least two variables) are one of the most useful tools for manipulating survey data.
        b. **Association** between variables - when the value of one variable changes with the value of the other. Examining the association of two variables within the category of a third variable, referred to as a **control variable**, which allows researchers to manipulate the data to remove the effect of a control variable from the original association.

F. Analysis of Existing Documents and Official Statistics
    1. Three types of existing documents sociologists have analyzed:
        a. Diaries
        b. Newspapers
        c. Published historical works.
    2. The most frequently used sources of official statistics:
        a. Census data
        b. Police crime reports (i.e. *Uniform Crime Reports*)
        c. Records of key life events.
    3. Four main advantages of existing documents and official statistics:
        a. Can save researchers time and money.
        b. Official statistics usually cover entire populations and are collected using rigorous and uniform methods, thus yielding high quality data.
        c. Useful for historical and comparative analysis.
        d. Reactivity is not a problem.
    4. One big disadvantage:
        a. Often contain biases that reflect the interests of the individuals and organizations that created the data, - and these data sources are not created with the researcher's needs in mind.

VIII. THE IMPORTANCE OF BEING SUBJECTIVE

A. Subjectivity leads, objectivity follows. Objective sociological knowledge has been enhanced as a result of subjective experiences.

Study Activity: Applying the Sociological Compass

After reading the chapter, studying the key terms and outline, re-read the section "A Sociological Compass." Identify and write down the key points of the "unresolved issues" and dilemmas. Write down possible questions and solutions from the points of view of functionalism, conflict theory, symbolic interactionism and feminist theory.

Equality Versus Inequality of Opportunity

Key Points:

Pressing Questions:

Functionalism:

1.

2.

3.

Conflict:

1.

2.

3.

Symbolic Interactionism:

1.

2.

3.

Feminist Theory

1.

2.

3.

Potential Solutions:

Functionalism:

1.

2.

3.

Conflict:

1.

2.

3.

Symbolic Interactionism:

1.

2.

3.

Feminist Theory

1.

2.

3.

<u>*Individual Freedom Versus Individual Constraint*</u>

Key Points:

Pressing Questions:

Functionalism:

1.

2.

3.

Conflict:

1.

2.

3.

Symbolic Interactionism:

1.

2.

3.

Feminist Theory

1.

2.

3.

Potential Solutions:

Functionalism:

1.

2.

3.

Conflict:

1.

2.

3.

Symbolic Interactionism:

1.

2.

3.

Feminist Theory

1.

2.

3.

InfoTrac College Edition Online Exercises

For the following exercises, log on to the online library of InfoTrac College Edition at http://www.infotrac-college.com/. Make note that InfoTrac has implemented a new registration system that will allow easier access to InfoTrac through the use of a personalized username and password.

Once you've created your username and password you may proceed directly to the Log On page. To create an account, register your passcode packaged with your textbook, and create a username and password, by following the online prompt. After you are logged in, click on "Infotrac College Edition." You will arrive at a screen that enables you to search topics.

Keyword: **social conflict**. Choose an article that discusses any example of social conflict of your interest. After reading the article, apply the functionalist and social conflict sociological perspectives to the content in the article, by contrasting how a functionalist versus a conflict theorist would explain the sources of conflict in the article.

Keyword: **symbolic interactionism**. Identify two specific topics or issues from at least two articles. Explain how these two topics can be explored from a symbolic interactionist perspective.

Keyword: **feminist sociology**. Identify three challenges feminist sociologists have faced in the past and face in the present, based on at least two of the articles.

Keyword: **theoretical paradigm**. Look for articles that deal with sociology. Why is it important to have theoretical paradigms? How does this relate to the sociological perspectives presented in this chapter? Explain the similarities and differences between those presented in the book and those found on the InfoTrac search.

Keyword: **nonverbal communication**. Find articles on how nonverbal communication influences our social interpretations. Is nonverbal communication reliable and accurate? Are there any gender differences in nonverbal communication?

Keyword: **virtual reality**. Look for articles that discuss how virtual reality influences our social experiences. How does this relate to sociology?

Keyword: **ecstasy**. Look for articles that provide information on how ecstasy is used socially. Is there anything specifically geared towards college students? What does this tell us about our methods of social interaction?

Keyword: **research ethics**. Select an article on research ethics and compare it to the American Sociological Association (ASA) Code of Ethics. Are there any similarities and differences? For example, you will find some things on the American Psychological Association (APA), the area of criminal justice and also for dealing with human subjects.

Keyword: **e-research**. The Internet is a growing source of research. Look for articles dealing with validity and reliability. How reliable is the research information provided. How can the accuracy and reliability of research information be assessed? In your opinion, do you think other students take the Internet as a "very" reliable source?

Internet Exercises

For a brief introduction to different sociologists and theorists visit the Work and Society: Sociology of Work and Occupation website at:

http://www.was.pe.kr/english1.htm Click on the links for sociologists. Which sociologists and theorists are discussed? Write a short paper discussing how Internet list compares to the sociologists and theorists that are presented in Chapter 1.

Visit the Annual Review of Sociology official website. This annual publication gives cutting edge articles on the different subfields within sociology. Go to: http://www.annurev.org. Read three different articles in the most recent Annual Review of Sociology and then write a short paper on how each article uses the sociology theories presented in Chapter 1.

For an overview of how sociology differs from common sense visit these search engines: www.metacrawler.com and www.megacrawler.com Write a small paper on how sociology differs from common sense.

Visit the official website for the American Sociological Association (ASA). http://www.asanet.org. ASA is the largest professional organization of sociologists in the United States. What issues does the ASA cover? What resources are available for students of sociology?

Go to the official website for the popular Gallup Poll at http://www.gallup.com and click on How Gallup polls are conducted for an overview of the research method and design the Gallup Poll institution uses. How does the research method and design used by the Gallup Poll compare to the research methods you learned from this chapter? What are the similarities? What are the differences?

Every professional organization that conducts research has a code of ethics or written guidelines on conducting research. Read the Code of Ethics for the American Sociological Association at this site: http://www.asanet.org/ecoderev.htm Do you think there are any ethical concerns that have been left out? If yes, what?

Practice Tests

Fill-In-The-Blank

Fill in the blank with the appropriate term from the above list of "key terms."

1. As a variant of symbolic interactionism, _____ argues that when people interact, they assume things are naturally what they seem to be.

2. Disruptive consequences of social structures are referred to as _____ .

3. The _____ which began about 1750, involved the citizens of the United States, France and other countries broadening their participation in government, and that human intervention can thus resolve social problems.

4. _____ are patterns of social relations that lie outside and above your circle of intimates and acquaintances.

5. The _____ which began in Europe about 1550, encouraged the view that sound conclusions about society must be based on solid evidence, not just speculation.

6. The _____ is the belief that religious doubts can be reduced, and a state of grace assured, if people work diligently and live ascetically.

7. According to Durkheim, the degree to which group members share beliefs, and the intensity and frequency of their interaction is referred to as _____ .

8. _____ is the struggle between classes.

9. _____ is the degree to which a measurement procedure yields consistent results.

10. _____ research involves attempts by researchers to observe a social milieu objectively and take part in the activities of the people they are studying.

11. _____ ask people questions about their knowledge, attitudes, or behavior, either in face-to-face or telephone interview or in a paper-and-pencil format.

12. _____ exists when research findings apply beyond the specific case examined.

13. _____ involves deciding which observations are to be linked to which variables.

Multiple-Choice Questions

Select the response that best answers the question or completes the statement:

1. Sociology is the social scientific study of human behavior in:
   a. the context of personality development.
   b. a social context.
   c. a psychological context.
   d. the context of human development.
   e. a biological context.

2. Which term refers to the degree to which group members share beliefs and the intensity and frequency of interaction.
   a. social forces
   b. social context
   c. social causes
   d. social solidarity
   e. social conflict

3. According to Durkheim's Theory of Suicide, as the level of social solidarity increases, the suicide rate:
   a. increases
   b. declines
   c. remains constant
   d. . All of the above.
   e. None of the above.

4. Which of the following is NOT a level of social structure?
   a. microstructures
   b. macrostructures
   c. global structures
   d. innate structures
   e. All of the above are levels of social structure.

5. The sociological imagination was born in the context of the following revolutions EXCEPT:
   a. the Scientific Revolution
   b. the Civil Rights Revolution
   c. the Democratic Revolution
   d. the Industrial Revolution
   e. Women's liberation in the United States

6. Who coined the term "sociology?"
   a. Auguste Comte
   b. Emile Durkheim
   c. Karl Marx
   d. Max Weber
   e. W.E.B. Du Bois

7. Functionalists refer to disruptive consequences of society produced by social structures as:
   a. manifest functions
   b. latent functions
   c. equilibrium
   d. dysfunctions
   e. social tensions

8. Which American sociological pioneer played a major role in the study of race and ethnic relations in the United States?
   a. Talcott Parsons
   b. Robert Merton
   c. W.E.B. Du Bois
   d. George Herbert Mead
   e. Emile Durkheim

9. Which term supports the idea that capitalism did not develop in the context of economic forces alone, but also depended on the meaning people attached to their work?
   a. the Protestant ethic
   b. class consciousness
   c. industrialization
   d. postindustrialism
   e. proletariat

10. Which is NOT a characteristic of feminist theory?
    a. focuses on various aspects of patriarchy.
    b. holds that male domination and female subordination are determined by structures of power.
    c. examines the operations of patriarchy in both micro and macro settings.
    d. contends that existing patterns of gender inequality should be changed exclusively for the benefit of women.

11. Who was among the first early sociologists to translate Comte's writing into English?
    a. W.E.B. Du Bois
    b. Karl Marx
    c. Harriet Martineau
    d. Robert Merton
    e. Emile Durkheim

12. Which sociological theoretical tradition found especially rich soil in the 19th and 20th century United States?
    a. functionalism
    b. conflict theory
    c. symbolic interactionism
    d. feminist theory
    e. All of the above.

13. Who noted the growth of the "service" sector with its many nonmanual workers and professionals?
    a. Max Weber
    b. Harriet Martineau
    c. Karl Marx
    d. Emile Durkheim
    e. Herbert Spencer

14. Brym and Lie refer to the ability of sociology to sketch the main unresolved issues confronting the postindustrial era as:
    a. thin soup with uncertain ingredients
    b. a sociological stepping stone
    c. a sociological compass
    d. a sociological looking-glass
    e. the sociological imagination

15. Which sociological perspective is especially concerned with the stable patterns of social relations?
    a. functionalism
    b. conflict
    c. symbolic interactionism
    d. feminist theory
    e. All of the above.

16. What is the first step in the research cycle?
    a. Review existing literature.
    b. Formulate a research question.
    c. Select a research method.
    d. Report the results.
    e. Analyze the data.
    f. Right to a fair trial.

17. Which type of research method involves attempts by researchers to observe a social milieu objectively and take part in the activities of the people they are studying?
    a. participant observation
    b. experiments
    c. surveys
    d. analysis of existing documents
    e. analysis of official statistics

18. _____ is often the initial step in participant observation research.
    a. Review existing literature.
    b. Analyze the data
    c. Select a research method
    d. Report the results
    e. Exploratory research

19. _____ are unverified but testable statements about the phenomenon in question.
    a. Variables
    b. Operationalizations
    c. Hypotheses
    d. Validity tests
    e. Reliability tests

20. _____ is the degree to which a measurement yields consistent results, while _____ is the degree to which a measure actually measures what it is intended to measure.
    a. Validity; reliability
    b. Reliability; validity
    c. Generalizability; validity
    d. Reliability; generalizability
    e. Validity; generalizability

21. Which type of variable is the presumed effect in the cause-and-effect relationship?
    a. dependent variable
    b. independent variable
    c. control variable
    d. the third variable
    e. spurious variable

22. Which of the following is a threat to the validity of survey research?
    a. undercounting
    b. nonresponse
    c. response bias
    d. wording effects
    e. All of the above

23. _____ occurs when the value of one variable changes with the value of the other.
    a. association
    b. causality
    c. contingency
    d. spuriousness
    e. control

24. As the saying in sociological research goes, "_____ leads, _____ follows."
    a. objectivity; subjectivity
    b. subjectivity; objectivity
    c. objectivity; common sense
    d. common sense; subjectivity
    e. None of the above.

25. Which is a main advantage of using existing documents and official statistics in sociological research?
    a. can save researchers money
    b. useful for historical and comparative analysis
    c. reactivity is not a problem
    d. None of the above.
    e. All of the above.

26. Which is a main way to administer a survey?
    a. self-administered
    b. face-to-face interviews
    c. telephone interviews
    d. None of the above.
    e. All of the above.

27. Researchers collect information using _____ by asking people in a representative sample as set of identical questions.
    a. field experiments
    b. laboratory experiments
    c. participant observations
    d. ethnographies
    e. surveys

28. A valuable lesson learned from the use of the Butterfly Ballot in the 2000 U.S. presidential election is that:
    a. the world of U.S. politics is entirely corrupt.
    b. voters are often incompetent.
    c. one must be careful to design self-administered questionnaires so that response categories are clear.
    d. All of the above.
    e. None of the above.

True False

1. Durkheim's research findings on suicide in the 1800s in France are outdated and inapplicable to here and now, since contemporary U.S. society has changed substantially since Durkheim's time.

    TRUE or FALSE

2. Since sociology has long been change-oriented, women and gender issues have always been at the center of sociological theory.

    TRUE or FALSE

3. Although Max Weber's contribution to conflict theory is big, his ideas also contributed to symbolic interactionism.

    TRUE or FALSE

4. Because women were excluded in the early history of sociology, the work of Harriet Martineau has had little impact on sociology today.

   TRUE or FALSE

5. In contrast to industrialization, sociologists agree that postindustrialism promises abundant opportunities to enhance the quality of life with few social barriers.

   TRUE or FALSE

6. A major weakness of participant observation research is that this method lacks depth of analysis.

   TRUE or FALSE

7. Variables are concepts that have only one value.

   TRUE or FALSE

8. Surveys often incorporate both closed-ended and open-ended questions.

   TRUE or FALSE

9. In survey research, smaller and more precise samples enhance statistical significance.

   TRUE or FALSE

10. Open-ended questions allow respondents to answer questions in their own words.

    TRUE or FALSE

11. A sample is the entire group in which the researcher wishes to generalize.

    TRUE or FALSE

12. Research involves taking the plunge from speculation to testing ideas against evidence.

    TRUE or FALSE

Short Answer

1. Briefly explain why sociology is a unique way of explaining social life, in spite of the fact that sociology is in some respects like other disciplines such as economics, political science, philosophy, drama, and abnormal psychology. (p. 1-5)

   _____

   _____

2. What is the "sociological imagination"? (p. 5)

   _____

   _____

3. Illustrate the difference between manifest and latent functions by providing an example of each function. (p. 10)

_____

_____

4. What do Brym and Lie mean by "a sociological compass?" (p. 29)

_____

_____

5. List and state the rights of research subjects. (p. 19)

_____

_____

6. Briefly explain the difference between validity and reliability. (p. 21-22)

_____

_____

7. List four advantages of analyzing existing documents and official statistics for sociological researchers. (p. 28)

_____

_____

Essay Questions

1. Contrast functionalism, conflict theory, and symbolic interactionism. Be sure to identify the key features of each sociological tradition. (p. 9-16)

2. Compare and contrast Karl Marx's and Max Weber's perspectives on social inequality and conflict. (p. 11)

3. Explain the transformation of society from industrialization to postindustrialism. (p. 29)

4. Compare and contrast participant observation, experiments, and surveys. In so doing, be sure to identify the major strengths and weaknesses of each research method. (p. 20-28)

5. Explain the statement "Subjectivity leads, objectivity follows," by describing the impact of feminism on sociological research. (p.15-18)

Solutions

Practice Tests

Fill-In-The-Blank

1. social constructionism
2. dysfunctional
3. Democratic Revolution
4. Macrostructures
5. Scientific Revolution
6. Protestant Ethic
7. social solidarity
8. Class conflict
9. Reliability
10. Participant observation
11. Surveys
12. Generalizability
13. Operationalization

Multiple-Choice Questions

1. B, (p. 2)
2. D, (p. 3)
3. B, (p. 3)
4. D, (p. 6)
5. B, (p. 8)
6. A, (p. 8)
7. D, (p. 10)
8. C, (p. 12)
9. A, (p. 13)
10. D, (p. 15)
11. C, (p. 15)
12. C, (p. 14)
13. A, (p. 11)
14. C, (p. 29)
15. A, (p. 9)
16. B, (p. 18)
17. A, (p. 20)
18. E, (p. 21)
19. C, (p. 21)
20. B, (p. 21-22)
21. A, (p. 23)
22. E, (p. 26)
23. A, (p. 27)
24. B, (p. 17)
25. E, (p. 28)
26. E, (p. 25)
27. E, (p. 24)
28. C, (p. 25)

True False

1. F, (p. 3)
2. F, (p. 15)
3. T, (p. 13)
4. F, (p. 15)
5. F, (p. 29)
6. F, (p. 20)
7. F, (p. 21)
8. T, (p. 25)
9. F, (p. 25)
10. T, (p. 25)
11. F, (p. 24)
12. T, (p. 17)

CULTURE

Student Learning Objectives

After reading Chapter 2, you should be able to:

1. Identify functions of culture to solve real-life problems.

2. Describe the origins of culture in terms of the three main tools of human survival.

3. Critique biological and evolutionary psychological perspectives on culture from a sociological point of view.

4. Explain the Sapir-Whorf thesis.

5. Explain the role of ethnocentrism, insider and outsider cultural perspectives on our sociological understanding of culture.

6. Contrast the notions of culture as freedom and culture as constraint.

7. Explain increasing cultural diversity in the contexts of globalization and postmodernism.

8. Explain the phenomena of rationalization and consumerism as sources of cultural constraint.

9. Identify aspects of postmodern culture that distinguish postmodernity from modernity.

10. Describe the cases of heavy metal and hip-hop as examples of the negative consequences of consumerism that limits expressions of freedom and change.

Key Terms

(defined on the indicated pages of the textbook, and in glossary)

culture (37)

society (38)

abstraction (39)

symbols (39)

cooperation (39)

norms (39)

production (39)

material culture (40)

nonmaterial culture (40)

sanctions (40)

social control (40)

language (41)

Sapir-Whorf thesis (41)

ethnocentrism (42)

multiculturalism (45)

cultural relativism (46)

rights revolution (46)

rites of passage (48)

globalization (48)

postmodernism (49)

cultural lag (56)

rationalization (58)

consumerism (58)

subcultures (59)

Detailed Chapter Outline

I. CULTURE AS PROBLEM SOLVING

A. **Culture** broadly defined refers to all the ideas, practices, and material objects that people create to deal with real-life problems.

B. Examples of real-life problems that culture helps us deal with:
1. Ease anxiety to maintain focus on tasks at hand (i.e. professional baseball players, college students writing a final exam).
2. How to build houses and plant.
3. Facing problems of death gives meaning to life.

C. Shared culture is *socially* transmitted. **Society** is a number of people who interact, usually in a defined territory, and share a culture.

D. Origins of Culture
1. Three main tools in human cultural survival kits:
a. **Abstraction** refers to the capacity to create general *ideas*, or ways of thinking that are not linked to particular instances, - and enables humans to learn and transmit knowledge in a way no other animal can.
i. **Symbols** are a type of idea that refers to things that carry particular meanings (i.e. languages, mathematical notations, and signs).
b. **Cooperation** is the capacity to create a complex social life, which is accomplished by establishing **norms**, or generally accepted ways of doing things.

      c. **Production** involves making and using tools and techniques, known as **material culture**, that improve our ability to take what we want from nature. **Nonmaterial culture** is composed of symbols, norms, and other nontangible elements of culture.

   2. **Sanctions** are the rewards and punishments aimed at ensuring conformity to cultural guidelines. The system of **social control** is the sum of sanctions in society.

II. CULTURE AND BIOLOGY

A. The Problem of Language
   1. Is Language Innate or Learned?
      a. A **language** is a system of symbols strung together to communicate thought.
      b. MIT cognitive scientist Steven Pinker concludes that language is not so much learned as it is grown. Should we believe him?
   2. The Sapir-Whorf Thesis and its Critics
      a. The proposition that experience, thought, and language interacts is known as the **Sapir-Whorf thesis.**
      b. Whorf saw speech patterns as "interpretations of experience."
      c. In what sense does language *in and of itself* influence the way we experience the world?
         i. By the 1970s, researchers concluded that speakers of different languages did not perceive color differently.
        ii. In the 1980s and 1990s, researchers found some effects of language on perception.
      d. Biological thinking about culture has benefits and dangers.
         i. Helps see the broad limits and potentials of human creativity.

III. CULTURE AND ETHNOCENTRISM

A. Culture is often invisible, because people tend to take their own culture for granted. Yet people tend to be startled when confronted by other cultures. In other words, culture is clearly visible from the margins.

B. **Ethnocentrism** is judging another culture exclusively by the standards of one's own culture (i.e. Western views of cow worship among Hindu peasants in India). Ethnocentrism impairs sociological analysis. If you refrain from taking your own culture for granted and ethnocentrism, you will have taken the important first steps towards a sociological understanding of culture.

IV. TWO FACES OF CULTURE

A. Two faces of culture:
   1. Culture as freedom
   2. Culture as constraint

B. Culture as Freedom
   1. Cultural Production
      a. Culture is like an *independent* variable. People do not just accept culture passively as previously argued by many sociologists until the 1960s.
      b. We actively produce and interpret culture, creatively fashioning it to suit our own needs.
   2. Cultural Diversity

a. American society, like most societies in the world, is undergoing rapid cultural diversification, partly due to a high rate of immigration, which is evident in every aspect of life.

b. Cultural diversity has become a source of political conflict, especially in the debates concerning curricula in the American educational system.

    i. Until recent years, the American educational system stressed the common elements of American culture, history, and society, as told from the perspective of European settlers overcoming great odds.

    ii. School curricula typically neglected the contributions of non-whites and non-Europeans to America's historical, literary, artistic, and scientific development, - and neglected the less savory aspects of American history, many of which involved the use of force to create a strict racial hierarchy that persists today.

3. Multiculturalism

a. Advocates of **multiculturalism** argue that the curricula of America's public schools and colleges should present a more balanced picture of American history, culture, and society that reflects the country's ethnic and racial diversity and recognizes the equality of all cultures.

b. Three criticisms of multiculturalism:

    i. Belief that multicultural education hurts minority students by forcing them to spend too much time on noncore subjects.

    ii. Belief that multicultural education causes political disunity and results in more interethnic and interracial conflict.

    iii. Complaint that multiculturalism encourages the growth of **cultural relativism**, which is the belief that all cultures and all cultural practices have equal value. This criticism lies in the assumption that some cultures oppose the most deeply held values of most Americans.

4. The Rights Revolution

a. The process by which socially excluded groups have struggled to win equal rights under the law and in practice is referred to as the **rights revolution.**

b. The rights revolution was in full swing by the 1960s.

c. The rights revolution fragments American culture by:

    i. Legitimizing the grievances of groups that were formerly excluded from full social participation and;

    ii. Renewing their pride in their identity and heritage.

5. From Diversity to Globalization

a. In *tribal societies*, culture tends to be homogeneous and organized based on **rites of passage** - cultural ceremonies that mark the transition from one stage of life to another.

b. Preindustrial Western Europe and North America were culturally fragmented by artistic, religious, scientific, and political forces.

c. Industrialization further fragmented culture, as the variety of occupational roles grew and new political and intellectual movements evolved.

      d.   In the postindustrial era, cultural fragmentation is quickening in pace due to globalization, the process by which formerly separate economies, states, and cultures are being tied together.

      e.   Roots of globalization:

          i.   Expansion of international trade and investment.

          ii.   Migration and sustained contact among different racial and ethnic groups.

          iii.   Transnational organizations are multiplying.

          iv.   Globalization of mass media.

6. Postmodernism

      a.   **Postmodernism** is characterized as an eclectic mixing of cultural elements and the erosion of consensus.

      b.   Some sociologists believe that this new term is needed to characterize the increasing cultural fragmentation and reconfiguration of our times.

      c.   Postmodernity is a distinct era following *modernity* – the era marked by the last half of the 19th century and the first half of the 20th century, and characterized by the belief in the inevitability of progress, respect for authority, and consensus around core values.

      d.   Aspects of postmodernism:

          i.   An eclectic mixing of elements from different times and places.

          ii.   The erosion of authority.

          iii.   The decline of consensus around core values.

          iv.   Voting patterns.

          v.   Big Historical Projects.

C. Culture as Constraint

  1. Value Persistence and Value Change

      a.   The World Value Survey (WVS) is the premier source of information on patterns, persistence and change in values.

      b.   Two Value Dimensions:

          i.   *The traditional/modern value dimensions.*

          ii.   *The materialist/postmaterialist value dimension.*

      c.   Two sets of social forces – economic and religious – influence where countries are located on the two value dimensions.

      d.   Level of economic development and direction of economic change are the main factors along the materialist-postmaterialist value dimension; and religion is the main factor that distinguishes them along the traditional-modern value dimension.

      e.   Two main reasons for interesting findings:

          i.   Values are not randomly distributed across populations, and people are not free to choose whatever values they want; instead clustering occurs along identifiable dimensions.

          ii.   Values *cluster* because they are influenced by powerful social forces.

      f.   The WVS findings say something about **cultural lag**, or the tendency of symbolic culture to change more slowly than material culture.

      i.   Cultural lag is less of an explanation, than many sociologists have suggested, and rather an invitation to search for additional variables that might account for the lag.

2. Rationalization and Time

    a. According to Max Weber, **rationalization** refers to the application of the most efficient means to achieve given goals, and the unintended, negative consequences of doing so.

3. Consumerism

    a. **Consumerism** is the tendency to define ourselves in terms of the goods we purchase. (i.e. the style of clothing and shoes you wear, and the display of clothing labels according to hip apparel advertisements).

    b. We can choose to purchase items that define us as members of a particular **subculture**, adherents of a set of distinctive values, norms, and practices within a larger culture.

    c. Regardless of our individual tastes, nearly all of us are good consumers.

4. Taming Subcultural Revolt

    a. Two examples from popular music subcultures:

        i.   Ozzy Osbourne - from the "Prince of Darkness" to *The Osbournes*

       ii. The development of Hip-Hop.

Study Activity: Applying the Sociological Compass

After reading the chapter, re-read the last section of the chapter, "Taming Subcultural Revolt" and review the functionalist and conflict sociological perspectives in Chapter 1. Accomplish the following tasks:

List the major social and political conditions in which heavy metal and hip-hop music was born out of.

1.

2.

3.

4.

Based on the conflict perspective, list the aspects of heavy metal and hip-hop as an expression of subcultural revolt and freedom.

1.

2.

3.

Based on the functionalist perspective, list the social forces that "tamed" the rebellious edge of heavy metal and hip-hop, and transformed each music subculture into a lucrative mainstream commodity.

1.

2.

3.

InfoTrac College Edition Online Exercises

For the following exercises, log on to the online library of InfoTrac College Edition at http://www.infotrac-college.com/. Make note that InfoTrac has implemented a new registration system that will allow easier access to InfoTrac through the use of a personalized username and password.

Once you've created your username and password you may proceed directly to the Log On page. To create an account, register your passcode packaged with your textbook, and create a username and password, by following the online prompt. After you are logged in, click on "Infotrac College Edition." You will arrive at a screen that enables you to search topics.

Keyword: **multicultural education** and/or **multiculturalism**. Identify at least one article that supports multiculturalism, and at least one article that critiques multiculturalism. After reading the articles, summarize the pros and cons of multiculturalism based on the articles. Identify the arguments from the articles that are consistent with Chapter 2 of the textbook.

Keyword: **deaf culture**. Look at the article called Transcending Revolutions: The Tsars, The Soviets, and Deaf Culture by Susan Burch. What issues does she present about deaf culture?

How similar or different are your comparisons of deaf culture and non-deaf culture?

Keyword: **tattoo parlor**. The tattoo has increased in popularity over recent years. Is there a specific culture that exists in the tattoo parlor? How does this culture compare to the larger American culture?

Keyword: **dowry**. What are the issues and concerns for being against the dowry? Research these by looking through the articles presented. What type of culture supports the notion of the dowry?

Keyword: **Holy War**. Recent events in the United States have caused there to be an increase awareness of Jihad: The Holy War for Muslims. Research the origins of this social phenomenon from a cultural standpoint. What sociological perspectives can you apply to this social phenomenon?

Internet Exercises

Go to http://www2.uchicago.edu/jnl-pub-cult for access to the home page of Public Culture: Study for Transnational Culture. You can browse and surf to your hearts content about culture. Look up some of your favorite topics. What types of topics are included in public culture? Are there some topics that you think should be included? If yes, what are they?

Read an article titled AJihad vs. McWorld@ at http://www.theatlantic.com/politics/foreign/barberf.htm written by Benjamin R. Barber. It discusses how the global culture is becoming more homogeneous. What points does Barber make to support his hypothesis? How does this relate to material covered in Chapter 2?

Link to http://www.h-net.org/~pcaaca/pca/pcahistory.htm the official website of the Popular Culture Association. You can research the history of the popular culture movement, read about the history of the American Culture Association and even link to academic discussion groups on culture. Make a list of five things that you learned from this short exercise.

Practice Tests

Fill-In-The-Blank

Fill in the blank with the appropriate term from the above list of "key terms."

1. The system of _____ is the sum of sanctions in society.

2. _____ is the tendency to define ourselves in terms of the goods we purchase?

3. A _____ is a system of symbols strung together to communicate thought.

4. _____ is a number of people who interact, usually in a defined territory, and share a culture.

5. Advocates of _____ argue that the curricula of America's public schools and colleges should present a more balanced picture of American history, culture, and society that reflects the country's racial and ethnic diversity.

6. _____ broadly defined refers to all the ideas, practices, and material objects that people create to deal with real-life problems.

7. Cultural ceremonies that mark the transition from one stage of life to another is referred to as _____ .

8. _____ is judging another culture exclusively by the standards of one's own culture.

9. The belief that all cultures and practices have equal value is referred to as _____ .

10. The process by which socially excluded groups have struggled to win equal rights under the law and in practice is referred to as the _____ .

Multiple-Choice Questions

Select the response that best answers the question or completes the statement:

1. Which of the following is NOT an example of real-life problems that culture helps people deal with in society?
   a. culture helps ease anxiety to maintain focus on tasks at hand.
   b. culture teaches how to build houses and plant.
   c. culture helps people face the problem of death.
   d. culture gives meaning to life.
   e. All of the above are examples of real-life problems that culture helps people deal with.

2. Which is NOT a main tool of the human cultural survival kit?
    a. abstraction
    b. cooperation
    c. production
    d. consumerism
    e. All of the above.

3. What is a sanction?
    a. The use of tools and techniques to improve our ability to take what we want from nature.
    b. The capacity to create complex social life.
    c. Generally accepted ways of doing things.
    d. A type of idea that carries particular meaning.
    e. A reward or punishment aimed at ensuring conformity to cultural guidelines.

4. The fact that people tend to get startled when confronted by other cultures suggests that:
    a. People tend to take their own culture for granted.
    b. People tend to be ethnocentric.
    c. Culture is visible from the margins.
    d. All of the above.
    e. None of the above.

5. Jim traveled to Indonesia for vacation and became shocked and judgmental toward the "foreign" practices. Which term best describes Jim's reaction?
    a. cultural relativism
    b. material culture
    c. ethnocentrism
    d. mass culture
    e. subcultural revolt

6. Which is NOT a critique of multicultural education?
    a. Belief that multicultural education hurts minority students by forcing them to spend
    b. too much time on noncore subjects.
    c. Belief that multicultural education causes political disunity.
    d. Belief that multicultural education results in more interethnic and interracial conflict.
    e. Complaint that multiculturalism discourages cultural relativism.
    f. All of the above are critiques of multicultural education.

7. In the postindustrial era, cultural fragmentation is increasing in pace due to:
    a. globalization.
    b. tribalization.
    c. increased homogeneity.
    d. the incline of consensus.
    e. None of the above.

8. _____ is characterized as an eclectic mixing of cultural elements and the erosion of consensus.
   a. Postmodernism
   b. Modernism
   c. Industrialization
   d. Preindustrialization
   e. Rationalization

9. Which of the following is NOT a source of globalization?
   a. expansion of international trade
   b. expansion of international investment
   c. migration and sustained contact among different ethnic groups
   d. growth of transnational organization
   e. All of the above are sources of globalization.

10. Which is an aspect of postmodernism?
    a. decline of consensus around core values
    b. belief in the inevitability of progress
    c. respect for authority
    d. homogeneity
    e. All of the above.

11. Bureaucracies exemplify _____, because of their level of institutional efficiency towards clear goals.
    a. consumerism
    b. postmodernism
    c. modernism
    d. rationality
    e. rites of passage

12. The idea that experience, thought, and language interacts is know as the:
    a. Sapir-Whorf thesis.
    b. cultural lag.
    c. abstraction.
    d. rationalization.
    e. None of the above.

13. _____ is a number of people who interact, usually in a defined territory, and share a _____.
    a. Culture; society
    b. Material culture; nonmaterial culture
    c. Symbols; language
    d. Society; culture
    e. Language; symbols

14. Which is the best sociological definition of language?
    a. A system of symbols strung together to communicate thought
    b. A means of communication biologically wired into our brains
    c. The biologically rooted human potential to communicate
    d. The vocal sounds that come out of our mouths as we speak
    e. None of the above.

15. American Indian sovereignty movements are examples of:
    a. rites of passage.
    b. material culture.
    c. rights revolution.
    d. taming a subcultural revolt.
    e. None of the above.

16. While _____ culture is consumed mainly by upper classes, _____ culture is consumed by all classes.
    a. popular; mass
    b. mass; popular
    c. mass; high
    d. high; mass
    e. popular; high

17. Based on the Sapir-Whorf Thesis model displayed in Chapter 2, which process comes second?
    a. conceptualization
    b. experience
    c. verbalization
    d. All of the above.
    e. None of the above.

18. A sociological view of cow worship in India might suggest that this practice is:
    a. bizarre.
    b. irrational.
    c. consumeristic.
    d. taming of subcultural revolt.
    e. rational.

19. The idea of globalization first gained prominence in marketing strategies in the:
    a. 1950s
    b. 1960s
    c. 1970s
    d. 1980s
    e. 1990s

20. Of the 216 countries, more than _____ of them lists English as an official or majority language.
    a. one half
    b. one third
    c. 75%
    d. one fourth
    e. 90%

21. In 2002, English usage accounted for _____ of languages used on the Internet.
    a. 25.5%
    b. 36.5%
    c. 75.5%
    d. 85.5%
    e. 15.5%

True False

1. Cooperation is the sum of sanctions in society.

   TRUE or FALSE

2. Due to technological innovation, industrialization lessened the fragmentation of culture.

   TRUE or FALSE

3. The fact that excessive consumption helps protect the environment is a function of consumerism.

   TRUE or FALSE

4. As the variety of jobs grew and the new political movements evolved, industrialization further fragmented culture.

   TRUE or FALSE

5. The need for educational curricula to reflect a more balanced story of America's inventors is an example of multiculturalism.

   TRUE or FALSE

6. Ethnocentrism is the belief that all cultures have equal value.

   TRUE or FALSE

7. Judging an ethnic group on the basis of its own cultural standards is an example of cultural relativism.

   TRUE or FALSE

8. Cultural diversity highlights the idea of culture as constraint.

   TRUE or FALSE

9. Norms are examples of material culture.

   TRUE or FALSE

10. Symbols are core elements of any culture.

    TRUE or FALSE

11. The United States continues to diversify culturally.

    TRUE or FALSE

12. A hallmark of postmodernism is the combining of cultural elements from different times.

    TRUE or FALSE

Short Answer

1. How does culture in general help you solve real-life problems? Identify three specific examples of functions of culture in your personal life. (p. 37-42)

    _____

    _____

2. List and define three main tools in human cultural survival kits. (p. 37-42)

    _____

    _____

3. Briefly explain the relationship between multiculturalism and cultural relativism. (p. 45-46)

    _____

    _____

4. List and describe two dysfunctions of consumerism. (p. 58).

    _____

    _____

5. Define Max Weber's notion of "rationalization." (p. 58)

    _____

    _____

Essay Questions

1. Explain the dysfunctional aspect of consumerism as obstacles of freedom in the case of Ozzy Osbourne. (p. 58-61)

2. Explain the impact of globalization on the ever-increasing cultural fragmentation of societies. (p. 48-53)

3. Explain the context of postmodern culture in terms of increasing individual freedom. Ironically, postmodern culture also places new constraints on contemporary culture. Contrast the idea of postmodern culture as a constraint versus freedom. (p. 48-53)

4. Explain how rationalization constrains culture by describing its relationship to time. (p. 58-60)

Solutions

Practice Tests

Fill-In-The-Blank

1. social control
2. Consumerism
3. language
4. Society

5. multiculturalism
6. Culture
7. rites of passage
8. Ethnocentrism

9. cultural relativism
10. rights revolution

Multiple-Choice Questions

1. E, (p. 37-38)
2. D, (p. 38-40)
3. E, (p. 40)
4. D, (p. 42-46)
5. C, (p. 42)
6. E, (p. 45)
7. A, (p. 48)

8. A, (p. 49)
9. E, (p. 48-54)
10. A, (p. 49)
11. D, (p. 58)
12. A, (p. 41)
13. D, (p. 37-38)
14. A, (p. 41)

15. C, (p. 46)
16. D, (p. 37)
17. A, (p. 41)
18. E, (p. 42)
19. C, (p. 48-49)
20. D, (p. 50)
21. B, (p. 50)

True False

1. F, (p. 39)
2. F, (p. 42-54)
3. F, (p. 58)
4. T, (p. 42-54)

5. T, (p. 45)
6. F, (p. 42)
7. T, (p. 46)
8. F, (p. 54-61)

9. F, (p. 39)
10. T, (p. 39)
11. T, (p. 44-54)
12. T, (p. 49)

SOCIALIZATION

Student Learning Objectives

After reading Chapter 3, you should be able to:

1. Understand the importance of socialization on the development of our human potentials and self-identity.

2. Compare and contrast the theoretical perspectives of Freud, Cooley, Mead, and Gilligan in terms of their contributions to our understanding of socialization.

3. Describe the significance of the family, schools, peer groups and the mass media as agents of socialization.

4. Explain the necessity of adult socialization.

5. Discuss the contradictory lessons among the agents of socialization that make childhood and adolescence more ambivalent and stressful today.

6. Explain the process of resocialization in the context of initiation rites and total institutions.

7. Describe the social factors that contribute to the fact that people's identities change faster, more often, and more completely, - and explain why the self has become more flexible.

8. Describe historical transformations of childhood and adolescence since the emergence of childhood as a distinct stage of socialization today.

9. Describe current dilemmas and problems for childhood and adolescent socialization today as a result of declining parental supervision, increasing adult responsibilities by youth, and declining participation in extracurricular activities.

Key Terms

(defined on the indicated pages of the textbook, and in glossary)

socialization (66)

roles (66)

self (68)

id (68)

superego (68)

ego (68)

unconscious (68)

looking glass self (69)

I (70)

me (70)

significant others (70)

generalized other (70)

primary socialization (71)

secondary socialization (72)

hidden curriculum (72)

self-fulfilling prophesies (74)

Thomas theorem (74)

peer groups (75)

status (75)

self-socialization (77)

gender roles (78)

resocialization (79)

initiation rite (79)

total institutions (79)

anticipatory socialization (81)

virtual communities (83)

Detailed Chapter Outline

I. SOCIAL ISOLATION AND THE CRYSTALIZATION OF SELF-IDENTITY

   A. Cases of socially isolated children suggest that the ability to learn culture and become human is only a potential. Socialization enables human potentials to be actualized.

   B. **Socialization** is the process by which people learn their culture (norms, values, and roles) and become aware of themselves as they interact with others.

   C. A **role** is the behavior expected of a person occupying a particular position in society.

   D. Socialization is also a life long process by which people develop a sense of self.

   E. Adolescence is a particularly crucial stage of the crystallization of self-identity, for "the central growth process in adolescence is to define the self through the clarification of experience and to establish self-esteem."

   F. In various institutional settings of socialization, referred to as "agents of socialization," we learn to control our impulses, think of ourselves as members of different groups, value certain ideals, and perform various roles.

II. THEORIES OF CHILDHOOD SOCIALIZATION

   A. Freud
      1. Main sociological contribution – the self emerges during early social interaction and early childhood experience exerts a lasting impact on personality development.
      2. Although infants initially are driven by elemental needs and gratifications, social interaction enables them to begin developing a self-image or sense of **self** – a set of ideas and attitudes about who they are as independent beings.
      3. Freud proposed the first social-scientific interpretation of self-emergence.
      4. Three parts of self:
         a. **Id** is the part of self that demands immediate gratification. Self-image emerges as soon as the id's demands are denied.

      b. **Superego** is the personal conscience, a moral sense of right and wrong and appropriate behavior.

      c. The **Ego**, in well-adjusted individuals, balances the conflicting needs of the pleasure-seeking id and the restraining superego.

5. The superego is a frustrating and painful process of repressed memories of denying the id, referred to as the **unconscious**.

6. Three criticisms of Freud:

      a. The connections between early childhood development and adult personality are more complex than Freud assumed.

      b. Many sociologists criticize Freud for gender bias in his analysis of male and female sexuality.

      c. Sociologists often criticize Freud for neglecting socialization after childhood.

B. Cooley

1. American sociologist, Charles Horton Cooley, introduced the idea of the "**looking glass self**." Like our physical body reflected in a mirror, we see our social selves reflected in people's gestures and reactions to us.

      a. When we interact with others, they gesture and react to us.

      b. This allows us to imagine how we appear to them.

      c. We judge how others evaluate us.

      d. From these judgments, we develop a **self-concept** (a set of feelings and ideas about who we are).

C. Mead

1. George Herbert Mead expanded Charles Horton Cooley's idea of the *looking glass self*, which suggests that our feelings about who we are depend on how we see ourselves judged by others.

2. Like Freud, Mead:

      a. Noted the presence of a subjective and impulsive aspect of self from birth, called the **"I"**.

      b. Highlighted importance of social interaction.

      c. Argued that an objective repository of culturally approved standards emerges as part of the self, referred to as the **"me"**.

3. Unlike Freud, Mead:

      a. Focused on the need to see yourself objectively – the *"me"*.

      b. Emphasized the unique human capacity to *take the role of the other* (seeing yourself from the points of view of other people) as the source of the *"me,"* and hence the self (in contrast to Freud's focus on the denial of the id's impulses).

      c. Argued that the self emerges from people using symbols, gradually during social interaction (not traumatic as Freud's ideas).

4. Four stages of role-taking:

      a. Children learn to use language and other symbols by *imitating* **significant others**, important people in their lives.

      b. Children use their imaginations to pretend and *role-play* in childhood games like "house," "school," and "doctor."

    c. Children learn to play complex games requiring simultaneous role taking with several other people called the **generalized other**, which involves the application of cultural standards to the self.

  D. Gilligan

    1. Carol Gilligan, likewise, emphasized the sociological foundations of moral development.

    2. She attributed differences in the moral development of boys and girls to the different cultural standards parents and teachers pass on to them.

III. AGENTS OF SOCIALIZATION

  A. The Family

    1. The family is the most important agent of **primary socialization**, which is the process of mastering the basic skills required to function in society during childhood.

    2. Characteristics of the family as an agent of socialization:

      a. Small group

      b. Frequent face-to-face contact

      c. High motivation of parents to care for children.

    3. The socialization function of the family was more pronounced in preindustrial societies, for many of its functions are performed by other institutions like schools and religion.

  B. Schools

    1. Public schools emerged in response to the need for better trained and educated employees by American industry

    2. Responsible for **secondary socialization**, or socialization outside the family after childhood.

    3. In addition to the more obvious role of schools to instruct students in academic and vocational subjects, a **hidden curriculum** teaches students what will be expected of them in the larger society after graduation (to be "good citizens," punctuality, respect for authority, the importance of competition). Many students of poor and racial minority families reject school authorities because they are skeptical about the school's ability to open job opportunities.

    4. **Self-fulfilling prophecies**, expectations that help cause what it predicts, can occur in terms of students' beliefs that school does not lead to economic success; and in terms of teachers' expectations of students.

    5. W.I. Thomas and Dorothy Swaine Thomas had a similar idea known as the **Thomas theorem** – "Situations we define as real become real in their consequences."

  C. Peer Groups

    1. **Peer groups** consist of individuals who are not necessarily friends but are about the same age and of similar status. **Status** refers to a recognized social position that an individual can occupy.

    2. Especially influential over lifestyle issues and the formation of an independent identity.

    3. Peer group values are often in conflict with values of the family, but families tend to be more influential and enduring.

    4. Peer groups nonetheless help integrate youth into the larger society.

D. The Mass Media

   1. The mass media include television, radio, movies, videos, CDs, audio tapes, newspapers, magazines, books, and the Internet.

   2. Used for stimulation and entertainment.

   3. Allows adolescents to engage in **self-socialization**, the choosing of socialization influences from the wide variety of mass media offerings.

   4. People tend to choose media influences that are most widespread, fit cultural standards, and are made appealing by those who control mass media. In other words, not all media influences are created equal.

     a. For example, the social construction of **gender roles** involves widely shared expectations about how males and females are supposed to act.

     b. Boys and girls, however, do not passively accept gendered messages, but often interpret them in unique ways and resist them.

E. Resocialization and Total Institutions

   1. **Resocialization** occurs when powerful socializing agents deliberately cause rapid change in people's values, roles, and self-conceptions, sometimes against their will.

     a. Example: staged **initiation rite** ceremonies signify the transition of the individual from one group to another and ensures his or her loyalty to the new group (i.e. fraternity, sorority, the marines, religious order).

     b. Three-stage ceremony:

       i. *Ritual rejection* involves separation from one's old status and identity.

       ii. *Ritual death* involves degradation, disorientation, and stress.

       iii. *Ritual rebirth* is the acceptance of the new group culture and status.

     c. **Total institutions** are settings where much resocialization occurs, and where people are isolated from the larger society and under the strict control and constant supervisions of a specialized staff.

     d. Example: Palo Alto experiment of a mock prison.

IV. ADULT SOCIALIZATION THROUGH THE LIFE COURSE

A. Adult socialization is necessary for four main reasons:

   1. Some adults are unpredictable.

     a. To learn a predictable new role, we typically engage in **anticipatory socialization**, which involves beginning to take on the norms and behaviors of the role to which we aspire.

   2. Adults change as we mature.

V. THE FLEXIBLE SELF

A. Older sociological perspectives on adult socialization underestimate the flexibility of the self, for today people's identities change faster, more often, and more completely.

B. Factors that contribute to the growing flexibility of the self:

   1. Globalization

2. Growing ability to change our bodies and hence our self-conception (i.e. bodybuilding, aerobic exercise, weight reduction, plastic surgery, sex-change operations, organ transplants, and whole-body transplants).
3. Growth of the Internet and **virtual communities**.

VI. THE DILEMMAS OF CHILDHOOD AND ADOLESCENT SOCIALIZATION

  A. The Emergence of Childhood and Adolescence
    1. In preindustrial societies:
      a. Children are perceived as small adults;
      b. Children are put to work as soon as they can contribute to the family;
      c. Achievement of adulthood is common by the age of 15 or 16.
    2. In the late 1600s, the idea of childhood as a distinct stage of life emerged among well-to-do Europeans and North Americans, who thought that boys should be allowed to play games and receive an education that would allow them to develop emotionally, physically and intellectually. Girls continued to be viewed as "little women."
    3. As we moved into the 20th century, social necessity and possibility influenced the emergence of the idea of childhood.
      a. Prolonged childhood was *necessary* in societies that required better educated adults to do complex work, because children needed a chance to prepare for adult life.
      b. Prolonged childhood was *possible* where improved hygiene and nutrition increased the human lifespan, which is more common in wealthier and more complex societies.

  B. Problems of Childhood and Adolescent Socialization Today
    1. The experience and meaning of childhood and adolescence seem to be changing radically today. Some analysts wonder if childhood and adolescence is disappearing.
    2. New developments are changing and creating problems for childhood and adolescence.
      a. Declining adult supervision and guidance.
      b. Increasing media influence.
      c. Declining extracurricular activities and increasing adult responsibilities.

Study Activity: Applying The Sociological Compass

Think about your experiences as a child, and consider how your childhood was different from your parents' (or guardian figure's) childhood. Contrast your childhood with your parents' (or guardian figure's) childhood by listing the social constraints you faced, and the new freedoms you enjoyed. List some of the social sources for the constraints and freedoms of your childhood. List the contradictions and problems of these "new" constraints and freedoms.

Be mindful of how your experiences affect (or will affect) the way you socialize your children. If you do not plan on having children, think about how you might socialize children you might be in contact with in the future (i.e. nieces and nephews, children in your work setting, etc.).

Childhood Social Constraints

Parent's/Guardian's constraints:

1.

2.

3.

4.

Your constraints:

1.

2.

3.

4.

Childhood Social Freedoms

Parent's/Guardian's freedoms:

1.

2.

3.

4.

Your freedoms:

1.

2.

3.

4.

Social Sources of Your Constraints and Freedoms

1.

2.

3.

4.

Social Problems Associated with Your Constraints and Freedoms

1.

2.

3.

4.

How might your childhood experiences affect how you socialize your children, or the children you may be in contact with?

Infotrac College Edition Online Exercises

For the following exercises, log on to the online library of InfoTrac College Edition at http://www.infotrac-college.com/. Make note that InfoTrac has implemented a new registration system that will allow easier access to InfoTrac through the use of a personalized username and password.

Once you've created your username and password you may proceed directly to the Log On page. To create an account, register your passcode packaged with your textbook, and create a username and password, by following the online prompt. After you are logged in, click on "Infotrac College Edition." You will arrive at a screen that enables you to search topics.

Keyword: **adolescence**. Identify and read at least four articles that discuss problems adolescence face today. Read the articles and compile a list of adolescent problems, and a list of good advice that might be useful to you personally.

Keyword: **hidden curriculum**. The education system is one of the agents of socialization. What role does the hidden curriculum play in the socialization process of humans? What role has the hidden curriculum played in your individual development?

Keyword: **cyber-language**. Cyber-language is an emerging language. Look for articles that deal with the impact of cyber-language in our society. What role do you think cyber-language will have on our socialization process?

Keyword: **sociobiology**. Look for articles that discuss the strengths and weaknesses of this argument. Read the articles and compile a list of the strengths and weaknesses of sociobiology.

After reading the evidence presented discuss if you personally think the sociological argument is valid.

Keyword: **cliques**. Look for articles that discuss the role of cliques in adolescent socialization.

What does your research conclude about the role of cliques in adolescent socialization? Explain how cliques would be viewed from the Marx perspective.

Keyword: **emotions**. Look for research on emotions from a global perspective. Find articles that deal with emotions from different cultural perspectives. For example, do some cultures not express emotion publicly?

Keyword: **symbols**. Look for articles that discuss how symbols are a part of the socialization process. Read the articles and compile a list of the ways symbols are part of the socialization process. Do symbols vary from culture to culture in the socialization process?

Internet Exercises

Read what the University of Minnesota's intellectual resources on issues important to children, youth and families are. Go to http://www1.umn.edu/pres/cyf.html. This is a report prepared by the President's Initiative on Children, Youth and Families. It discusses important concerns in socialization. What key ideas do they suggest for sharing intellectual resources with children and families?

What impact has the National Vietnam Memorial had on American society? For a look at its impact link to http://www.saed.kent.edu/Architronic/v2n2/v2n2.05.html

and read the article titled *Ritual and Monument*. Make a list of 5 ways that this memorial has impacted American society.

The Boy Scouts of America and Girl Scouts of America are an important agent of socialization for many boys and girls in American society. Go to their respective websites for their views on socialization. http://www.bsa.scouting.org/ and http://www.girlscouts.org/

Compare and contrast the purpose of each organization, their sponsors, and where they receive their funding.

Go to http://www.nbcdi.org/ which is the web site of The National Black Child Development Institute (NBCDI). Their mission statement states they exist "to improve and protect the quality and life of African American children and their families." Look over the web site and discuss what you learn about socialization in a short paragraph.

Practice Tests

Fill-In-The-Blank

Fill in the blank with the appropriate term from the above list of "key terms."

1. _____ occurs when powerful socializing agents deliberately cause rapid change in people's values, roles, and self-conceptions, sometime against their will.

2. Socialization outside the family after childhood is referred to as _____ .

3. _____ is the process by which people learn their culture, and become aware of themselves as they interact with others.

4. According to Freud, the _____ is the personal conscience that provides a moral sense of right and wrong.

5. According to Mead, the presence of a subjective and impulsive aspect of self from birth is referred to as _____ .

6. _____ is a set of feelings and ideas about who we are.

7. Based on Mead's first stage of role-taking, children learn by imitating _____ .

8. _____ refers to a recognized social position that an individual can occupy.

9. To learn a predictable new role, individuals engage in _____ , which involves the process of beginning to take on the norms and behaviors of the role to which one aspires.

10. _____ are settings where much resocialization occurs, whereby people are isolated from the larger society under strict control.

Multiple-Choice Questions

Select the response that best answers the question or completes the statement:

1. Cases of extremely socially isolated children described in the book, suggest that:
   a. we are born with our self-conceptions.
   b. the ability to learn culture and become human is only a potential.
   c. we are fully human at birth.
   d. the ability to use culture can develop in social isolation.
   e. All of the above.

2. Self-identity crystallizes:
   a. during early childhood.
   b. at birth.
   c. during old age.
   d. during adolescence.
   e. None of the above.

3. Institutional settings of socialization are referred to as:
   a. socialization encounters.
   b. interaction settings..
   c. back-stage socialization regions
   d. agents of socialization.
   e. None of the above.

4. _____ are expected behaviors of a person occupying a particular position in society.
   a. Roles
   b. Self-socialization
   c. Sanctions
   d. Self-conceptions
   e. Self-fulfilling prophecies

5. Which theorist proposed the first social-scientific interpretation of self-emergence?
   a. Freud
   b. Mead
   c. Piaget
   d. Kohlberg
   e. Vygotsky

6. According to Mead, children learn to apply cultural standards when they:
   a. learn to role-take with the generalized other.
   b. imitate significant others.
   c. first use their imaginations to role-play.
   d. first acquire the use of language.
   e. All of the above.

7. The _____ is the part of the self that demands immediate gratification, according to Freud.
   a. id
   b. ego
   c. superego
   d. me
   e. None of the above

8. Which is a criticism of Freud?
    a. The connections between early childhood development and adult personality are more complex than Freud assumed.
    b. Freud is criticized for gender bias in his analysis of male and female sexuality.
    c. Freud is criticized for neglecting socialization after childhood.
    d. All of the above.
    e. None of the above.

9. Which concept is an expansion of Cooley's idea of the "looking-glass self?"
    a. superego
    b. unconscious
    c. cognitive development
    d. moral reasoning
    e. None of the above.

10. The ability of us to see ourselves objectively involves:
    a. the development of the self.
    b. the "me."
    c. taking the role of the other.
    d. All of the above.
    e. None of the above.

11. The _____ is the most important agent of primary socialization.
    a. family
    b. schools
    c. peer groups
    d. mass media
    e. All of the above.

12. Which is a characteristic of the family as an agent of socialization?
    a. small group
    b. frequent face-to-face interaction
    c. high motivation of parents to care for children
    d. enduring influence on individuals over time
    e. All of the above.

13. Which is an expectation that helps cause what it predicts?
    a. primary socialization
    b. secondary socialization
    c. tertiary socialization
    d. self-fulfilling prophecy
    e. self-socialization

14. _____ is a latent function of schools, because it teaches what will be expected of individuals in the larger society after graduation.
    a. The hidden curriculum
    b. The Thomas theorem
    c. Self-socialization
    d. None of the above.
    e. All of the above.

15. The Palo Alto experiment described in the book is an example of:
    a. virtual communities
    b. initiation rites
    c. the hidden curriculum
    d. total institutions
    e. None of the above

16. Which is NOT one of the stages of resocialization ceremonies?
    a. ritual rejection
    b. ritual death
    c. ritual rebirth
    d. ritual connection
    e. All of the above are stages of resocialization ceremonies.

17. Which agent of socialization is most influential and long-lasting to individuals?
    a. family
    b. schools
    c. peer groups
    d. mass media
    e. team sports

18. Which is a factor that contributes to the growing flexibility of the self?
    a. globalization
    b. growth of the domestic economy
    c. declining adult supervision
    d. All of the above.
    e. None of the above.

19. The research of Harry and Margaret Harlow on monkeys concluded that:
    a. emotional development requires affectionate cradling.
    b. baby monkeys raised with an artificial mother made of wire mesh without a soft cover were later unable to interact normally with other monkeys.
    c. when baby monkeys interacted with an artificial mother covered with a soft terry cloth, they revealed less emotional distress.
    d. All of the above.
    e. None of the above.

20. Carol Gilligan has made a major sociological contribution to our understanding of:
    a. childhood development.
    b. internal conversation.
    c. the interplay between the "I" and the "me."
    d. total institutions.
    e. extreme isolation.

21. Which occupational sector do adolescents prefer?
    a. Service including food, cleaning, and personal.
    b. Teachers, counselors, librarians, social workers, and religious workers.
    c. Lawyers and judges.
    d. Engineers, architects, natural and social scientists.
    e. Sales.

22. Sociological research has shown that gender segregation during schoolyard play:
    a. no longer exists in the United States.
    b. has been erased since the Women's Movement in the United States.
    c. has long existed in U.S. schools.
    d. All of the above.
    e. None of the above.

23. According to the U.S. Department of Health and Human Services, which substance used by Americans age 12-17 showed the sharpest decline in percentage between 1990 and 1997?
    a. Cocaine
    b. Marijuana
    c. Alcohol
    d. Cigarettes
    e. None of the above.

24. Which school age cohort spent the greatest number of hours watching television per day in 2000?
    a. Students with 0-11 years of schooling.
    b. Students with 12 years of schooling.
    c. Students with 13-14 years of schooling.
    d. Students with 15-16 years of schooling.
    e. Students with 17-20 years of schooling.

25. Which was the top waking activity for American women and men ages 18-24 from 1993 to 1995?
    a. television
    b. school
    c. visiting
    d. travel
    e. All of the above.

True False

1. Socialization is a process that ends at adulthood.

   TRUE or FALSE

2. According to Mead, the "me" is an objective repository of culturally approved standards that emerges as part of the self.

   TRUE or FALSE

3. Primary socialization occurs outside the family after childhood.

   TRUE or FALSE

4. Self-socialization occurs when powerful socializing agents deliberately cause rapid change in people's values, roles, and self-conceptions, some against their will.

   TRUE or FALSE

5. Public schools emerged in response to the need for better-trained and educated employees by American industry.

   TRUE or FALSE

6. In the late 1600s, the idea of childhood as a distinct stage of life emerged among both the rich and poor, and for boys and girls.

   TRUE or FALSE

7. Improved hygiene and nutrition played a role in the emergence of the idea of childhood in the 20th century.

   TRUE or FALSE

8. Children were viewed as small adults during a significant part of human history.

   TRUE or FALSE

9. Although it was believed in the 1600s that boys should be allowed to play games and receive an education that would allow them to develop emotionally, physically and intellectually, girls continued to be treated as "little women."

   TRUE or FALSE

Short Answer

1. Provide an example of a self-fulfilling prophecy in schooling that illustrates the Thomas theorem. (p. 74)

    _____

    _____

2. How does mass media allow adolescents to engage in self-socialization? (p. 76)

    _____

    _____

3. List three factors that contribute to the growing flexibility of the self. (p. 68)

    _____

    _____

4. Explain the difference between primary and secondary socialization. (p.71-72)

    _____

    _____

Essay Questions

1. Describe the central historical factors that led to the notion of childhood as a unique stage of socialization. (p. 83-84)

2. Some social scientists wonder if childhood and adolescence are disappearing today. Explain the rationale of this position by discussing the current sources of problems and dilemmas associated with childhood and adolescence. (p. 82-86)

3. Compare and contrast Freud and Mead's theories of the "self." How is Mead's theory more sociological? (p. 68-70)

Solutions

Practice Tests

Fill-In-The-Blank

1. Resocialization
2. secondary socialization
3. Socialization
4. superego
5. the "I"
6. Self-concept
7. significant others
8. Status
9. anticipatory socialization
10. Total institutions

Multiple-Choice Questions

1. B, (p. 65-66)
2. D, (p. 66-67)
3. D, (p. 71)
4. A, (p. 66)
5. A, (p. 68)
6. A, (p. 70)
7. A, (p. 68)
8. D, (p. 69)
9. E, (p. 69)
10. D, (p. 70)
11. A, (p. 71)
12. E, (p. 71)
13. D, (p. 74)
14. A, (p. 72)
15. D, (p. 79)
16. D, (p. 79-80)
17. A, (p. 71)
18. A, (p. 80-87)
19. D, (p. 66)
20. A, (p. 70-71)
21. D, (p. 74)
22. C, (p. 78)
23. C, (p. 76)
24. B, (p. 78)
25. A, (p. 77)

True False

1. F, (p. 66)
2. T, (p. 70)
3. F, (p. 71)
4. F, (p. 77)
5. T, (p. 72)
6. F, (p. 83)
7. T, (p. 83-84)
8. T, (p. 83-84)
9. T, (p. 83-84)

SOCIAL INTERACTION

Student Learning Objectives

After reading Chapter 4, you should be able to:

1. Explain the fundamental processes and concepts of social interaction.

2. Describe the historical context of emotions, and the role of emotions in social interaction in terms of emotion management and emotion labor.

3. Identify and explain the three modes of interaction.

4. Describe the manipulative aspects of social interaction in terms of impression management.

5. Describe the role of verbal and nonverbal communication in the use and acquisition of language in a social and cultural context.

6. Explain the major points of interaction in terms of exchange/rational choice theory, symbolic interactionism, dramaturgical analysis, ethnomethodology, and conflict theory.

7. Discuss the ways of maintaining social interaction in the context of differential power.

8. Explain the relationship between micro-level interactions and higher-level structures.

Key Terms

(defined on the indicated pages of the textbook, and in glossary)

social interaction (91)   emotion management (98)

status set (92)   emotion labor (98)

ascribed status (92)   exchange theory (100)

achieved status (92)   rational choice theory (101)

roles (92)   dramaturgical analysis (102)

role conflict (94)   role distance (102)

role strain (94)   ethnomethodology (102)

Detailed Chapter Outline

I. WHAT IS SOCIAL INTERACTION?

    A. **Social interaction** involves people communicating face-to-face, acting and reacting in relation to each other, and is structured around statuses, roles, and norms.

        1. While *status* refers to recognized positions occupied by interacting people (i.e. flight attendants and passengers), a **status set** is the entire ensemble of statuses occupied by an individual (i.e. a flight attendant, a wife, and a mother at the same time. If a status is involuntary, it is an **ascribed status** (i.e. daughter). If it is involuntary, it is an **achieved status** (i.e. flight attendant). One's **master status** is the status that is most influential in shaping one's life over time.

        2. While people *occupy* statuses, they *perform* **roles**, which are sets of expected behaviors. A **role set** is a cluster of roles attached to a single status (i.e. in-flight safety expert and server).

        3. *Norms* are generally accepted ways of doing things that change over time. Some norms are *prescriptive*, whereby they suggest what a person is expected to do while performing a role. Other norms are *proscriptive*, whereby they suggest what a person is *not* to do.

    B. *The changing role of the stewardess.*

    C. *The enforcement of norms.*

        1. **Role conflict** occurs when two or more statuses held at the same time place contradictory role demands on a person.

        2. **Role strain** occurs when incompatible role demands are placed on a person in a single status.

    D. Change in status.

II. THE SOCIOLOGY OF EMOTIONS

    A. Laughter and Humor

        1. Robert Provine's research on laughing in public places.

            a. Speakers laugh more often than listeners do (79.8 percent vs. 54.7 percent).

            b. Women laugh more than men do, especially when the speaker is a woman, and the listener is a man.

        2. Laugher is unevenly distributed across the status hierarchy.

            a. People with higher status get more laughs, and people with lower status laugh more.

            b. When social interaction takes place between status equals, they often direct their humor at perceived social inferiors.

                i. For example, "put down" jokes have the effect of excluding outsiders, making you feel superior, and reinforcing group norms and the status hierarchy itself.

        3. Disadvantaged people often laugh at the privileged majority, and also laugh at themselves.

4. The more repressive a government, the more widespread are antigovernment jokes.
5. Sometimes, humor has a political edge, and sometimes humor has no political content; yet all jokes are "little revolutions" as remarked by George Orwell.
6. Sociologically, jokes enable us to see the structure of society that lies beneath our laughter, for they suddenly and momentarily let us see beyond the serious, taken-for-granted world.

B. Emotion Management
1. We *control* our emotions, for emotions don't just happen to us; we manage them.
2. When we manage our emotions, we tend to follow cultural "scripts."
3. Sociologist Arlie Hochschild is one of the leading figures in the study of what she coined **emotion management**, which involves people obeying "feeling rules" and responding appropriately to the situations they find themselves.

C. Emotion Labor
1. **Emotion labor** is emotion management that many people do as part of their job and for which they are paid, while emotion management is done by everyone in their personal life.
   a. Different occupations require different types of emotion labor (i.e. the flight attendant vs. the bill collector).
   b. Emotion labor become a commodity, while the emotional life of workers is increasingly governed by organizations, and is therefore less and less spontaneous and authentic.

D. Emotions in Historical Perspective
1. Feeling rules take different forms under different social conditions, which vary historically.
2. Three examples from social history of emotions.
   a. *Grief.*
   b. *Anger.*
   c. *Disgust.*

III. THREE MODES OF INTERACTION

A. Interaction as Competition and Exchange
1. Conversation and exchange:
   a. Conversation typically involves the *exchange* of attention, and can involve subtle competition for attention.
2. Exchange and Rational Choice Theories
   a. **Exchange theory** proposes that social interaction involves trade in valued resources.
   b. **Rational choice theory** is a variant of exchange theory that focuses less on the resources and more on the way interacting individuals weigh the benefits and costs of interaction.
   c. Types of interaction that cannot be explained in terms of exchange and rational choice theories.
      i. Altruistic and heroic acts.
      ii. When people behave altruistically, they interact on the basis of *norms* that say they should act justly and help others in need, despite the substantial costs of doing so.

B. Interaction as Symbolic
1. Dramaturgical Analysis

a. Haas and Shaffir's study of professional socialization.
b. *Impression management* is the process of manipulating the way people present themselves so they appear in the best possible light.
c. Three principles of *symbolic interactionism* according to Herbert Blumer:
    i. "Human beings act toward things on the basis of the meaning these things have for them."
    ii. "The meaning of a thing" emerges from the process of interaction.
    iii. "The use of meanings by the actors occurs through a process of interpretation."
d. **Dramaturgical analysis** is a distinct approach to symbolic interactionism first developed by Erving Goffman, which views social interaction as a sort of play in which people present themselves so as to appear in the best possible light.
    i. We are constantly engaged in *role-playing*, as most clearly evident when we are "front stage."
    ii. When backstage, people can relax, prepare and discuss the front stage with fellow actors.
e. If a role is stressful, we may engage in **role distancing**, which involves giving the impression that we are just "going through the motions" but actually lack serious commitment to a role.

2. Ethnomethodology
    a. **Ethnomethodology** is the study of the methods ordinary people use during everyday interaction, often unconsciously, to make sense of what others do and say.
    b. Everyday interaction could not take place without *pre-existing* shared norms and understandings.

3. Verbal and Nonverbal Communication
    a. Language is used in its *social and cultural context*. People are assisted in the task of learning the social and cultural contexts of language, and the meanings of words by *nonverbal* cues.

4. Facial Expressions, Gestures, and Body Language
    a. Social interaction involves a complex mix of verbal and nonverbal messages including facial expressions, gestures, body language, and manipulation of "personal space" or "intimate zones."
    b. *Cosmopolitan* example "How to reduce otherwise evolved men to drooling, panting fools."

5. Status Cues
    a. **Status cues** are a type of nonverbal communication that involves visual indicators of other people's social position.
    b. Example—Profiling strangers on the basis of skin color, age, gender, companions, clothing, jewelry, and objects to determine their "dangerousness."
    c. Status cues can degenerate into **stereotypes,** rigid views of how members of various groups act, regardless of whether individual group members really behave that way.

C. Power and Social Interaction
    1. Summary of four main points of interaction:
        a. Competitive exchange of valued resources is one of the most important forces that cement social interaction (exchange and rational choice theories).

b. We mold values, norms, roles, and statuses to suit us as we interact with others (symbolic interactionism and dramaturgical analysis).

c. Norms do not necessarily emerge spontaneously during interaction, for in general form they exist before any given interaction takes place (ethnomethodology).

d. Nonverbal mechanisms of communication facilitate interaction.

2. A Fifth Point: Power

    a. **Conflict theories of social interaction** emphasize that when people interact, their statuses are often arranged in a hierarchy, with those at the top enjoying more power.

    b. The degree of inequality affects the character of social interaction between the interacting parties.

    c. According to Weber, **power** is "the probability that one actor within a social relationship will be in a position to carry out his [or her] own will despite resistance." (male-female interaction).

3. Domination, Competition, and Cooperation

    a. **Domination** represents one extreme type of interaction, whereby nearly all power is concentrated in the hands of people of similar status while people of different status enjoy almost no power (i.e. guards vs. inmates, landowners vs. slaves in the antebellum South).

    b. **Cooperation** represents another extreme type of interaction whereby power is more or less equally distributed between people of different status, often based on feelings of trust (i.e. happy marriages where housework and child-care are shared).

    c. **Competition** a type of interaction between the two extremes whereby power is unequally distributed, but the degree of inequality is less that in systems of domination.

      i. Randall Collins' work on cooperative work environments.

IV. BIG STRUCTURES AND SMALL PROCESSES

A. It is within small structures where individuals interpret, negotiate, and modify their surrounding social settings. This, in turn, gives big structures their dynamism and their life.

Study Activity: Applying the Sociological Compass

As you interact in your natural everyday settings, such as at work, at school, shopping at the mall, etc., pay close attention to your interaction experiences with others, and take notes on your observations. You may recall from Chapter 1 that what you will engage in is an example of participant observation research. In so doing, accomplish the following tasks:

Based on your observations and interpretations, make a list of examples of

Emotion labor:

1.

2.

3.

Impression management:

1.

2.

3.

Status cues:

1.

2.

3.

Additionally during your everyday interactions, behave quite a bit nicer and more giving than usual. Perhaps, offer to help someone with a task, offer your place in line, offer your parking space on campus during rush hour, give a nice complement, and so forth. In other words, engage in altruistic behavior beyond the perceived norms. Behave very nicely and give without expecting anything in return, to the point of "disrupting" the situational norms, despite how people act around you. Make a list of reactions of people to your altruistic acts, as you keep in mind the principles of *ethnomethodology*. In other words, breach interaction by behaving overly altruistic, and list your observations of how others react to you.

1.

2.

3.

4.

Finally, make a list of explanations for: a) the reasons behind others' *frontstage* behaviors, and the reactions of people to your altruistic acts. Base you explanations on any relevant theories and concepts from Chapter 4.

Front stage behaviors?

1.

2.

3.

Reactions to altruism?

1.

2.

3.

InfoTrac College Edition Online Exercises

For the following exercises, log on to the online library of InfoTrac College Edition at http://www.infotrac-college.com/. Make note that InfoTrac has implemented a new registration system that will allow easier access to InfoTrac through the use of a personalized username and password.

Once you've created your username and password you may proceed directly to the Log On page. To create an account, register your passcode packaged with your textbook, and create a username and password, by following the online prompt. After you are logged in, click on "Infotrac College Edition." You will arrive at a screen that enables you to search topics.

Keyword: **dramaturgical analysis**. How is dramaturgical analysis used in research by sociologists? Compile a list of at least 5 ways that sociologists use this approach.

Keywords: **exchange theory** and **rational choice theory**. Identify and read at least 4 articles that provide research findings from an exchange or rational choice perspective. Read the articles and compile a list of evidence in support of the major principles of exchange and rational choice theories, and a list of criticisms.

Keyword: **community service**. Look for articles on how service learning is related to the community at large? What information do these articles bring to light about the interaction between the individual and the larger society?

Internet Exercises

For a choice example of cyberspace social interaction go to The MUD Connector at http://www.mudconnect.com/

How is cyberspace social interaction different from face-to-face interaction?

Visit the Society of Social Interaction Web site at http://sun.soci.niu.edu/~sssi. This is a professional organization for sociologists who study social interaction. Search their web site and compile a list of 10 things that you learned.

To become aware of the emotional and sociological implications of social interaction on the Internet go to: http://www.levity.com/julian/bungle.html and read the article "A Rape in Cyberspace," by Julian Dibbell. Make a list of the emotional and sociological implications of social interaction that Dibbell proposes.

Practice Tests

Fill-In-The-Blank

Fill in the blank with the appropriate term from the above list of "key terms."

1. A(An) _____ is the entire ensemble of statuses occupied by an individual.

2. One's _____ is the most influential status in shaping one's life over time.

3. _____ is a behavior people engage in as part of their job.

4. _____ proposes that social interaction involves trade in valued resources.

5. The process of manipulating the way people present themselves so they appear in the most favorable light is referred to as _____ .

6. _____ is a distinct approach to symbolic interactionism first developed by Erving Goffman, which views social interaction like a theatrical performance.

7. If a role is stressful, we may engage in _____ , which involves giving the impression that we are just "going through the motions" but actually lack serious commitment to the role.

8. _____ represents one extreme type of interaction, whereby nearly all power is concentrated in the hands of people of similar high powered status.

9. _____ involves people communicating face-to-face, acting and reacting in relation to each other.

Multiple-Choice Questions

Select the response that best answers the question or completes the statement:

1. Interacting individuals:
   a. tend to conform to specific norms.
   b. act according to role expectations.
   c. assume a certain status.
   d. None of the above.
   e. All of the above.

2. Role conflict occurs when:
   a. two or more statuses held at the same time place contradictory role demands on an individual.
   b. incompatible role demands are placed on a person in a single status.
   c. individuals have difficulty with frontstage impression management.
   d. individuals are incapable of role distancing.
   e. All of the above.

3. Which is NOT a characteristic of interaction according to Goffman's dramaturgical analysis?
   a. We are constantly engaged in role-playing during frontstage interaction.
   b. People can relax in the backstage.
   c. We become aware of our public roles and our "true" selves.
   d. Interaction involves a trade in valued resources.
   e. We engage in role-distance during interaction.

4. _____ focuses less on resources and more on the way interacting individuals weigh the benefits and costs of interaction.
   a. Psychoanalytic theory
   b. Rational choice theory
   c. Symbolic interactionism
   d. Dramaturgical analysis
   e. Ethnomethodology

5. Which type of interaction can NOT be explained in terms of exchange or rational choice theory?
   a. altruism
   b. heroic acts
   c. a conversation between individuals competing for attention
   d. All of the above.
   e. a and b

6. Status cues can degenerate into _____ as in the example of racial profiling.
   a. role distance
   b. impression management
   c. backstage behavior
   d. stereotypes
   e. cooperation
   f. theorists

7. A _____ is a type of nonverbal communication that involves visual indicators of other people's social position.
   a. role distance
   b. social category
   c. social role
   d. status cue
   e. backstage status

8. Which type of status do we assume involuntarily?
    a. Occupation status
    b. Achieved status
    c. Ascribed status
    d. Status conflict
    e. Status strain

9. Which term refers to a cluster of roles attached to a single status?
    a. Status set
    b. Status cluster
    c. Role achievement
    d. Role strain
    e. Role set

10. Who coined the term "emotion management"?
    a. Harold Garfinkel
    b. Erving Goffman
    c. Herbert Blumer
    d. Arlie Hochschild
    e. William Shaffir

11. Which is NOT one of the modes of interaction discussed in the Brym and Lie textbook?
    a. Interaction as internal meditation.
    b. Interaction as competition and exchange.
    c. Interaction as symbolic.
    d. Power and social interaction.
    e. All of the above are modes of interaction discussed in the Brym and Lie text.

12. Which of the following statements is true of the role and status of the airline stewardess of the 1950s to the late 1970s?
    a. Stewardesses were not considered sex objects as they are today.
    b. Stewardesses of the 1950s to the late 1970s made relatively high incomes compared to today.
    c. The role of the stewardess of the 1950s to the late 1970s was certainly glamorous.
    d. All of the above.
    e. None of the above.

13. Robert Provine's research on conversations of people laughing in public places, found that, in general:
    a. speakers laugh more often than listeners do.
    b. listeners laugh more often than speakers do.
    c. speakers and listeners spend about equal time laughing.
    d. All of the above.
    e. None of the above.

14. According to the Brym and Lie textbook, which is true about "put down" jokes?
    a. It excludes outsiders.
    b. It makes one feel superior.
    c. It reinforces group norms and the status hierarchy itself.
    d. All of the above.
    e. None of the above.

15. The emotional life of workers seems to be:
    a. more and more spontaneous.
    b. increasingly governed by the organizations they work for.
    c. more and more authentic.
    d. All of the above.
    e. None of the above.

16. Which is NOT one of the examples from the social history of emotions discussed in the Brym and Lie text?
    a. Grief
    b. Anger
    c. Disgust
    d. All of the above.
    e. None of the above.

17. Who state that, "Every joke is a tiny revolution?"
    a. Erving Goffman
    b. Arlie Hochschild
    c. George Orwell
    d. Albert Einstein
    e. Herbert Blumer

18. The multiple difficulty of meeting the role expectations associated with being a mother, flight attendant, and wife is an example of:
    a. role conflict.
    b. role strain.
    c. master status.
    d. status set.
    e. role set.

19. The contradictory roles of stewardesses to be suggestive on the one hand, yet polite on the other hand, is an example of:
    a. role conflict.
    b. role strain.
    c. master status.
    d. status set.
    e. role set.

20. According to Robert Provine's research, the biggest discrepancy in laughing occurs when:
    a. the speaker is a woman and the listener is a man.
    b. the speaker is a man, and the listener is man.
    c. the speaker has greater status than the listener.
    d. All of the above.
    e. None of the above.

21. The examples of Chris Rock's on stage jokes illustrated in the Brym and Lie textbook indicate that:
    a. disadvantaged people often laugh at the privileged majority.
    b. disadvantaged people laugh at themselves.
    c. although disadvantaged people often laugh at the privileged majority, they do not always do so.
    d. All of the above.
    e. None of the above.

22. Manners in Europe during the Middle Ages were:
    a. quite acceptable by U.S. standards today.
    b. utterly disgusting based on the social norms of the Middle Ages in general.
    c. utterly disgusting by U.S. standards today.
    d. All of the above.
    e. None of the above.

23. According to "Sociology at the Movies" in Chapter 4, Miss Congeniality is:
    a. an unsuccessful film because it fails to provide consumers with an entertaining escape from reality.
    b. an entertaining escape from reality's messiness.
    c. a poor guide to life as we actually live it.
    d. All of the above.
    e. Both 'B' and 'C'.

True False

1. Interaction as exchange especially emphasizes the use of methods to make sense of what others do and say by ordinary people during everyday interaction.

    TRUE or FALSE

2. A job interview is an example of the frontstage.

    TRUE or FALSE

3. Nonverbal mechanisms of communication facilitate interaction.

    TRUE or FALSE

4. The assumption that the use of meanings by the actors occurs through the process of interaction is a major principle of symbolic interactionism according to Harold Garfinkel.

    TRUE or FALSE

5. Dramaturgical analysis is a distinct approach to symbolic interactionism first developed by Herbert Blumer.

   TRUE or FALSE

6. Cooperation is a type of interaction whereby power is unequally distributed, but not to the degree as in a system of domination.

   TRUE or FALSE

7. From the late 1950s to the late 1970s, both the role and pay of stewardesses were glamorous.

   TRUE or FALSE

8. In social situations where people of different statuses interact, laughter is unevenly distributed across the status hierarchy.

   TRUE or FALSE

9. People of higher status tend to laugh more, while people with lower status get more laughs.

   TRUE or FALSE

10. Disadvantaged people often laugh at the privileged majority, but not always.

    TRUE or FALSE

11. We virtually have no control over our emotions, which is a trademark of human beings as emotional beings.

    TRUE or FALSE

12. Politicians should be well versed in the vocation of impression management because their success depend heavily on voter's opinions and perceptions of them.

    TRUE or FALSE

13. Body language is a rare mode of communication that does not reflect gender roles.

    TRUE or FALSE

14. In a relationship marked by cooperation, the imbalance of interpersonal power between superordinate persons and subordinate persons is greater than in relations of competition.

    TRUE or FALSE

15. Domination, as a mode of interaction, yields the highest level of inequality and highest level of efficiency.

    TRUE or FALSE

Short Answer

1. List and define three ways of maintaining social interaction in the context of power. (p. 108)

    _____

    _____

2. Describe examples of impression management, frontstage behavior, and back stage behavior. (p. 102)

    _____

    _____

3. What is the similarity and difference between the terms emotion management and emotion labor? (p. 97-98)

    _____

    _____

4. What is the difference between role conflict and role strain? Provide a brief example for each term. (p. 94)

    _____

    _____

5. Describe an example of role distancing. (p. 102)

    _____

    _____

Essay Questions

1. Compare and contrast exchange theory and dramaturgical analysis. (p.100-104)

2. Compare and contrast symbolic interactionism and ethnomethodology in terms of their respective views on the role of social norms during social interaction. (p.101-104)

3. Explain the cultural evolution of grief, anger, and disgust as examples of the social history of emotions. (p. 98-99)

4. Compare and contrast exchange theory and conflict theories of social interaction. (p. 100-104, 108-110)

Solutions

Practice Tests

Fill-In-The-Blank

1. status set
2. master status
3. Emotion labor

4. Exchange theory
5. impression management
6. Dramaturgical analysis

7. role distancing
8. Domination
9. Social interaction

Multiple-Choice Questions

1. E, (p. 92)
2. A, (p. 94)
3. D, (p. 102)
4. B, (p. 101)
5. E, (p. 100-101)
6. D, (p. 107)
7. D, (p. 106)
8. C, (p. 92)

9. E, (p. 92)
10. D, (p. 98)
11. A, (p. 99-109)
12. C, (p. 93)
13. A, (p. 95)
14. D, (p. 96)
15. B, (p. 98)
16. D, (p. 98-99)

17. C, (p. 97)
18. A, (p. 94)
19. B, (p. 94)
20. A, (p. 95-96)
21. D, (p. 96)
22. C, (p. 99)
23. E, (p. 103)

True False

1. F, (p. 99-101)
2. T, (p. 102)
3. T, (p. 104-106)
4. F, (p. 102-104)
5. F, (p. 102)

6. F, (p. 109)
7. F, (p. 93)
8. T, (p. 95-97)
9. F, (p. 95-97)
10. T, (p. 95-97)

11. F, (p. 97)
12. T, (p. 102)
13. F, (p. 105)
14. F, (p. 109)
15. F, (p. 109)

NETWORKS, GROUPS, AND ORGANIZATIONS

Student Learning Objectives

After reading Chapter 5, you should be able to:

1. Understand the influential role of networks, groups, and bureaucracies on individual behavior.

2. Describe the far-reaching connection between individuals through the dynamics of social networks.

3. Identify and discuss the building blocks of social networks.

4. Describe the range of social group experience.

5. Explain the power of conformity and "groupthink" in a social group context.

6. Discuss the group boundaries in terms of inclusion and exclusion.

7. Understand the human ability to interact with others in the imagination.

8. Describe the major sources of bureaucratic inefficiency from a sociological perspective.

9. Explain the importance of social networks to the operation of bureaucracies.

10. Discuss three types of leadership styles in terms of their effectiveness or lack thereof for bureaucracies.

11. Explain the influence of organizational environments on leadership characteristics and functions of bureaucratic organizations.

12. Explain the function of networks, groups, and organizations as foundations of constraint as well as sources of freedom.

Key Terms

(defined on the indicated pages of the textbook, and in glossary)

bureaucracy (119)   triad (124)

social network (120)   social groups (125)

dyad (124)   social categories (125) primary groups (125)

secondary groups (126)

groupthink (127)

in-group (128)

out-group (128)

reference groups (129)

formal organizations (130)

dehumanization (132)

bureaucratic ritualism (132)

oligarchy (132)

bureaucratic inertia (132)

laissez-faire leadership (135)

authoritarian leadership (135)

democratic leadership (135)

organizational environment (137)

Detailed Chapter Outline

I. BEYOND INDIVIDUAL MOTIVES

A. The Holocaust
1. The Experience of Robert Brym's Father in the 1940s—Nazi Genocide
    a. How was it possible for many thousands of ordinary Germans to systematically murder millions of defenseless and innocent Jews, Roma ("Gypsies"), homosexuals, and mentally disabled people in death camps?

B. The Social Origins of Evil
1. *Norms of solidarity demand conformity.*
2. *Structures of authority tend to render people obedient.*
3. *Bureaucracies are highly effective structures of authority.*
    a. As Max Weber defined the term, **bureaucracy** is a large, efficient, impersonal organization composed of clearly defined positions arranged in a hierarchy.

II. NETWORKS

A. It's a Small World
1. The *Internet Movie Database* (2003).
    a. The example of Kevin Bacon.
2. Jeffrey Travers and Stanley Milgram (1969) study.

B. Network Analysis
1. A **social network** is a bounded set of individuals linked by the exchange of material or emotional resources, from money to friendship. The patterns of exchange determine the boundaries of the network. Member exchange resources more frequently with each other than with nonmembers. They also think of themselves as a network of members. Social networks may be formal or informal.
2. The "nodes" (units of analysis) in a social network can be individuals, groups, organizations, and countries; thus social network analysts have examined everything from intimate relationships to diplomatic relations.

3. In contrast to organizations, most networks lack names and offices. Networks lie beneath the more visible social collectivities.

C. Finding a Job
   1. Mark Granovetter (1973) found that mere acquaintances are more likely to provide useful information about employment opportunities than friends and family members, because acquaintances are connected to diverse networks.

D. Urban Networks
   1. Urban acquaintances tend to be few and functionally specific.
   2. According to German sociologist Ferdinand Tonnies, a "community" is marked by intimate and emotionally intense social ties, whereas a "society" is marked by impersonal relationships held together by self-interest. Tonnies focuses on only sparse functionally specific ties, whereas network analysts found elaborate social networks, some functionally specific and some not.
   3. Network analysis helped to show that the characterization of HIV/AIDS as a "gay disease" was an oversimplification. It spread along friendship and acquaintanceship networks of people first exposed. In India and parts of Africa, it did not spread among gay men, but rather through a network of long-distance truck drivers and the prostitutes who catered to them.
   4. Regarding health in general, People who are well integrated into cohesive social networks of family, extended kin, and friends are less likely to suffer heart attacks, complications during pregnancy, and so forth.
   5. Research shows that you are less likely to come down with an infectious disease the more social contact you have.

E. The Building Blocks of Social Networks
   1. The **dyad** is the most elementary network form, which is a social relationship between two nodes or social units.
   2. A **triad** is a social relationship among three nodes.
   3. As Georg Simmel showed early in the 20th century, the social dynamics of these two network forms are fundamentally different. When a third person enters the picture, relationships tend to be less intimate and intense.

III. GROUPS

A. Love and Group Loyalty
   1. Group loyalty is often more powerful than romantic love.

B. Varieties of Group Experience
   1. **Social groups** are composed of one or more networks of people who identify with one another and adhere to defined norms, roles, and statuses.
   2. **Social categories** consist of people who share similar status but do not identify with one another.
   3. In **primary groups**, norms, roles, and statuses are agreed upon but are not put into writing. Social interaction creates strong emotional ties, extends over a long period, and involves a wide range of activities.
   4. **Secondary groups** are larger and more impersonal than primary groups, which creates weaker emotional ties, extends over a shorter period and involves a narrow range of activities.

C. Conformity and "Groupthink"
  1. Conformity is an integral part of group life, and primary groups generate more pressure to conform than secondary groups.
  2. Samuel Stouffer's (1945) classic study showed that primary group cohesion was the main factor motivating soldiers to engage in combat.
  3. Social psychologist Solomon Asch's (1955) famous experiment demonstrates how group pressure creates conformity.
  4. Research shows that several factors affect the likelihood of conformity.
    a. The likelihood of conformity increases as *group size* increases to three or four members.
    b. As *group cohesiveness* increases, so does the likelihood of conformity.
    c. *Social status* affects the likelihood of conformity. People with low status are less likely to dissent.
    d. The *appearance of unanimity* affects the likelihood of conformity. One dissenting voice increases the chance that others will dissent.
  5. **Groupthink** is group pressure to conform despite individual misgivings.
    a. The dangers of groupthink are greatest in high-stress situations.
  6. "Bystander apathy" – as the number of bystanders increases, the likelihood of any one bystander helping decreases because the greater the number of bystanders, the less responsibility any one individual feels.

D. Inclusion and Exclusion
  1. **In-group** members are people who belong to a group. **Out-group** members are people who are excluded from the in-group. Members of an in-group typically draw a boundary separating themselves from out-group members, and they try to keep out-group members from crossing the line.
  2. Why do group boundaries crystallize?
    a. One theory is that group boundaries emerge when people compete for scarce resources.
    b. Another theory is that group boundaries emerge when people are motivated to protect their self-esteem.
    c. *The Robber's Cave Study* (1961), a classic experiment on prejudice, supports both theories.
  3. Dominant groups construct group boundaries to further their goals.

E. Groups and Social Imagination
  1. People interact with other group members in their imagination, through **reference groups**, which are composed of people against whom an individual evaluates his or her situation or conduct. Reference group members function as "role models."
    a. Theodore Newcomb's (1843) study of students at Bennington College is a classic example of a reference group.
  2. Most people highly value the opinions of in-group members.
  3. We have to exercise our imagination because much social life in a complex society involves belonging to secondary groups without knowing or interacting with most group members.
  4. **Formal organizations** are secondary groups designed to achieve explicit objectives.

IV. BUREAUCRACY

    A. Bureaucratic Inefficiency
        1. Contradiction of Weber's view of bureaucratic efficiency and the realities of bureaucratic inefficiency.
        2. Four main sociological criticisms against bureaucracies:
            a. **Dehumanization** occurs when bureaucracies treat clients as standard cases and personnel as cogs in a giant machine, which frustrates and lowers morale.
            b. **Bureaucratic ritualism** is the preoccupation by bureaucrats with rules and regulations that make it difficult for the organization to fulfill its goals.
            c. **Oligarchy** is the "rule of the few" that results from the tendency for power to become concentrated in the hands of a few people at the top of the organizational hierarchy.
            d. **Bureaucratic inertia** occurs when bureaucracies become so large and rigid that they lose touch with reality and continue their policies even when their clients' needs change.
        3. *Size* and *social structure* underlie bureaucratic inefficiency. Problems multiply with the increasing size of groups, and the increasing number and complexity of levels in bureaucratic structures.

    B. Bureaucracy's Informal Side
        1. A social network is important for the operation of bureaucracies. The patterns of exchange determine the boundaries of the network.
        2. Examples:
            a. 1930s Hawthorne plant of the Western Electric Company near Chicago.
            b. Rosabeth Kanter's landmark 1970s study on the informal social relations in bureaucracies.
            c. Socializing, business dinners.

    C. Leadership
        1. Leadership style affects bureaucratic performance.
        2. Three types of leadership:
            a. *Laissez-Faire* **leadership**—The least effective form of leadership that allows subordinates to work things out largely on their own, with almost no direction from above.
            b. **Authoritarian leadership**—Authoritarian leaders demand strict compliance from subordinates. Effective in a crisis, and earn grudging respect for achieving goals, but rarely win popularity contests.
            c. **Democratic leadership** offers more guidance than the *laissez-faire* type, but less control than the authoritarian type. Usually the most effective except for crisis situations, because democratic leaders attempt to include all group members in the decision-making process toward an integrated strategy.

    D. Overcoming Bureaucratic Inefficiency
        1. Smaller innovative firms are often more effective because they have flatter, more democratic and network-like organizational structures, and multiple lines of communication, which produces more satisfied workers, happier clients, and bigger profits.

    E. Organizational Environments

1. An **organizational environment** is composed of a host of economic, political, and cultural factors that lie outside an organization and affect the way it works.
2. Japanese versus American business bureaucracies in the 1970s.
   a. *Japanese workers were in a position to demand efficiency in Japan.*
   b. *International competition encouraged bureaucratic efficiency in Japan.*
   c. *The availability of external suppliers allowed Japanese firms to remain lean.*

V. FREEDOM AND CONSTRAINT IN SOCIAL LIFE

   A. Social collectivities are constraining.

   B. Paradoxically, to succeed in challenging social collectivities, people must sometimes form a new social collectivity.
   1. Seymour Martin Lipset, Martin A. Trow, and James S. Coleman's (1956) classic sociological study of the International Typographical Union.

Study Activity: Applying the Sociological Compass

On your next visit to the bank, the department of motor vehicles, admissions and records at your college, or your college major department, pay close attention to how employees interact and perform their roles. Take notes on your observations. In so doing, accomplish the following tasks:

Based on your observations, make a list of examples of

Dehumanization:

1.

2.

3.

Bureaucratic ritualism:

1.

2.

3.

Bureaucratic inertia:

1.

2.

3.

Finally, make a list of explanations for the reasons behind the bureaucratic behaviors you might have observed, based on what your learned from Chapter 5 of the Brym and Lie textbook.

1.

2.

3.

InfoTrac College Edition Online Exercises

For the following exercises, log on to the online library of InfoTrac College Edition at http://www.infotrac-college.com/. Make note that InfoTrac has implemented a new registration system that will allow easier access to InfoTrac through the use of a personalized username and password.

Once you've created your username and password you may proceed directly to the Log On page. To create an account, register your passcode packaged with your textbook, and create a username and password, by following the online prompt. After you are logged in, click on "Infotrac College Edition." You will arrive at a screen that enables you to search topics.

Keyword: **tokenism**. In what ways is tokenism portrayed? Look for articles that give evidence that tokenism is a problem in the corporate world. Cite five articles that deal with this issue.

Keyword: **employment discrimination**. Identify and read at least three articles that deal with employment discriminations. Compile a list of patterns of employment discrimination that are similar in the three articles.

Keyword: **group service** and **community service**. Look for articles on how service learning is related to the community at large. What information do these articles bring to light about the interaction between groups and the larger society?

Keyword: **networks**. Identify four articles that discuss how networking helps to find employment. After reading the articles compile a list of things you can do now right now to apply the research findings of networking to your future job search. Why is it important for you to develop a "network" in your career area?

Internet Exercises

For a look at the Ray Mine Pilot Study (dealing with hazardous waste), put out by the Environmental Protection Agency go to: http://epa.www.ciesin.org/raymine. Write a short paper discussing the role of organization in this operation.

Go to: http://www.dannen.com/decision/targets.html

This article discusses the atomic bomb decision. Read the article and write a short paper on how Michel's' Iron Law of Oligarchy was at work in this situation.

Go to: http://www.geocities.com/mcdonaldization/

This site explores the meaning of McDonaldization in our society. Look over the site and then write a short opinion paper stating whether you agree or disagree with the McDonaldization of society in general.

Practice Tests

Fill-In-The-Blank

Fill in the blank with the appropriate term from the above list of "key terms."

1. As Max Weber defined the term, _____ is a large, efficient, impersonal organization composed of clearly defined positions arranged in a hierarchy.

2. The _____ is the most elementary network form.

3. _____ are composed of one or more networks of people who identify with one another and adhere to defined norms, roles, and statuses.

4. _____ are larger, more impersonal, and create weaker emotional ties.

5. People interact with other group members in their imagination, through _____ , which are composed of people against whom an individual evaluates his or her situation or conduct.

6. _____ are secondary groups designed to achieve explicit objectives.

7. _____ occurs when bureaucracies become so large and rigid that they lose touch with reality and continue their policies even when their client's needs change.

8. Although effective in a crisis, _____ earn grudging respect from subordinates, and rarely win popularity contests.

9. A(An) _____ is a bounded set of individuals linked by the exchange of material or emotional resources.

10. _____ is the preoccupation by bureaucrats with rules and regulations that make it difficult for the organization to fulfill its goals.

Multiple-Choice Questions

Select the response that best answers the question or completes the statement:

1. In _____ social interactions lead to strong, more enduring emotional ties.
   a. primary groups
   b. secondary groups
   c. tertiary groups
   d. social categories
   e. None of the above.

2. Which concept refers to "rule of the few" in bureaucracies?
   a. dehumanization
   b. bureaucratic inertia
   c. bureaucratic ritualism
   d. competition
   e. oligarchy

3. One evening after being in a traffic accident, Kiana was rushed to the nearest emergency room for moderate injuries. It took nearly two hours to be seen by a medical doctor because much time was spent by staff members following hospital procedure to determine if Kiana possessed medical insurance, and whether her insurance policy would indeed pay for care at the hospital in question. In short, the emergency room staff members lost site of the goals of the emergency room in favor of following regulations and procedures. Which terms best captures this scenario?
   a. bureaucratic inertia
   b. bureaucratic ritualism
   c. oligarchy
   d. monopolization
   e. None of the above.

4. Which type of leadership is most effective during times of crisis?
   a. *laissez-faire* leadership
   b. democratic leadership
   c. egalitarian leadership
   d. authoritarian leadership
   e. rational leadership

5. If a supervisor allows his or her subordinates to settle disputes and conflict without direction, he or she would be described as what type of leader?
   a. *laissez-faire* leadership
   b. democratic leadership
   c. egalitarian leadership
   d. authoritarian leadership
   e. rational leadership

6. The distinctions between Japanese and American corporations in the 1970s illustrate the impact of _____________ on the way economic organizations operate.
   a. organizational deviance
   b. authoritarian leadership
   c. organizational environments
   d. social networks
   e. None of the above.
   f. The function of business dinners and reservations to play golf with business associates illustrates the importance of_____________ for the operation of economic bureaucracies.
   g. social encounters
   h. social networks
   i. competition
   j. domination
   k. ethnomethods

7. According to Mark Granovetter's research, which social network is more likely to provide useful information about employment opportunities?
   a. friends
   b. family members
   c. former supervisors
   d. former spouses
   e. acquaintances

8. Based on the research literature, which factor affects the likelihood of conformity?
   a. Group size
   b. Group cohesiveness
   c. Social status
   d. Appearance of unanimity
   e. All of the above.

9. The dangers of groupthink are greatest in:
   a. high-stress situations.
   b. low-stress situations.
   c. democratic situations.
   d. low anxiety situations.
   e. None of the above.

10. __________ members are people who belong to a group, whereas __________ members are people who are excluded from that group.
   a. Primary group; secondary group
   b. Secondary group; primary group
   c. In-group; out-group
   d. Out-group; in-group
   e. In-group; reference group

11. Which of the following is NOT a basis of criticism of bureaucracies?
    a. Dehumanization
    b. Efficiency
    c. Bureaucratic ritualism
    d. Oligarchy
    e. Bureaucratic inertia

12. The movie *Schindler's List* turns the history of Nazism into a play of morality of good against evil Which of the following statements is true of this movie according to the Brym and Lie textbook?
    a. It does not probe into the sociological roots of good and evil.
    b. As a rare case of a motion picture, it probes into the sociological roots of good and evil.
    c. It provides an authentic representation of many altruistic Nazis during the Holocaust.
    d. All of the above.
    e. None of the above.

13. In 2002, corporate whistle blowers were widely _____ as news of corporate and bureaucratic scandals proliferated in the mass media.
    a. shunned
    b. dismissed
    c. ignored
    d. celebrated
    e. None of the above.

14. Which is one of the main sociological points of "Social Policy: What Do You Think? Group Loyalty or Betrayal" in Chapter 5, p. 118 of the Brym/ Lie textbook?
    a. The essence of romantic love tends to outweigh group loyalty.
    b. The subordination of women tends to be lower in situations where there is high level of group loyalty.
    c. In social situations where there is much tolerance of male misconduct, compassion for the weak tends to be greater.
    d. An important question to consider is where we ought to draw the line between group loyalty and group betrayal.
    e. None of the above.

15. In the classic Milgram experiment on obedience to authority, which laboratory setting yielded the greatest percentage of subjects who administered "maximum shocks" to others?
    a. Same room; hand forced.
    b. Same room.
    c. Different rooms; see and hear.
    d. Different rooms; hand forced.
    e. Different rooms; see but not hear.

16. The 1968 movie, *The Graduate*, as mentioned in the Brym and Lie textbook, illustrates the fact that:
    a. social networking does not necessarily lead to employment opportunities.
    b. parents can help their graduating children find jobs by plugging them into the right social networks.
    c. formal organizations are more effective than informal social networks at helping graduates find jobs.
    d. All of the above.
    e. None of the above.

17. Which of the following is NOT a characteristic of a triad?
    a. No "free riders" are possible.
    b. Intensity and intimacy are reduced.
    c. Coalitions are possible.
    d. A divide-and-conquer strategy is possible.
    e. It is possible to shift responsibility to the larger collectivity.

18. Which is NOT true of primary groups?
    a. Strong emotional ties.
    b. Extends over a long period of time.
    c. Narrow range of activities.
    d. Group members know each other well.
    e. The family is the most important primary group.

19. Which of the following is considered a social origin of evil according to Brym and Lie?
    a. Norms of solidarity demand conformity.
    b. Structures of authority tend to render people obedient.
    c. Bureaucracies are highly effective structures of authority.
    d. All of the above.
    e. None of the above.

20. Network analysis helped to show that the characterization of HIV/AIDS as "gay disease" was:
    a. true in the United States, although false in other countries.
    b. entirely true.
    c. an oversimplification.
    d. true in other countries, but false in the United States.
    e. None of the above.

21. "Nodes" of a social network are:
    a. the resources exchanged.
    b. the larger social structures.
    c. the bureaucracies themselves.
    d. monetary units of exchange.
    e. None of the above.

22. Which term captures the idea of people sharing similar status but do not identify with one another?
    a. Primary group
    b. Social category
    c. Social group
    d. Reference group
    e. None of the above.

23. Which type of leadership is least effective in a crisis?
    a. Authoritarian leadership
    b. Democratic leadership
    c. Charismatic leadership
    d. Tyrannical leadership
    e. *Laissez-Faire* leadership

24. Which of the following statements is true regarding the differences between Japanese and American business in the 1970s?
    a. Japanese workers were in a position to demand efficiency in Japan.
    b. International competition encouraged bureaucratic efficiency in Japan.
    c. The availability of external suppliers allowed Japanese firms to remain lean.
    d. All of the above.
    e. None of the above.

True False

1. Social groups and social categories are indistinguishable.

   TRUE or FALSE

2. Because bureaucracies tend to take on a life of their own in the form of enduring social patterns, the size and social structure of bureaucracies have little to do with their efficiency.

   TRUE or FALSE

3. Contemporary realities of bureaucratic inefficiency contradict Max Weber's view of bureaucratic efficiency.

   TRUE or FALSE

4. In the business world, smaller innovative firms are often more effective in producing more satisfied workers, happier clients, and bigger profits than larger firms.

   TRUE or FALSE

5. Nearly a quarter of all people who ever acted in a movie are separated from Kevin Bacon by just one or two links.

   TRUE or FALSE

6. Natural boundaries, such as rivers, mountains, highways, and railroad tracks, typically separate groups or communities.

    TRUE or FALSE

7. In contrast to organizations, most networks lack names and offices.

    TRUE or FALSE

8. A triad is fundamentally the same as a dyad, since only one person is added to the relations.

    TRUE or FALSE

9. Romantic love is often more powerful than group loyalty.

    TRUE or FALSE

10. Although social networks are useful in finding jobs within a bureaucracy, social networks are not important for the operation of bureaucracies.

    TRUE or FALSE

11. An organizational environment is composed of economic, political, and cultural factors that lie outside an organization and affect the way it works.

    TRUE or FALSE

Short Answer

1. Chapter 5 opens with a narrative describing the experiences of Robert Brym's father with Nazi genocide in the 1940s. A perplexing question that struck Robert Brym's father was "How was it possible for many thousands of ordinary Germans − products of what he regarded as the most advanced civilization on earth − to systematically murder millions of defenseless and innocent Jews, Roma ("Gypsies"), homosexuals, and mentally disabled people in death camps?" Briefly answer this question based on what you learned about structures of bureaucratic authority. (p. 115-120)

    _____

    _____

2. Explain the relationship between social status and conformity. (p. 125-130)

    _____

    _____

3. List and define three types of leadership. (p.135)

    _____

    _____

4. Illustrate the concepts of bureaucratic ritualism and democratic leadership by briefly describing the transformation of the character "Kanji Watanabe" in the 1952 film *Ikiru* described in Chapter 5, box 5.3. (p. 131)

_____

_____

Essay Questions

1. Explain the influence of organizational environments on bureaucratic structures by contrasting Japanese and American businesses in the 1970s. (p. 135-138).

2. Consider your occupation, or your future occupation (in other words engage in anticipatory socialization) for this question. Draw a bureaucratic structure of the organization in which you work (or hope to work). In so doing, identify each node, or group. Next, explain the nature of secondary group relations, and possible types of leadership. (p. 130-135)

3. Explain four sociological criticisms against bureaucracies, and at least two strategies to overcome bureaucratic inefficiency. (p. 119-120, 130-135)

4. Conduct a "mini" network analysis on your potential to find a job through networking with family, friends, and acquaintances. In your analysis, be sure to list the number of different possible job leads from family, friends, and acquaintances, respectively. Determine which social network (family, friends, or acquaintances) has the greatest potential of leading you to a job, and explain why. (p. 120-125)

Solutions

Practice Tests

Fill-In-The-Blank

1. bureaucracy
2. dyad
3. Social groups
4. Secondary groups
5. reference groups
6. Formal organizations
7. Bureaucratic inertia
8. authoritarian leaders
9. social network
10. Bureaucratic ritualism

Multiple-Choice Questions

1. A, (p. 125)
2. E, (p. 132)
3. B, (p. 132)
4. D, (p. 135)
5. A, (p. 135)
6. H, (p. 137) (p. 120)
7. E, (p. 122)
8. E, (p.126)
9. A, (p. 127)
10. C, (p. 128)
11. B, (p. 136)
12. A, (p. 116)
13. D, (p. 117)
14. D, (p. 118)
15. E, (p. 117)
16. B, (p. 122)
17. A, (p. 125)
18. C, (p. 125)
19. D, (p. 116-120)
20. C, (p. 123)
21. E, (p. 121)
22. B, (p. 125)
23. E, (p. 135)
24. D, (p. 137)

True False

1. F, (p. 125)
2. F, (p. 130-132)
3. T, (p. 130-132)
4. T, (p. 135-138)
5. T, (p. 121)
6. T, (p. 129)
7. T, (p. 120)
8. F, (p. 124)
9. F, (p. 127)
10. F, (p. 122-124)
11. T, (p. 137)

DEVIANCE AND CRIME

Student Learning Objectives

After reading Chapter 6, you should be able to:

1. Explain why definitions of crime and deviance vary across cultures, history, and social contexts.

2. Identify the general categories of deviance and crime.

3. Explain the social construction of crime and deviance in the context of differential social power.

4. Describe the major data sources of crime and delinquency, and their strengths and weaknesses.

5. Describe recent demographic characteristics (i.e. gender, age, and race) of crime and deviance.

6. Identify the major sociological theories of crime and deviance, their central features and key exemplars.

7. Compare and contrast motivational and constraint theories of crime and deviance.

8. Discuss the historical and contemporary trends in social control and punishment.

9. Identify and explain the major views on the function of prisons.

10. Describe the impact of moral panics on criminal justice policies and crime prevention.

11. Discuss the pros and cons of alternative forms of punishment.

Key Terms

(defined on the indicated pages of the textbook, and in glossary)

deviance (144)

crime (144)

informal punishment (144)

stigmatization (144)

formal punishment (144)

social diversions (146)

social deviations (146)

conflict crimes (146)

consensus crimes (146)

white-collar crimes (147)

street crimes (147)

victimless crimes (149)

self-report surveys (149)

social control (157)

motivational theories (1154)

constraint theories (154)

strain theory (155)

subcultural theory (155)

techniques of neutralization (155)

differential association theory (155)

labeling theory (157)

master status (157)

control theory (157)

conflict theory (158)

moral panic (161)

Detailed Chapter Outline

I. THE SOCIAL DEFINITION OF DEVIANCE AND CRIME

    A. Crime and Punishment in the United States
        1. Considering television, cable, local, daytime, and late-night shows, one might conclude that the United States is a society obsessed with crime.
        2. Punishment is also a big issue in the United States
            a. The United States has more people behind bars than any other country on earth, - and the number is increasing by 50,000-80,000 per year.

    B. Definitions of deviance and crime change over time and vary across people.
        1. Examples:
            a. 1872 Susan B. Anthony and voting rights
            b. Late 1950s and early 1960s Martin Luther King Jr. and civil rights

    C. Types of Deviance and Crime
        1. **Deviance** involves breaking a norm.
        2. **Informal punishment** is mild, and may involved raised eyebrows, gossip, ostracism, shaming, or **stigmatization** (negative evaluation because of a marker that distinguishes them from others).
        3. **Formal punishment** results from people breaking *laws*, which are norms stipulated and enforced by government bodies.
        4. Three dimensions of the various types of deviance (John Hagan):
            a. *Severity of social response.*

b. *Perceived harmfulness.*

c. *Degree of public agreement.*

5. Four types of deviance and crime:

   a. **Social diversions** are minor acts of deviance such as participating in fads or fashions like dyeing one's hair purple. Usually perceived as harmless.

   b. **Social deviations** are more serious acts, large proportions of people agree they are deviant and somewhat harmful, and they are usually subject to institutional sanction.

   c. **Conflict crimes** are deviant acts that the state defines as illegal, but the definition is controversial in the wider society.

   d. **Consensus crimes** are widely recognized to be bad in and of themselves, and there is little controversy over their seriousness.

D. Power and the Social Construction of Crime and Deviance

1. *Social constructionism* is the school of sociological thought that emphasizes that various social problems, including crime, are not inherent in certain actions themselves. *Powerful* groups are in positions to create norms and laws that suit their interests and stigmatize other people, while the *powerless* often struggle against stigmatization.

2. Crimes Against Women

   a. Has the law been biased against women?

   b. Many types of crimes against women were largely ignored in the United States and most parts of the world (i.e. rape, physical violence against women, sexual harassment).

   c. The situation has improved today. Why?

      i. Women's position in the economy, the family, and other social institutions has improved.

      ii. Women's rights movement.

      iii. Increased public awareness.

      iv. Shift in the distribution of power.

3. White-Collar Crime

   a. **White-collar crimes** refer to illegal acts "committed by a person of respectability and high social status in the course of his [or her] occupation" (i.e. embezzlement, false advertising, tax evasion, insider stock trading, fraud, unfair labor practices, copyright infringement, conspiracy to fix prices and restrain trade, and environmental degradation). Disproportionately committed by middle and upper classes.

   b. **Street crimes**, by contrast, include arson, burglary, assault, and other illegal acts disproportionately committed by people from lower classes.

   c. Many sociologists argue that white-collar crimes are *more costly* than street crimes.

   d. White-collar crime is underreported.

   e. White-collar crimes result in few prosecutions and fewer convictions. Why?

      i. Much white-collar crime occurs in private and is therefore difficult to detect.

      ii. Corporations can afford legal experts, public relations firms, and advertising agencies that advise their clients on how to bend laws, build up their corporate image in the public mind, and influence lawmakers to pass laws "without teeth."

   f. Governments also commit serious crimes, and are also hard to punish.

E. Crime Rates
   1. A word about *official crime statistics*
      a. Much crime is not reported to the police (i.e. common assaults and rape).
      b. Authorities and the wider public decide which criminal acts to report and which to ignore.
      c. Many crimes are not incorporated in major crime indexes published by the FBI, such as **victimless crimes** (violations of law in which no victim steps forward and is identified, such as white-collar crimes, prostitution and illegal drug use).
   2. **Self-report surveys** are used to supplement official crime statistics in light of reporting problems. Respondents are asked to report their involvement in criminal activities, either as perpetrators or victims.
      a. The National Crime Victimization Survey is the main source of self-report victimization data in the United States.
   3. What does the official record show?
      a. Every hour in 2002, law enforcement agencies in the United States received verifiable reports on average of nearly 2 murders or nonnegligent manslaughter, 11 rapes, 72 robberies, 102 aggravated assaults, 142 motor vehicle thefts, 245 burglaries, and 800 larceny-thefts.
      b. 500% increase in the rate of violent crime, and a 150% increase in the rate of major property crimes, between 1960 and 1992.
      c. However the long crime wave that began its upswing in the early 1960s eased in the 1980s and fell in the 1990s.
      d. Four factors usually mentioned for the decline in crime rate:
         i. Governments put more police in the streets and many communities established their own systems of surveillance and patrol.
         ii. America is aging and the number of young men in the population has declined.
         iii. 1990s economic boom.
         iv. Controversially, some researchers noted that the decline in crime started 19 years after abortion was legalized in the United States, thus proportionately fewer unwanted children in the population beginning in 1992.
      e. Note: The authors have not claimed that putting more people in prison and imposing tougher penalties for crime help account for lower crime rates. The authors explain why these actions do not generally result in lower crime rates later in the chapter when they discuss **social control** (methods of ensuring conformity) and punishment.
F. Criminal Profiles
   1. Gender
      a. 77% of all persons arrested in the United States in 2002 were men.
      b. Men account for 83% of arrests.
      c. Women are catching up.
      d. Men are still six times more likely than women to be arrested.
   2. Age
      a. Most crime is committed by people who have not reached middle age.
      b. The 15- to 24-year-old age cohort is the most crime prone.
   3. Race

    a.   In 2000 whites accounted for 75.1% of the U.S. population, but only 70.7% of arrests.

    b.   African Americans accounted for 26.9% of arrests but made up only 12.3% of the population in 1998.

    c.   Why the disproportionately high arrest, conviction, and incarceration rates of African Americans?

        i.   Bias in the way crime statistics are collected (i.e. absence of data on white-collar crime which are disproportionately committed by whites).

        ii.   The low class position of blacks in American society.

        iii.   Racial discrimination in the criminal justice system.

G. Explaining Deviance and Crime

   1. Explanations can be categorized into two basic types.

     a.   **Motivational theories** identify the social factors that *drive* people to commit deviance and crime.

     b.   **Constraint theories** identify the social factors that impose deviance and crime (or conventional behavior) on people.

   2. Motivational Theories

     a.   Strain Theory

        i.   Robert Merton's **strain theory** argues that people may turn to deviance when they experience strain. Strain results when a culture teaches people the value of material success, and society fails to provide enough legitimate opportunities for everyone to succeed.

        ii.   Five adaptations to strain:

        iii.   *Conformity;*

        iv.   *Innovation;*

        v.   *Ritualism;*

        vi.   *Retreatism;* and

        vii.   *Rebellion.*

     b.   Subcultural Theory

        i.   **Subcultural theory** argues that gangs are a collective adaptation to social conditions. Distinct norms and values that reject the legitimate world crystallize in gangs.

        ii.   Three features of criminal subcultures:

        iii.   Delinquent youths turn to different types of crime, depending on the availability of different subcultures in their neighborhoods.

        iv.   Members of criminal subcultures spin out a whole series of rationalizations for their criminal activities, called **techniques of neutralization**, or the creation of justifications and rationalizations that make deviance and crime seem normal, and enable criminals to clear their consciences and get on with the job.

        v.   Members of criminal subcultures are strict conformists to the norms of their own culture.

     c.   Learning Theory

        i.   Edwin Sutherland's **differential association theory** holds that people learn to value deviant or nondeviant lifestyles depending on whether their social environment leads them to associate more with deviants or nondeviants.

      ii. Differential association theory holds for people in all social class positions including white-collar crime.

   3. Constraint Theories

     a. Labeling Theory

       i. **Labeling theory** argues that deviance results not so much from the actions of the deviant as from the response of others, who label the rule breaker a deviant.

       ii. Labeling may lead to immersion of the stigmatized juvenile into a deviant subculture and adopt "delinquent" as his [or her] **master status**, or one's overriding public identity.

       iii. Labeling may act as a self-fulfilling prophecy.

     b. Control Theory

       i. **Control theory** proposes that the rewards of deviance and crime are ample; therefore, most of us would commit deviant and criminal acts if we could get away with it. The reason deviants and criminals break norms and laws are that social controls are insufficient to ensure their conformity.

       ii. Four types of social control according to Travis Hirschi and Michael Gottfredson: *attachments, opportunities, involvement;* and *beliefs.*

     c. Conflict Theory

       i. **Conflict theory** maintains that the rich and powerful impose deviant and criminal labels on the less powerful members of society, especially those who challenge the existing social order. Conflict theory holds the view that the law applies differently to the rich and poor. The rich and powerful are also able to use their money and influence to escape punishment for their own deviant acts.

       ii. Examples: Thieves challenge private property, thus theft is a crime; "Bag ladies" and drug addicts drop out of society, thus are labeled deviant because of their refusal to engage in productive labor; Militant trade unionists represent threat to the social order, thus are defined as deviant or criminal; White-collar crimes are less severely punished than street crimes, regardless of the relative harm to society.

II. TRENDS IN CRIMINAL JUSTICE

  A. Social Control

   1. The *degree* and *form* of *social control* varies over time and from one society to the next.

  B. The Prison

   1. Prisons are *agents of socialization*, and new inmates often become more serious offenders as they adapt to the culture of the most hardened, long-term prisoners.

   2. In preindustrial societies, criminals were publicly humiliated, tortured, or put to death. Prisons emerged with industrialization, and were seen as less harsh and more "civilized."

   3. Four views of prisons

     a. *Rehabilitation* involves the belief that prisoners can be taught how to become productive citizens, which was a predominant view in the United States in the 1960s and early 1970s.

     b. *Deterrence* involves a view that people will be less inclined to commit crimes if they know they are likely to get caught and serve long and unpleasant prison terms.

    c. *Revenge* involves a view that depriving criminals their freedom and forcing them to live in poor conditions is fair retribution for their illegal acts.

    d. *Incapacitation* involves the view that the chief function of the prison is simply to keep criminals out of society as long as possible to ensure they can do no harm.

C. Moral Panic

    1. A **moral panic** occurs when wide sections of the public, including lawmakers and criminal justice officials, believe that some form of deviance or crime poses a profound threat to society's well being.

    2. Examples of consequences in criminal justice:

        a. war on drugs

        b. "three strikes and you're out" law

        c. popularity of the death penalty

    3. Crime prevention

        a. walls built around neighborhoods

        b. hiring of private security police to patrol

        c. security systems and steel bars

        d. handguns

        e. laws allowing concealed handguns in some states

    4. The moral panic of the 1980s and 1990s occurred when crimes stabilized and dramatically declined.

    5. Why the panic and who benefits?

        a. Mass media profits.

        b. Crime prevention and punishment industry profits.

        c. Some formerly depressed rural regions of the United States have become dependent on prison construction for economic well being of their citizens.

        d. The criminal justice system benefits because of increased spending on crime prevention, control and punishment.

        e. "Get tough" policies used for political gain.

D. Alternative Forms of Punishment

    1. Capital Punishment

        a. The United States is one of the few industrial societies to retain capital punishment for the most serious offenders.

        b. The death penalty ranks high as a form of *revenge*, but is questionable as a *deterrent*. Why?

            i. Since murder is often committed in irrational rage, the murderer is unlikely to coolly consider the costs of his or her actions.

            ii. If rational calculation occurs, the perpetrator is likely to know that very few murders result in death sentences.

           iii. Capital punishment is hardly a matter of blind justice (racial bias), and mistakes are common (mistrial).

2. Incarcerating Less Serious Offenders in Violent, "No Frills" Prisons
   a. Most of the increase in the prison population over the past 20 years is due to the conviction of nonviolent criminals, based on the hypothesis that imprisonment lowers the crime rate.
   b. Data shows a weak relationship between imprisonment and the crime rate.
   c. Prison teaches inmates to behave more violently.
   d. Reasonable alternatives?
      i. Anecdotal evidence suggests that institutions designed to rehabilitate and reintegrate prisoners into society can work, especially for less serious offenders.
      ii. Cost-effective and workable alternative.

Study Activity: Applying the Sociological Compass

After reading the chapter, make a list of the motivational and constraint theories, and a list of key assumptions of each theory. Critically observe a motion picture from the "gangster" genre (*The Godfather* series, *Boys in the Hood*, *Menace to Society*, *Goodfellas*, and so forth). Apply relevant theories to the motion picture by accomplishing the following tasks. The tasks are divided by motivational and constraint theories. In applying the motivational theories, you are to describe the portrayal of the motion picture. In applying the constraint theories, you are to critique the portrayals.

Applying Motivational Theories

Make a list of causes and motivations of deviance and crime as portrayed in the motion picture in terms of strain theory, subcultural theory, and differential association.

Strain theory

1.

2.

3.

4.

Subcultural theory

1.

2.

3.

4.

Differential association

1.

2.

3.

4.

Applying Constraint Theories

In applying constraint theories, interpret the motion picture from a more critical point of view. Make a list of stereotypical portrayals. Then, in your interpretation, make a list of negative social consequences of the portrayals in terms of labeling. In other words, what are the negative consequences of the socially constructed stereotypes on the racial or ethnic group in question? Finally, make a list of reasons why the stereotypes are constructed in the manner in which they are from a conflict perspective.

Stereotypical portrayals

1.

2.

3.

4.

Labeling theory

1.

2.

3.

4.

Conflict theory

1.

2.

3.

4.

Infotrac College Edition Online Exercises

For the following exercises, log on to the online library of InfoTrac College Edition at http://www.infotrac-college.com/. Make note that InfoTrac has implemented a new registration system that will allow easier access to InfoTrac through the use of a personalized username and password.

Once you've created your username and password you may proceed directly to the Log On page. To create an account, register your passcode packaged with your textbook, and create a username and password, by following the online prompt. After you are logged in, click on "Infotrac College Edition." You will arrive at a screen that enables you to search topics.

Keyword: **Hazing**. Do a search for articles dealing with hazing. Is hazing considered a crime or an act of deviance? Assess the current trends in hazing.

Keyword: **Computer crime**. Look for articles on computer crime. What are the different types of computer crime? How can our society curtail computer crime?

Keyword: **crimes without victims**. Examine articles on victimless crime. What types of crimes are considered victimless crimes? Why?

Keyword: **deviant behavior**. Do a search for articles on deviant behavior. Select one area of interest and do an in-depth search in this area. Present your findings to the class.

Keyword: **Fraternity or Sorority Parties**. Look for articles that deal with binge drinking. What factors cause binge drinking?

Keyword: **Moral Panic**. Identify and read at least 2 articles that discuss a social issue involving a moral panic (i.e. war on drugs, child abuse in day-care centers, terrorism, three strikes initiative, get tough on crime initiatives, etc.). Read the articles and list the major findings of each article. What similarities and differences do you see in the different studies?

Internet Exercises

For statistics and information from The Drug Enforcement Administration go to http://www.usdoj.gov/dea/index.htm

Look up statistics in your state or area. What drugs are most likely to be used in your area or state?

The Federal Bureau of Investigation (FBI) website is found at http://www.fbi.gov/

Locate information about the Uniform Crime Reports. Locate information from your hometown. How often does auto theft occur in your hometown compared to the area where you are currently living?

The United States Government Bureau of Justice Statistics provides statistics, reports and other information about all areas of justice. Give an oral report on your findings. http://www.ojp.usdoj.gov/bjs/

For information on United States execution methods go to Amnesty International at http://www.amnesty-usa.org/abolish/methus.html

Write a short paper about your views on capital punishment execution methods.

Practice Tests

Fill-In-The-Blank

Fill in the blank with the appropriate term from the above list of "key terms."

1. _____ is defined as negative evaluation because of a marker that distinguishes groups and their members from others, which becomes the basis of labeling.

2. _____ are more serious acts that are usually subject to institutional sanctions.

3. Deviant acts that the state defines as illegal, which is however controversial in the wider society, are referred to as _____ .

4. In light of the reporting problems associated with official crime statistics, _____ are used to supplement official crime statistics.

5. _____ argues that gangs are a collective adaptation to social conditions.

6. Members of criminal subcultures often express a whole series of rationalizations for their criminal activities, which is referred to as _____ .

7. Labeling may lead to the immersion of a stigmatized juvenile into a deviant subculture, and therefore lead him or her to adopt "delinquent" as his or her _____ .

8. A(An) _____ occurs when wide sections of the public believe that some form of deviance or crime poses a profound threat to society's well being.

9. _____ results from breaking laws.

10. Arson, burglary, and assault are examples of _____ .

Multiple-Choice Questions

Select the response that best answers the question or completes the statement:

1. The experience of Martin Luther King Jr. at the hands of law enforcement in the late 1950s and early 1960s illustrates that:
   a. definitions of deviance and crime change over time.
   b. definitions of deviance and crime vary across social contexts.
   c. deviance and crime are socially constructed.
   d. All of the above.
   e. None of the above.

2. Raised eyebrows, shaming, and ostracism are examples of:
   a. deviance
   b. informal punishment
   c. formal punishment
   d. social diversions
   e. social deviations

3. Which is NOT a type or category of deviance and crime according to Brym and Lie?
   a. social diversions
   b. social deviations
   c. conflict crimes
   d. consensus crimes
   e. formal stigmatization

4. _____ is the school of sociological thought that emphasizes that various social problems, including crime, are not inherent in certain actions themselves, but are rather socially created.
   a. Functionalism
   b. Conflict criminology
   c. Social constructionism
   d. Social control theory
   e. Anomie theory

5. Women's situations involving their treatment at the hands of the criminal justice system has improved today. Which is a social source of this improvement?
   a. Women's position in the economy has improved.
   b. Women's rights movement.
   c. Increased public awareness.
   d. All of the above.
   e. None of the above.

6. _____ crimes are widely recognized to be bad in and of themselves, and there is little controversy over them.
   a. Conflict
   b. Consensus
   c. Dysfunctional
   d. Functional
   e. Constructive

7. White collar crimes are disproportionately committed by:
   a. middle and upper classes
   b. lower classes
   c. the working class
   d. white ethnic groups
   e. None of the above.

8. Which is NOT a criticism of official crime statistics?
   a. Much white-collar crime is not reported to the police.
   b. Authorities and the wider public decide which criminal acts to report and which to ignore.
   c. Many crimes are not incorporated in major crime indexes such as victimless crimes.
   d. All of the above are criticisms of official crime statistics.
   e. None of the above is a criticism of official crime statistics.

9. The long crime wave that began its upswing in the early 1960s eased in the 1980s and _____ in the 1990s.
   a. increased
   b. reached its climax
   c. fell
   d. remained consistent
   e. None of the above.

10. The _____ is the main source of self-report victimization data in the United States.
   a. Uniform Crime Report
   b. National Crime Victimization Survey
   c. U.S. Census
   d. Delinquency Index
   e. Index Crimes

11. Men accounted for _____ of arrests for violent crimes in 2002.
   a. 99%
   b. 77%
   c. 40%
   d. 29%
   e. 13%

12. Statistics indicate that African Americans have disproportionately high arrest, conviction, and incarceration rates. Which is an explanation of this pattern?
   a. Biases in the way crime statistics are collected.
   b. Absence of data on white-collar crime, which is disproportionately committed by whites.
   c. The disproportionate representation of African Americans in the lower classes.
   d. Racial discrimination in the criminal justice system.
   e. All of the above.

13. Which type of criminological theories identify the social factors that drive people to commit deviance and crime?
   a. motivational theories
   b. constraint theories
   c. control theories
   d. conflict theories
   e. None of the above.

14. Which is NOT an adaptation to strain according to Robert Merton?
    a. innovation
    b. ritualism
    c. retreatism
    d. rebellion
    e. stigmatization

15. Drug dealing is an example of:
    a. conformity
    b. innovation
    c. ritualism
    d. retreatism
    e. rebellion

16. According to Merton's typology of adaptations to anomie, an individual who accepts society's goals may be:
    a. an innovator or retreatist
    b. a conformist or ritualist
    c. a retreatist or ritualist
    d. an innovator or conformist
    e. a ritualist or innovator

17. Which theory proposes that deviance is tempting to everyone, thus social bonds with legitimate authority figures need to be established at an early age?
    a. differential association
    b. labeling theory
    c. strain theory
    d. control theory
    e. None of the above.

18. The theory of deviance that argues that deviant behavior is caused by the gap between culturally acceptable goals and the legitimate means of achieving them is:
    a. control theory
    b. labeling theory
    c. strain theory
    d. conflict theory
    e. differential association theory

19. hich is NOT a type of social control according to Travis Hirschi and Michael Gottfredson?
    a. attachments
    b. opportunities
    c. self-fulfilling prophecies
    d. involvements
    e. beliefs

20. Which criminological theory especially highlights the reasons why white-collar crimes are less severely punished than street crimes, regardless of the relative harm to society?
    a. strain theory
    b. control theory
    c. differential association theory
    d. conflict theory
    e. motivational theories

21. Which view of prisons believes that the chief function of the prison is simply to keep criminals out of society as long as possible to ensure they can do no harm?
    a. rehabilitation
    b. deterrence
    c. revenge
    d. incapacitation
    e. None of the above.

22. In regards to the relationship between prisons and crime, data shows a _____ relationship between imprisonment and the crime rate.
    a. weak
    b. strong
    c. moderate
    d. positive
    e. None of the above.

23. Until the early part of the 20th century, people considered cocaine as a(an):
    a. medicine.
    b. hallucinogen.
    c. aphrodisiac.
    d. All of the above.
    e. None of the above.

24. Which type of violent crime remained relatively constant from 1978-1999, according to U.S. FBI statistics?
    a. aggravated assault
    b. rape
    c. murder
    d. All of the above.
    e. Both 'B' and 'C.'

25. Which age cohort accounted for the highest percentage of arrests in 2001?
    a. 10-14 years of age.
    b. 15-19 years of age.
    c. 25-29 years of age.
    d. 30-34 years of age.
    e. 35-39 years of age.

26. Which is a major policy implication in box 6.1 "Social Policy: What Do You Think? The War on Drugs" on p. 154 in the Brym and Lie text?
    a. Drug policy needs to be discussed in a serious way in the United States.
    b. The "just say no" campaign has been highly effective.
    c. Spending most of the drug-control budget on trying to curb the supply of illegal drugs has been effective.
    d. All of the above.
    e. None of the above.

27. As depicted in *The Sopranos*, having family members and friends in the Mafia predisposes one to Mafia involvement. Which theory best captures this likelihood?
    a. conflict theory
    b. social control theory
    c. anomie theory
    d. labeling theory
    e. differential association theory

28. From around 1995 to 2000, belief in capital punishment in the United States has:
    a. increased.
    b. declined.
    c. remained constant.
    d. All of the above.
    e. None of the above.

True False

1. The United States has more people behind bars than any other country on earth.

   TRUE or FALSE

2. The number of people behind bars in the United States has leveled off in recent years.

   TRUE or FALSE

3. Because women have long been perceived as in need of chivalrous protection, the law has often been biased in favor of protecting women.

   TRUE or FALSE

4. White collar crimes are equally stigmatized as street crimes.

   TRUE or FALSE

5. Many sociologists argue that white collar crimes are more costly than street crimes.

   TRUE or FALSE

6. Whites accounted for 69.5% of arrests in 2001.

   TRUE or FALSE

7. According to conflict theory, thieves challenge private property, thus theft is a crime.

   TRUE or FALSE

8. The degree and form of social control tends to remain consistent over time.

   TRUE or FALSE

9. The more complex a society, the less likely many norms will be widely shared.

   TRUE or FALSE

10. The moral panic regarding the crime problem of the 1980s and 1990s occurred when crimes reached epidemic proportions.

    TRUE or FALSE

Short Answer

1. Briefly identify and explain three dimensions of the various types of deviance according to John Hagan. (p. 144)

   _____

   _____

2. Explain the premise of social constructionism in terms of the creation of deviance and crime in the context of social power. (p. 146)

   _____

   _____

3. List and define Hirschi and Gottfredson's four types social control. (p. 157)

   _____

   _____

4. Explain the major premise of labeling theory. Be sure to mention the concept of "self-fulfilling prophecy." (p. 156-157)

   _____

   _____

5. List and define four views of prison. (p. 160-161)

   _____

   _____

6. Define "moral panic" and provide an example of a moral panic. (p. 161-162)

_____

_____

Essay Questions

1. Contrast a motivational and constraint theory of your choice. Be sure to provide a substantive example to illustrate the differences between the theories. (p. 153-159)

2. Explain why white-collar crimes are less stigmatized and result in fewer prosecutions in comparison to street crimes according to labeling theory and conflict theory. Be sure to integrate both theories. (p. 156-159)

3. Compare and contrast the strengths and weaknesses of official crime statistics and self-report surveys. (p. 148-149)

4. Explain the concept "techniques of neutralization" in terms of delinquent subcultures. Illustrate the concept by describing the process of delinquent gang formation. (p. 155-156)

Solutions

Practice Tests

Fill-In-The-Blank

1. Stigmatization
2. Social deviations
3. conflict crimes
4. self-report surveys

5. Subcultural theory
6. techniques of neutralization
7. master status
8. moral panic

9. Formal punishment
10. street crimes

Multiple-Choice Questions

1. D, (p. 144)
2. B, (p. 144)
3. E, (p. 144)
4. C, (p. 146)
5. D, (p.147)
6. B, (p. 146)
7. A, (p. 147)
8. D, (p. 149-153)
9. C, (p. 150)
10. B, (p. 149)

11. B, (p. 151)
12. E, (p. 152)
13. A, (p. 154)
14. E, (p. 155)
15. B, (p. 155)
16. D, (p. 155)
17. D, (p. 157)
18. C, (p. 155)
19. C, (p. 157)
20. D, (p. 158)

21. D, (p. 161)
22. A, (p. 161)
23. A, (p. 145)
24. E, (p. 150)
25. B, (p. 152)
26. A, (p. 154)
27. E, (p. 156)
28. B, (p. 161)

True False

1. T, (p. 143)
2. F, (p. 143)
3. F, (p. 147)
4. F, (p. 147)

5. T, (p. 147)
6. T, (p. 152)
7. T, (p. 158)
8. F, (p. 157-158)

9. T, (p. 157-158)
10. F, (p. 161)

SOCIAL STRATIFICATION: UNITED STATES AND GLOBAL PERSPECTIVES

Student Learning Objectives

After reading Chapter 7, you should be able to:

1. Define stratification in terms of the gap between the rich and poor in the United States.

2. Describe the trends involving income and wealth inequality in the United States.

3. Identify and describe the categories of the upper class—that is the upper-upper class versus the lower-upper class, and "Old Money" versus "New Money."

4. Explain the impact of high-tech industries in the 1990s on the economy and social stratification in the United States.

5. Explain global inequality and discuss cross-national variations in internal stratification.

6. Describe the development of internal stratification in terms of societal development in general.

7. Discuss and contrast the contribution of Karl Marx and Max Weber to the sociological understanding of inequality and stratification.

8. Explain stratification and mobility according to the functionalist perspectives of Kingsley Davis and Wilbert Moore, and Peter Blau and Otis Dudley Duncan.

9. Contrast functionalist and contemporary class theories of stratification.

10. Describe the role of noneconomic dimensions of social class, including prestige, taste, and politics.

11. Explain the impact of government policy initiatives on poverty rates and perceptions of poverty.

12. Describe American perceptions of social class inequality in the United States based on cited research.

13. Dispel the myths of poverty and poor people based on sociological research.

Key Terms

(defined on the indicated pages of the textbook, and in glossary)

social stratification (172)

vertical social mobility (175)

global inequality (178)

cross-national variations in
internal stratification (178)

The Gini index (178)

ascription (181)

achievement (181)

caste (181)

apartheid (182)

class consciousness (183)

class (183, 185)

bourgeoisie (183)

proletariat (183)

status groups (186)

parties (186)

the functional theory of stratification (184)

socioeconomic index of
occupation status (SEI) (187)

socioeconomic status (SES) (187)

intragenerational mobility (188)

intergenerational mobility (188)

structural mobility (188)

poverty rate (190)

Detailed Chapter Outline

I. PATTERNS OF STRATIFICATION

   A. Shipwrecks and Inequality

      1. Stories of shipwrecks and survivors provide space to make a point of social inequality—that allows the sweeping away of social convention and privilege.

      2. Examples:

         a. 1719 *Robinson Crusoe* portrays capitalism favorably, and the importance of hard work and inventiveness to get rich.

         b. Three messages in 1875 *Swept Away*:

            i.   It is possible to be rich without working hard because one can inherit wealth.

            ii. One can work hard without becoming rich.

            iii. Something about the structure of society causes inequality.

         c. 1997 *Titanic* shows, on the one hand that class differences are important. On the other hand, the movie suggests that class is insignificant in its optimistic tale of the American Dream.

      3. **Social stratification** is the way society is organized in layers or strata.

   B. Economic Inequality in the United States

      1. Wealth

         a. *Wealth* is what you own.

         b. The gap between the rich and poor in the United States is tremendous.

            i. In the mid-1990s, the richest 1% of American households owned nearly 39% of all national wealth, while the richest 10% owned almost 72%. The poorest 40% of

American households owned a meager 0.2% of all national wealth. The bottom 20% has a negative net worth, which means they owed more than they owned.

    c. Wealth inequality has been increasing since the early 1980s. Sixty-two percent of the increase in national wealth in the 1990s went to the richest 1% of Americans, 99% of the increase went to the richest 20%. The United States has surpassed all other highly industrialized countries in wealth inequality.

    d. Only a modest correlation exists between wealth and income.

2. Income

    a. *Income* is what you earn in a given period.

    b. Stratification is often divided into two categories of inequality:

       i. *Income classes*--differ in lifestyle.

       ii. *Income strata*—equal-sized statistical categories.

    c. Two important facts about stratification:

       i. Inequality has been rising in the United States for more than a quarter of a century. In 1974 the top fifth of households earned 9.8 times more than the bottom fifth. By 2001, the top fifth earned 14.3 times more than the bottom fifth. For the first time since data became available on the subject, the top 20% of households earned more than half of all of the national income, in 2001.

       ii. The middle 60% of income earners have been "squeezed" during the past 25 years, with their share of national income falling from 52.5% to 46.4% of the total.

C. How Green is the Valley?

    1. Two categories of the upper class include the *upper-upper class* and *lower-upper class*.

    2. "Old Money"

       a. Comprises 1% of the U.S. population.

       b. Inherited wealth earned in older industries such as banking, insurance, and oil.

       c. Inhabited elite East Coast neighborhoods.

    3. "New Money"

       a. Substantial amount of "new money" entered the upper-upper class in the 1990s—booming high-tech industries.

       b. Concentrated in high-tech meccas in the West, such as San Francisco, San Mateo County, and Santa Clara County.

       c. Still overwhelmingly white and non-Hispanic.

    4. Although high-tech industries witnessed the longest economic boom in the 1990s it changed the pattern of social stratification in the United States, encouraged upward mobility, and increased the median income. However, the changes were not always positive. It increased the cost of living and widened the gap between the rich and the poor.

    5. High-technology industry helped to create a new division in the lower-upper class—the "Poor Rich."

    6. High-technology industry squeezed the middle class and encouraged downward mobility

       a. This is referred to as **vertical social mobility**, or the movement up the stratification system ("upward mobility").

    7. High-technology industry lowered the value of unskilled work, swelling the rank of the poor.

II. INTERNATIONAL DIFFERENCES

    A. Global Inequality

        1. There is also a gap in income and wealth *between* countries, as there is a gap *within* countries. (i.e. United States, Canada, Japan, Australia, Germany, France, and Britain versus Angola, Africa, South Africa, South America, and Asia).

           a. **Global inequality** refers to the differences in the economic ranking of countries.

           b. **Cross-national variations in internal stratification** are differences between countries in their stratification systems.

           c. Inequality between rich and poor countries is staggering.

              i. Nearly a fifth of the world's population lack adequate shelter, and over a fifth lacks safe water.

              ii. About a third of the world's people are without electricity and over two-fifths lack adequate sanitation.

              iii. While the annual health expenditure in the United States is $2,765 per person, it is $4 for Tanzania and Sierra Leone, and $3 for Vietnam.

              iv. Poor countries are more likely to experience mass suffering

        2. Internal Stratification

           a. The **Gini index** is the measure of income inequality. Its value ranges from zero (which means that every household earn exactly the same amount of money) to one (which means that all income is earned by a single household).

           b. The United States has the highest percentage of people living below the low-income line and the highest level of income inequality, among wealthy postindustrial countries.

    B. Development and Internal Stratification

        1. What accounts for cross-national differences in internal stratification—*political factors* and *socioeconomic development*?

        2. Socioeconomic development and internal stratification: over human history, as societies became richer and more complex, the level of social inequality first increased, then tapered off, then began to decline, and finally began to rise again.

           a. Foraging Societies

              i. First 90,000 years of human existence.

              ii. Hunting and foraging.

              iii. Shared food to ensure survival and subsistence.

              iv. No rich and poor.

           b. Horticultural and Pastoral Societies

              i. About 12,000 years ago.

              ii. First agricultural settlements.

              iii. Based on horticulture (the use small hand tools to cultivate plants), and pastoralism (the domestication of animals).

              iv. Production of wealth and surplus beyond subsistence.

              v. Significant social stratification emerged.

           c. Agrarian Societies

     i. About 5,000 years ago.

     ii. Plow agriculture.

     iii. Surpluses grew.

     iv. Religious beliefs justified growing inequality (i.e. "divine right")

     v. Stratification was based on **ascription** (allocation of rank depends on the features a person is born with) than **achievement** (allocation of rank depends on one's accomplishments), - and there was little social mobility.

     vi. Agrarian India was nearly purely ascriptive, and was divided into **castes** (occupation and marriage partners assigned on the basis of caste membership).

     vii. **Apartheid** (caste system based on race) in South Africa is an example of caste systems in industrial times.

  d. Industrial Societies

     i. The tendency of industrialism to lower the level of stratification was not apparent in the first stages of industrial growth.

     ii. Improvements in technology and social organization of manufacturing raised the living standards of the entire population, thus stratification declined.

     iii. Birth was no longer destiny, and merit and talent became important for mobility.

     iv. Political pressure also played a role in reducing inequality (i.e. labor unions).

     v. Gender inequality began to break down.

  e. Postindustrial Societies

     i. In the United States and the United Kingdom, social inequality has been increasing for the last quarter century. The concentration of wealth in the hands of the top 1% is higher today than anytime in the past 100 years. The gap between the rich and the poor is greater today than is has been for at least 50 years. Other postindustrial societies, such as Germany, France, and Canada, social inequality has remained constant since the mid-1970s.

     ii. Many high-tech jobs have been created at the top of the stratification system over the past few decades, which pay well. At the same time, new technologies make jobs routine, require little training, and pay poorly. Because the number of routine jobs is growing faster than the number of jobs at the top, the overall effect of technology today is to increase social inequality.

III. THEORIES OF STRATIFICATION

  A. Classical Perspectives

    1. Marx

     a. The capitalist class grew richer and smaller, while the workers grew larger and more impoverished.

     b. Marx thought that workers would enhance their sense of **class-consciousness**, or become more aware of belonging to the same exploited class, which would lead to the growth of labor unions and political parties to the point of creating a *communist system* based on shared wealth.

      c.   Several points of Marx's theory:

          i.   The **bourgeoisie** are members of the capitalist class who own the means of production, including factories, tools, and land, and are in position to make profit. The **proletariat** are members of the working class who do physical labor, and do not own the means of production—and earn wages.

          ii. Some of Marx's predictions about the development of capitalism turned out to be wrong.

  2. A Critique of Marx

      a.   Industrial societies did not polarize into two opposed classes engaged in bitter conflict. Instead, a large heterogeneous middle class of "white-collar" workers emerged, who have acted as a stabilizing force of capitalism.

      b.   Marx did not expect investment in technology to make higher wages and toil fewer hours under less oppressive conditions for workers.

      c.   Communism took root not where industry was most highly developed, but in semiindustrialized countries such as Russia in 1917 and China in 1947. And new forms of privilege emerged under communism, not a classless society of shared wealth (i.e. nomenklatura in communist Russia).

  3. Weber

      a.   For Weber, *class position* is determined by "market situation," including the possession of goods, opportunities for income, level of education, and degree of technical skill.

      b.   Four main classes:

          i.   Large property owners.

          ii. Small property owners.

          iii. Propertyless, but relatively highly educated and well-paid employees.

          iv. Propertyless manual workers.

      c.   Two types of groups other than class:

          i.   **Status groups** are distinguishable in the prestige and social honor they enjoy and in their life-style.

          ii. **Parties** are organizations that seek to impose their will on others, not just political groups.

B. American Perspectives

  1. Functionalism

      a.   Kingsley Davis and Wilbert Moore's **functional theory of stratification** argues that:

          i.   Some jobs are more important than others,

          ii. People have to make sacrifices to train for important jobs, and

          iii. Inequality is required to motivate people to undergo these sacrifices.

      b.   Chief flaws of Davis and Moore's theory.

          i.   The question of which occupations are most important is not as clear-cut as Davis and Moore suggest. From a historical perspective, *none* of the jobs regarded by Davis and Moore as "important" would exist without the physical labor done by people in "unimportant" jobs through the ages.

          ii. Functional theory ignores the pool of talent lying undiscovered *because of* inequality.

          iii. Functional theory fails to examine how advantages are passed from generation to generation.

  2. Social Mobility

      a. Peter Blau and Otis Dudley Duncan's *The American Occupational Structure.*

          i. Claimed stratification in America is based mainly on individual achievement and merit versus ascription and inheritance.

          ii. Stratification system is not made up of distinct groups or classes, but rather a continuous hierarchy of occupations with hundreds of rungs.

          iii. Saw little if any potential for class-consciousness and action in the United States.

          iv. Created a **socioeconomic index of occupation status (SEI)**, which combines for each occupation, average earnings and years of education of men employed full-time in the occupation. Other researchers then combined income, education, and occupational prestige data to construct an index of **socioeconomic status (SES)**.

      b. Peter Blau and Otis Dudley Duncan's subsequent findings:

          i. Confirmed that the rate of social mobility for men in the United States is high and that most has been upward.

          ii. Since the early 1970s, substantial downward mobility has occurred.

          iii. Mobility for men within a single generation (**intragenerational mobility**) is modest, while mobility for men over more than one generation (**intergenerational mobility**) can be substantial.

          iv. Most social mobility is due to change in the occupational structure, which became known as **structural mobility**.

          v. There are only small differences in rates of social mobility among the highly industrialized countries.

IV. NONECONOMIC DIMENSIONS OF CLASS

  A. Prestige and Taste

    1. Elaborating on Weber, *status groups* distinguish their rank by means of material and symbolic culture in addition to prestige and honor, such as "taste" in fashion, food, music, literature, manners, travel, and so forth.

  B. The Role of Politics and the Plight of the Poor

    1. Politics has a profound impact on the distribution of opportunities and rewards in society (i.e. changing laws governing people's right to own property, entitlements to welfare benefits, and redistributing income through tax policies).

    2. Two main currents of American opinion on poverty, which correspond to the Democratic and Republican positions.

      a. Most Democrats want the government to play a role in helping to solve the problem of poverty.

      b. Most Republicans want to reduce government involvement with the poor so people can solve the problem themselves.

3. Fluctuations in the **poverty rate** (the percentage of people living below the poverty threshold, which is three times the minimum food budget established by the United States Department of agriculture) reveals the impact of government policy on poverty.

4. Three policy initiatives that have been directed at the problem of poverty.

   a. Introduction of Social Security, Unemployment Insurance, and Aid to Families with Dependent Children (AFDC) by President Franklin Roosevelt in response to the Great Depression in the mid-1930s.

   b. President Lyndon Johnson's "War on Poverty" in the mid-1960s, in response to a new wave of social protest. Millions of southern blacks that migrated to the northern and western cities in the 1940s and 1950s were unable to find jobs.

   c. President Ronald Reagan from the 1980s cut government services and taxes that fund poor relief (i.e. AFDC budget, expenditures for employee training), based on the rationale that claims that relief worsens the problem of poverty.

   d. Research in the 1990s showed the inaccuracy of many beliefs of Reagan's so-called "war against the poor."

      i. *Myth 1: The overwhelming majority of poor people are African- or Hispanic-American single mothers with children.*

      ii. *Myth 2: People are poor because they don't want to work.*

      iii. *Myth 3: Poor people are trapped in poverty.*

      iv. *Myth 4: Welfare encourages married women with children to divorce so they can collect welfare, and it encourages single women on welfare to have more children.*

      v. *Myth 5: Welfare is a strain on the federal budget.*

C. Politics and the Perception of Class Inequality

   1. Surveys show that few Americans have trouble placing themselves in the class structure when asked to do so (i.e. General Social Survey).

   2. If Americans see the stratification system as divided by class, they also know that the gaps between classes are relatively large.

   3. Most Americans do not think big gaps between classes are needed to motivate people to work hard.

   4. Based on the 18-nation survey, most Americans agreed with the statement "inequality continues because it benefits the rich and powerful."

   5. Americans tend to be opposed to the government playing an active role in reducing inequality.

   6. Attitudes vary by class position.

Study Activity: Applying the Sociological Compass

After reading the chapter, study the classical, functionalist, and revived class theories of stratification—and re-read the first paragraph under "Politics and the Perception of Class Inequality." The authors ask you a set of questions to consider, which are listed below. Answer the questions as suggested in the textbook. In addition, take it a step further and attempt to explain and support your answers based on the various theories and research evidence you learned in Chapter 7.

"Do you think the gaps between the classes in American society are big, moderate, or small?" Why?

"How strongly do you agree or disagree with the view that big gaps between classes are needed to motivate people to work hard and maintain national prosperity? What is the theoretical and research evidence to support your position?"

"How strongly do you agree or disagree with the view that inequality persists because ordinary people don't join together to get rid of it?" Why?

InfoTrac College Edition Online Exercises

For the following exercises, log on to the online library of InfoTrac College Edition at http://www.infotrac-college.com/. Make note that InfoTrac has implemented a new registration system that will allow easier access to InfoTrac through the use of a personalized username and password.

Once you've created your username and password you may proceed directly to the Log On page. To create an account, register your passcode packaged with your textbook, and create a username and password, by following the online prompt. After you are logged in, click on "Infotrac College Edition." You will arrive at a screen that enables you to search topics.

Keyword: **Social mobility** and **poverty**. Identify and read a few articles that discuss recent trends in mobility and poverty. Read the articles and make note of the major trends. Are the findings consistent with the research cited in Chapter 7? Make a list of supporting and refuting evidence.

Keyword: **American Dream**. What are the different ways that this term is used? How do the different ways relate to stratification?

Keyword: **global poverty**. Do a search under this topic. What are the key issues concerning global poverty? How do they relate to stratification in the United States?

Keyword: **black market**. What are the different ways that this term is used in the research literature? How do the different ways reflect stratification in our society?

Keyword: **runaways**. Look for ways that runaways earn their living. What are their main occupations? What are the economic issues facing runaways?

Internet Exercises

For information on the 400 richest people in America, visit the annual compilation of *Forbes* business magazine at: http://www.forbes.com/2002/09/13/rich400land.html

Look at the characteristics that the 400 richest people have. What commonalities and differences do you see? Compile a list of the differences and similarities.

Look up http://www.unicef.org/ to see how this United Nations Organization views global stratification. Compare it to the Karl Marx perspective of stratification.

Human trafficking has been a major news event in recent years. Children and women are most often sold into slavery. The Commission on Human Rights has issued a State Human Rights Report for 2001 in Thailand. Go to http://www.humanrights-usa.net/reports/thailand.html and write a short paper about what they found in Thailand about this phenomenon.

The Bureau Labor Statistics provides current statistics for economic issues. Their Economy at a Glance page provides regional and state date. Go to http://www.bls.gov/eag

and find information about your state and region. Write a short paper discussing your findings.

To read about wage inequality go to: http://www.aei.org/cs/cs6931.htm

This takes you to a report called *Wage Inequality: International Comparisons of Its Sources* published by The American Enterprise Institute for Public Policy Research. Compare the United States to other countries on wage inequality. Discuss your findings in the class.

Practice Tests

Fill-In-The-Blank

Fill in the blank with the appropriate term from the above list of "key terms."

1. _____ are differences between countries in their stratification systems.

2. Fluctuations in the _____ reveals the impact of government policy on poverty.

3. Social mobility within a single generation is referred to as _____ .

4. _____ combines, for each occupation, average earnings and years of education in the occupation.

5. _____ is the measure of income inequality, and its value ranges from zero to one.

6. Stratification based on _____ depends on one's accomplishments.

7. _____ are organizations that seek to impose their will on others.

8. Social mobility due to change in the occupational structure is called _____ .

9. _____ in South Africa is an example of a caste system in industrial times.

Multiple-Choice Questions

Select the response that best answers the question or completes the statement:

1. _____ is the way society is organized in layers or strata.
   a. Social status
   b. Social mobility
   c. Social stratification
   d. Economic inequality
   e. Income strata

2. Which is an important fact about stratification in the United States?
   a. Inequality has been rising for the past quarter of a century.
   b. By 2001, the top fifth of households earned 14.3 times more than the bottom fifth.
   c. During the past 25 years, the middle 60% of income earners have been "squeezed," with their share of national income falling from 52.5% to 46.4% of the total population.
   d. All of the above.
   e. None of the above.

3. The emergence of "new money" in the United States in the 1990s is attributable to:
   a. inherited wealth.
   b. wealth earned in industries such as banking, insurance, and oil.
   c. booming high-tech industries.
   d. All of the above.
   e. None of the above.

4. Which is NOT a way that high-tech industries have widened the gap between the rich and the poor?
   a. High-technology industry helped to create a new division in the lower-upper class—the "poor rich."
   b. High-technology industry squeezed the middle class and encouraged downward mobility.
   c. High-technology industry lowered the value of unskilled work, swelling the rank of the poor.
   d. High-technology industry decreased the cost of living.
   e. All of the above are ways the high-tech industry widened the gap between the rich and poor.

5. _____ is the movement up the stratification system.
   a. Vertical social mobility
   b. Horizontal social mobility
   c. Lateral social mobility
   d. Enhance social mobility
   e. None of the above.

6. Which term refers to the differences in the economic ranking of countries?
   a. cross-national variations in internal stratification
   b. Gini index
   c. intragenerational mobility
   d. global inequality
   e. None of the above.

7. Which is a fact regarding inequality between rich and poor countries?
   a. Nearly a fifth of the world's population lack adequate shelter, and over a fifth lacks safe water.
   b. About a third of the world's people are without electricity and over two-fifths lack adequate sanitation.
   c. While the annual health expenditure in the United States is $2,765 per person, it is $3 for Vietnam.
   d. Poor countries are more likely to experience mass suffering.
   e. All of the above.

8. Which type of society is characterized by sharing for survival and subsistence with no rich and poor?
   a. foraging societies
   b. horticultural societies
   c. pastoral societies
   d. agrarian societies
   e. industrial societies

9. Evidence shows that inequality has been _____ in postindustrial societies like the United States.
    a. remaining constant
    b. tapering off
    c. increasing
    d. decreasing
    e. None of the above.

10. With industrialization, improvements in technology and social organization of manufacturing led to a(an) _____ in stratification in comparison to the agrarian period.
    a. increase
    b. dramatic climax
    c. decline
    d. All of the above.
    e. None of the above.

11. According to Marx, a crucial determinant of one's class position is one's:
    a. possession of cultural capital.
    b. occupation in powerful positions.
    c. political influence.
    d. relationship to the means of production.
    e. degree of upward mobility.

12. Which term did Marx refer to as the working class who do physical labor?
    a. bourgeoisie
    b. proletariat
    c. petty bourgeoisie
    d. parties
    e. status groups

13. Which is NOT a major criticism of Marx's theory of social class?
    a. Marx failed to recognize that investment technology would make high profits for capitalists possible.
    b. Industrial societies did not polarize into two opposed classes in the way Marx predicted.
    c. Marx did not expect investment in technology to make higher wages and less oppressive conditions for workers.
    d. Communism did not take root where industry was most highly developed.
    e. All of the above are major criticisms.

14. Weber referred to _____ as distinguishable based on their prestige and social honor.
    a. class position
    b. expert managers
    c. parties
    d. status groups
    e. bourgeoisie

15. Which theorist(s) argued that inequality is necessary to motivate people to make sacrifices and work hard?
    a. Marx and Engels
    b. Weber
    c. W.E.B. Du Bois
    d. Davis and Moore
    e. Comte

16. Who created the "socioeconomic index of occupation status" (SEI)?
    a. Weber
    b. Blau and Duncan
    c. Davis and Moore
    d. Marx
    e. Engels

17. Taste in fashion, food and music are indicators of:
    a. class
    b. status groups
    c. political parties
    d. proletariats
    e. None of the above.

18. In the 1980s, President Ronald Reagan:
    a. enhanced social security, unemployment insurance, and Aid to Families with Dependent Children.
    b. continued the "War on Poverty" that Lyndon Johnson initiated in response to a contemporary wave of social protest from the working class.
    c. expanded government services and taxes to aid the poor.
    d. Cut government services and taxes to fund relief for the poor.
    e. None of the above.

19. The 1997 movie *Titanic* depicts a story of stratification and love, which:
    a. proves the sociological idea that love can overcome inequality.
    b. concludes that social stratification has no effect on love.
    c. suggests that social class overcomes love, and doesn't allow it to blossom.
    d. All of the above.
    e. None of the above.

20. Horatio Alger's books from the post-Civil War era to the end of the 19th century:
    a. depicted the brutal realities of social inequality in America.
    b. inspired Americans with tales of how courage, faith, honesty, hard work, and a little luck could help young people rise from rags to riches.
    c. inspired young readers to fight for social justice and social change toward an equal society.
    d. All of the above.
    e. None of the above.

21. Michael Dell was the _____ richest person in the United States, in 2003.
    a. 2nd
    b. 9th
    c. 18th
    d. 10th
    e. 38th

22. In 2001, the annual household income of the lower-upper class was:
    a. $1 million.
    b. $100,000-$999,999
    c. $57,500-$99,999
    d. $37,500-$57,499
    e. $20,000-$37,499

23. As a real-life indicator of the concentration of wealth at the top of the social hierarchy in the United States, Bill Gates, the world's richest man, lives in a house that is valued at:
    a. more than $53 million.
    b. around $23 million.
    c. between $10 million and $17 million.
    d. around $8 million.
    e. None of the above.

True False

1. The debt of a significant proportion of Americans is greater than their assets.

   TRUE or FALSE

2. Income inequality has been increasing in the United States since the mid-1970s.

   TRUE or FALSE

3. The emergence of "new money" in the United States created proportionate representation of Hispanics in the upper-upper class.

   TRUE or FALSE

4. Within agrarian societies, stratification is based on ascription.

   TRUE or FALSE

5. Apartheid is a class system based on race.

   TRUE or FALSE

6. In contrast to Karl Marx, Max Weber's multidimensional approach to stratification negated the idea of classes as economic categories.

   TRUE or FALSE

7. Weber's theory is considered a functionalist approach to stratification among most contemporary sociologists.

   TRUE or FALSE

8. Most Americans want to reduce government involvement with the poor so people can help themselves.

   TRUE or FALSE

9. Most Americans think big gaps between classes are needed to motivate people to work hard.

   TRUE or FALSE

10. The Gini index indicates that the United States has the highest level of income inequality, among wealthy postindustrial countries.

    TRUE or FALSE

Short Answer

1. Distinguish between intragenerational and intergenerational mobility. (p. 188)

    _____

    _____

2. What is apartheid? Be sure to explain how apartheid in South Africa is a contemporary form of a caste system based on race. (p. 182)

    _____

    _____

3. Identify three flaws of Davis and Moore's functional theory of stratification. You must first briefly articulate their major assumptions. (p. 184)

    _____

    _____

4. List three prevailing perceptions of class inequality among Americans based on major research findings. (p. 192-195)

    _____

    _____

Essay Questions

1. Describe the development and transformation of internal stratification in terms of the socioeconomic development of societies across foraging, horticultural and pastoral societies, agrarianism, and industrialization. (p. 179-183)

2. Compare and contrast the following stratification theorists—Marx and Weber. (p. 183-187)

3. Many sociologists claim that the United States took several steps backwards in the quest to alleviate problems of poverty, largely as a result of President Ronald Reagan's approach to the problem of poverty. Identify the five myths of Reagan's so-called "war against the poor,"—and describe the research that dispelled these myths in the 1990s. (p. 190-195)

Solutions

Practice Tests

Fill-In-The-Blank

1. Cross-national variations in internal stratification
2. poverty rate
3. intragenerational mobility
4. Socioeconomic index of occupation status (SEI)
5. The Gini index
6. achievement
7. Parties
8. structural mobility
9. Apartheid

Multiple-Choice Questions

1. C, (p. 172)
2. D, (p. 173-177)
3. C, (p. 175)
4. D, (p. 174-177)
5. A, (p. 175)
6. D, (p. 178)
7. E, (p. 177-180)
8. A, (p. 180)
9. C, (p. 182-183)
10. C, (p. 182)
11. D, (p. 183)
12. B, (p. 183)
13. A, (p. 183-184)
14. D, (p. 185-186)
15. D, (p. 184)
16. B, (p. 187)
17. B, (p. 186)
18. D, (p. 192)
19. E, (p. 172)
20. B, (p. 172)
21. D, (p. 173)
22. B, (p. 175)
23. A, (p. 174)

True False

1. T, (p. 173)
2. T, (p. 173)
3. F, (p. 175)
4. T, (p. 181)
5. T, (p. 182)
6. F, (p. 185-186)
7. F, (p. 185-186)
8. T, (p. 195)
9. F, (p. 194-195)
10. T, (p. 178)

GLOBALIZATION, INEQUALITY, AND DEVELOPMENT

Student Learning Objectives

After reading Chapter 8, you should be able to:

1. Describe the historical evolution of globalization.

2. Discuss the advantages and disadvantages of globalization.

3. Explain the influence of globalization on the everyday lives of people.

4. Explain the importance of technology, politics, and economics on globalization.

5. Discuss the degree to which globalization is homogenizing the world on the one hand, and strengthening differences on the other hand.

6. Discuss rising antiglobalization and anti-Americanism.

7. Explain the concept of "development" in the context of global inequality.

8. Contrast modernization theory and dependency theory as explanations of global inequality, development, and underdevelopment.

9. Identify and explain the new means of exploitation of poor countries by rich countries, according to dependency theory.

10. Explain Immanuel Wallerstein's "world system" approach to capitalist development and global inequality.

11. Identify and describe the three types of countries according to the world system approach.

12. Describe and explain the differences between semiperipheral and peripheral countries.

13. Debate the advantages and shortcomings of neoliberal globalization.

14. Discuss the prospects for democratic globalization, and the contradictory support by the U.S. government of both antidemocratic and democratic regimes in the developing world.

Key Terms

(defined on the indicated pages of the textbook, and in glossary)

imperialism (204)

global commodity chain (205)

transnational corporations (207)

McDonaldization (209)

glocalization (210)

regionalization (211)

modernization theory (216)

dependency theory (217)

colonialism (218)

core (219)

peripheral (219)

semiperipheral (219)

neoliberal globalization (221)

Detailed Chapter Outline

I.   INTRODUCTION

    A.   The Creation of the Global Village

        1.   The world seems a much smaller place today than it did 25 years ago. Some people say that we have created a "global village." Is this uniformly beneficial, or does it have a downside too?

    B.   The Triumphs and Tragedies of Globalization

        1.   People throughout the world are now linked together as never before. Facts and indicators of globalization.

            a.   Tourism.

            b.   International organizations and agreements.

            c.   International telecommunication.

            d.   International trade and investment.

        2.   There are benefits of the rapid movement of capital, commodities, culture, and people across national boundaries.

        3.   Yet not everyone is happy. Inequality between rich and poor countries remains staggering, and in some respects is increasing. Many people oppose globalization because of its hurtful effect on local cultures and the natural environment. Antiglobalization activists suggest that globalization is a form of **imperialism**, the economic domination of one country by another. It contributes to the "homogenization" of the world, the cultural domination of less powerful by more powerful countries.

II.   GLOBALIZATION

    A.   Globalization in Everyday Life

        1.   Everything influences everything else in a globalized world.

            a.   Barbara Garson (2001) traced a small sum of money she invested in the Chase Manhatten Bank. Her money got caught up in the globalization of the world.

2. Most of us do not often appreciate that our actions have implications for people far away. When we buy a commodity we often tap into a **global commodity chain**, which is "a world-wide network of labor and production processes, whose end result is a finished commodity."

    a. For example, athletic shoes like Nike as a commodity binds consumers and producers. *The new international division of labor* yielded high profits for Nike. When someone buys a pair of Nike athletic shoes they insert themselves in a global commodity chain.

3. Sociology makes us aware of the complex web of social relations and interactions in which we are embedded. *The sociological imagination* allows us to link our biography with history and social structure.

B. The Sources of Globalization

1. Technology

    a. Technological progress has made it possible to move things and information over long distances quickly and inexpensively - for example, commercial jets and various means of communication.

2. Politics

    a. Politics is important in determining the level of globalization – for example, North Korea versus South Korea relations to the United States.

3. Economics

    a. Economics is an important source of globalization. Capitalist competition has been a major spur to international integration.

    b. **Transnational corporations** – also called multinational or international corporations – are the most important agents of globalization in the world today. They are different from traditional corporations in five ways.

        i. Traditional corporations rely on domestic labor and domestic production. Transnational corporations depend increasingly on foreign labor and foreign production.

        ii. Traditional corporations extract natural resources or manufacture industrial goods. Transnational corporations increasingly emphasize skills and advances in design, technology, and management.

        iii. Traditional corporations sell to domestic markets. Transnational corporations depend increasingly on world markets.

        iv. Traditional corporations rely on established marketing and sales outlets. Transnational corporations depend increasingly on massive advertising campaigns.

        v. Traditional corporations work with or under national governments. Transnational corporations are increasingly autonomous from national governments.

4. Technological, political, and economic factors do not work independently in leading to globalization. Governments often promote economic competition to help transnational corporations win global markets.

    a. For example, in the 1970s Phillip Morris and other tobacco companies pursued globalization as a way out of slumping domestic sales.

C. A World Like the United States?

1. Much evidence supports the view that globalization homogenizes societies.

      a. For instance, transnational organizations such as the World Bank and the International Monetary Fund have imposed economic guidelines for developing countries that are similar to those governing advanced industrial countries.

      b. In the realm of politics, the United Nations (UN) engages in global governance whereas Western ideas of democracy, representative government, and human rights have become international ideals.

      c. In the domain of culture, American icons circle the planet.

2. **McDonaldization**, as defined by George Ritzer, is a form of rationalization. Specifically, it refers to the spread of the principles of fast-food restaurants, such as efficiency, predictability, and calculability, to all spheres of life.

      a. McDonald's has turned lunch preparation into a model of rationality.

      b. McDonald's now does most of its business outside the United States.

      c. McDonaldization has come to stand for the global spread of values associated with the United States and its business culture.

3. Some analysts find fault with the view that globalization is making the world a more homogeneous place based on American values. They argue that people always interpret globalizing forces in terms of local conditions and traditions – in fact, it sharpens some local differences. **Glocalization** is the simultaneous homogenization of some aspects of life and the strengthening of some local differences under the impact of globalization.

4. **Regionalization** is the division of the world into different and often competing economic, political, and cultural areas.

      a. World trade is not evenly distributed around the planet or dominated by just one country.

      b. Politically, regionalization can be seen in the growth of the European Union.

      c. The expansion of Islam has become a unifying religious, political, and cultural force over Asia and Africa, and is a form of regional integration especially in its politically active form.

D. Globalization and Its Discontents: Antiglobalization and Anti-Americanism

1. In his book *Jihad vs. McWorld* published in 1992, Benjamin Barber book argued that globalization ("McWorld") was generating an antiglobalization reaction (*jihad*).

      a. Traditionally, Muslims use the term, *jihad,* to mean perseverance in achieving a high moral standard.

      b. The term can also suggest the idea of a holy war against those who harm Muslims. It represents an Islamic fundamentalist reaction to globalization. September 11, 2001 was the most devastating manifestation of fundamentalist Islamic *jihad*.

2. Another example involves Mexican peasants in the southern state of Chiapas, who staged an armed rebellion against the Mexican government in the 1990s.

3. As an example of the antiglobalization movement in the advanced industrial countries, when the WTO met in Seattle in December 1999, 40,000 union activists, environmentalists, supporters of worker and peasant movements in developing countries, and other opponents of transnational corporations protested, which caused property damage and threatened to disrupt the meetings.

4. The antiglobalization movement has many currents - some extremely violent, some nonviolent, some in rejection of the excesses of globalization, and other in rejection of globalization in its entirety.

III. DEVELOPMENT AND UNDERDEVELOPMENT

A. Levels and Trends in Global Inequality
1. We find an even more dramatic gap between rich and poor at the global level, than the national level.
2. The total worth of the world's 358 billionaires equals that of the world's 2.3 billion poorest people (45% of the world's population). The three richest people in the world own more than the combined GDP of the 48 least-developed countries. The richest 1% of the world's population earns as much income as the bottom 57%. The top 10% of U.S. income earners earn as much as the poorest 2 billion in the world.
3. According to the UN, 800 million people in the world are malnourished and 4 billion people (2/3 of the world's population) are poor. A fifth of the developing world's population goes hungry every night. The citizens of the 20 or so rich, highly industrialized countries spend more on cosmetics, alcohol, ice cream or pet food, respectively, than it would take to provide basic education, water and sanitation, or basic health and nutrition for everyone in the world.
4. Of the 1.3 billion people living on $1 a day or less around the world, 1 billion are women. Sixty-four percent of illiterate adults in the world are women. Racial and other minority groups often fare worse than their majority-group counterparts in the developing countries.
5. Between 1975 and 2000, the annual income gap between the 20 or so richest countries and the rest of the world grew enormously.

B. Theories of Development and Underdevelopment
1. Modernization Theory
   a. According to **modernization theory**, global inequality and economic underdevelopment results from poor countries lacking Western attributes including Western values, business practices, level of investment capital, and stable governments. Thus, rich countries can help by transferring Western culture and capital to poor countries to invigorate their cultural, political and economic development.
2. Dependency Theory
   a. Criticisms of modernization theory:
      i. For more than 500 years, the most powerful countries in the world deliberately impoverished the less powerful countries.
      ii. Focusing on internal characteristics blames the victim rather than the perpetrator.
   b. **Dependency theory** views global inequality and economic underdevelopment as the result of exploitive relations between rich and poor countries.
   c. Less global inequality existed in 1500 and even 1750 than today.
      i. However, beginning around 1500, the world's most power countries subdued and annexed or colonized most of the rest of the world. Around 1780, the Industrial Revolution began, which enabled the Western European countries, Russia, Japan, and the United States to accumulate enormous wealth, and extend globally. The colonies became sources of raw materials, cheap labor, investment opportunities, and markets for conquering nations. Colonizers prevented industrialization and locked the colonies into poverty.

d. Despite the political independence of nearly all colonies in the decades following World War II, exploitation by direct political control was replaced by new means of: substantial foreign investment, support for authoritarian governments, and mounting debt.

   i. *Substantial Foreign Investment.* Although they created some low-paying jobs, multinational corporations invested heavily in the poor countries to siphon off wealth in the form of raw materials and profits, which created more high-paying jobs in the rich countries where the raw materials were use to produce manufactured goods. Multinational corporations sold part of the manufactured goods back to the poor, unindustrialized countries for additional profit.

   ii. *Support for Authoritarian Governments.* Multinational corporations and rich countries continued to exploit poor countries in the postcolonial period by giving economic and military support to local authoritarian governments, which keep their populations subdued most of the time. Western governments have also sent in their own troops and military advisors, when authoritarian governments were unable to subdue their populations, which is called "gunboat diplomacy." The United States has been particularly active in using gunboat diplomacy in Central America, such as the case of Guatemala in the 1950s.

   iii. *Mounting Debt.* In order for the governments of poor countries to build transportation infrastructures, education systems, safe water systems, and basic health care, they had to borrow money from Western banks and governments. By 1999, poor countries owed rich countries more than 2.6 trillion dollars, which is 54% more than in 1992. Crushing interest payments leave governments in poor countries with too little money for development. At the end of the 20th century, poor countries were paying about two and a half times more interest to Western banks and governments than they were receiving in foreign aid. Providing foreign aid to compensate for centuries of injustice ranks last on Americans' list of priorities according to GSS data. The United States spends a small and declining amount on foreign aid.

C. Effects of Foreign Investment
   1. Almost all sociologists agree with dependency theory on one point. Since about 1500, Spain, Portugal, Holland, Britain, France, Italy, the United States, Japan, and Russia treated the world's poor with brutality to enrich themselves. **Colonialism** did have a devastating economic and human impact on poor countries. In the postcolonial era, the debt has crippled the development efforts of many poor countries.
   2. Do foreign investment and liberalized trade policies have positive or negative effects today?
      a. Modernization theorists want more foreign investment in poor countries and freer trade to promote economic growth and general well-being for everyone.
      b. Dependency theorists think foreign investment drains wealth out of poor countries. They want the poor countries to revolt against the rich countries, throw up barriers to free trade and investment, and find their own path to economic well being.
      c. A recent summary of research in this area cautiously reaches two conclusions.
         i. First, in the 1980s and 1990s but not in the 1960s and 1970s, openness to international trade and investment generally seems to have stimulated economic growth.

ii. Second, in most well documented cases, openness to international trade and foreign investment also increased inequality.

d. These findings suggest that it is a mistake to lump all periods of history and all countries together when considering the effects of openness on economic growth and inequality.

D. Core, Periphery, and Semiperiphery

1. Immanuel Wallerstein argues that capitalist development has resulted in the creation of a "world system" composed of three tiers.

a. **Core** capitalist countries, are rich such as the United States, Japan, and Germany that are the major sources of capital and technology.

b. **Peripheral** countries are former colonies that are poor and are major sources of raw materials and cheap labor.

c. **Semiperipheral** countries consist of former colonies that are making considerable headway in their attempts to become prosperous, such as South Korea, Taiwan, and Israel.

2. The semiperipheral countries differ from the peripheral countries in four main ways: type of colonialism, geopolitical position, state policy, and social structure.

3. Type of Colonialism

a. In contrast to European colonizers of Africa, Latin America, and other parts of Asia, the Japanese built up the economies of their colonies, Taiwan and Korea, and established transportation networks and communication systems.

b. The Japanese-built infrastructure served as a springboard to development for Korea and Taiwan.

4. Geopolitical Position

a. Countries with significant strategic importance to the United States receive more help.

b. By the end of World War II, the United States began to feel its dominance threatened in the late 1940s by the Soviet Union and China, therefore poured unprecedented aid into South Korea and Taiwan in the 1960s fearing these countries might fall to the communists. Israel also received economic assistance for its strategic position in the Middle East.

5. State Policy

a. The Taiwanese and South Korean states developed on the Japanese-model: low worker's wages, restricted trade union growth, quasi-military discipline in the factories, high taxes on consumer goods, limitations on the import of foreign goods, and prevention of citizens to invest abroad.

b. This encourages their citizens to put their money in the bank, which created a large pool of capital that the state made available for industrial expansion.

c. From the 1960s on, South Korean and Taiwanese states gave subsidies, training grants, and tariff protection to export-based industries.

6. Social Structure

a. Social cohesion and solidarity in Taiwan and South Korea is strong and based partly on two main factors.

i. The sweeping land reforms in the late 1940s and early 1950s redistributed land to small farmers, eliminated the class of large owners, and thus eliminated a major source of conflict. In contrast, many countries in Latin America and Africa have not undergone land reform, whereby the United States has often intervened militarily to prevent land reform based on U.S. commercial interests in large plantations.

    ii.   Taiwan and South Korea are both ethnically homogeneous, thus limiting the ability of colonizers to instigate antagonism among the colonized. In contrast, British, French, and other West European colonizers kept tribal tensions alive to make it easier for imperial rule in Africa.

IV. NEOLIBERAL VERSUS DEMOCRATIC GLOBALIZATION

A. Globalization and Neoliberalism

    1. Resembling the modernization theorists of a generation ago, **neoliberal globalization** is a policy that promotes private control of industry, minimal government interference in the running of the economy, the removal of taxes, tariffs, and restrictive regulations that discourage the international buying and selling of goods and services, and the encouragement of foreign investment..

    2. Many social scientists are skeptical of neoliberal prescriptions. Nobel Prize-winning economist and former Chief Economist of the World Bank, Joseph E. Stiglitz argues that the World Bank and other international economic organizations often impose outdated policies on the developing countries, putting them at a disadvantage *vis-à-vis* developed countries.

    3. With the exception of Great Britain, neoliberalism was *never* a successful development strategy in the early stages of industrialization. Typically, it is only after industrial development is well under way and national industries can compete on the global market that countries begin to advocate neoliberal globalization to varying degrees.

        a. Great Britain is the exception, as it needed less government involvement to industrialize because it was the first industrializer and had no international competitors.

        b. The United States, one of the most vocal advocates of neoliberalism today, invested a great deal of public money subsidizing industries and building infrastructure. Today, the United States still subsidizes large corporations in a variety of ways and maintains substantial tariffs on a whole range of foreign products.

B. Foreign Aid, Debt Cancellation, and Tariff Reduction

    1. If you think that we have a responsibility to compensate for centuries of injustice and that we are spending too little on foreign aid, you are in a minority. According to the GSS, foreign aid ranks a distant last on American's list of priorities. Most U.S. foreign aid goes for economic and military support to strategically important friends: Israel, Egypt, Jordan, and Colombia.

    2. Foreign aid as presently delivered is not an effective way of helping the developing world.

    3. Brym and Lie conclude that foreign aid is often beneficial. Poor countries need more of it. But strict government oversight is required to ensure that foreign aid is not wasted and that it is directed to truly helpful projects, such as improving irrigation and sanitation systems and helping people acquire better farming techniques.

    4. Many analysts argue that the world's rich countries and banks should simply write off the debt owed to them by the developing countries in recognition of historical injustices. This proposal of blunting the worst effects of neoliberal globalization may be growing in popularity among politicians in developed countries.

5. A third reform proposed in recent years involves the elimination of tariffs by the rich countries. However, there is little room for optimism in this regard to date.

C. Democratic Globalization
    1. A final reform involves efforts to help spread democracy throughout the developing world. A large body of research shows that democracy lowers inequality and promotes economic growth, for several reasons.
        a. Democracies make it more difficult for elite groups to misuse their power and enhance their wealth and income at the expense of the less well-to-do.
        b. They increase political stability, thereby providing a better investment climate.
        c. Because they encourage broad political participation, democracies tend to enact policies that are more responsive to people's needs and benefit a wide range of people from all social classes.
    2. Although democracy has spread in recent years, by 2002 only 80 countries with 55% of the world's population were considered fully democratic by one measure. The United States has supported as many antidemocratic as democratic regimes in the developing world. The CIA refers to the unexpected and undesirable consequences of these actions as "blowback."
        a. For example, in the 1980s the U.S. government supported Saddam Hussein when it considered Iraq's enemy, Iran, the greater threat to U.S. security interests.
        b. The United States also funded Osama bin Laden when he was fighting the Soviet Union in Afghanistan.
        c. Only a decade later, these so-called allies turned into the United States' worst enemies.

Study Activity: Applying the Sociological Compass

After reading Chapter 8 of the textbook, re-read the sections "Development and Underdevelopment" and "Neoliberal Versus Democratic Globalization." As you re-read these sections, make a list of evidence cited in the textbook, in support of modernization theory, neoliberal globalization, dependency theory, and democratic globalization. Which theory implies the greatest potential of "freeing individuals" and which theory most implies that the world's poor people (which are the numerical majority of the world population) will likely experience greater constraints in the future. Which theory or theories seem most plausible based on the cited evidence? Explain why?

Modernization Theory:

Neoliberal Globalization:

Dependency Theory:

Democratic Globalization:

InfoTrac College Edition Online Exercises

For the following exercises, log on to the online library of InfoTrac College Edition at http://www.infotrac-college.com/. Make note that InfoTrac has implemented a new registration system that will allow easier access to InfoTrac through the use of a personalized username and password.

Once you've created your username and password you may proceed directly to the Log On page. To create an account, register your passcode packaged with your textbook, and create a username and password, by following the online prompt. After you are logged in, click on "Infotrac College Edition." You will arrive at a screen that enables you to search topics.

Keyword: **dependency theory**. Locate the article by Alex Dupuy called, "*Thoughts on globalization, Marxism, and the left*." Read the article and look for specific evidence to support and refute Marx's theory. How does the evidence, or lack of evidence, compare with the section in this chapter on Marx's theory?

Keywords: **Development Peru**. Look at all of the articles. There are not too many. What development issues are currently facing Peru? Make a list of all the issues pertaining to development. How does your list compare to development issues discussed in the chapter?

Keywords: **Global village**. Find the article called, ***Toronto A global village,*** by Mary Vincent. Read the article. How does evidence of a "global village" in the article compare to the section of a global village in this chapter? Do you agree or disagree with the idea of a global village?

Internet Exercises

The United Nations has many statisticians who have created indicators of human development for every country in the world. The indicators for the 2003 Human Development Indicators are available at:

http://www.undp.org/hdr2003/indicator/index_indicators.html

Make a list of the indicators that you think are the most important. Why did you include each item on your list?

Go to: http://www.nologo.org/ for Namoi Klein's *No Logo: Taking Aim at the Brand Bullies*. This site is against the globalization movement. Look over the site and then list specific reasons why Klein is anti-globalization.

At this site: http://www.worldbank.org you will be able to find many reports and date on the state of the global economy and many other nations. This is the World Bank site. Look over a report of interest to you. Write a brief description stating its purpose and what information it contains.

Practice Tests

Fill-In-The-Blank

Fill in the blank with the appropriate term from the above list of "key terms."

1. Multinational corporations are also called _____ .

2. _____ is the simultaneous homogenization of some aspects of life and the strengthening of some local differences under the impact of globalization.

3. _____ is the economic domination of one country by another.

4. _____ views global inequality and economic underdevelopment as the result of exploitive relations between rich and poor countries.

5. A(An) _____ is a world-wide network of labor and production processes, whose end result is a finished commodity.

6. As defined by George Ritzer, _____ is a form of rationalization.

7. _____ is the division of the world into different and often competing economic, political, and cultural areas.

8. _____ countries consist of former colonies that are making considerable headway in their attempts to become prosperous.

Multiple-Choice Questions

Select the response that best answers the question or completes the statement:

1. Antiglobalization activists suggest that globalization is a form of:
   a. modernization.
   b. imperialism
   c. development.
   d. All of the above.
   e. None of the above.

2. Transnational corporations are different from traditional corporations in what way?
   a. Traditional corporations extract natural resources or manufacture industrial goods. Transnational corporations emphasize skills and advances in design, technology, and management.
   b. Traditional corporations work with or under national governments. Transnational corporations are increasingly autonomous from national governments.
   c. Traditional corporation sell to domestic markets. Transnational corporations depend increasingly on world markets.
   d. Traditional corporations rely on domestic labor and domestic productions. Transnational corporations depend increasingly on foreign labor and foreign production.
   e. All of the above.

3. The fact that world trade is not evenly distributed around the planet or dominated by just one country is an example of:
   a. regionalization.
   b. glocalization.
   c. underdevelopment.
   d. development.
   e. None of the above.

4. Which theory suggests that global inequality is a result of poor countries lacking Western attributes such as Western values and business practices?
   a. dependency theory
   b. modernization theory
   c. world system theory
   d. All of the above.
   e. None of the above.

5. Which tier of what Immanuel Wallerstein refers to as the world system, is a major source of raw materials and cheap labor?
   a. core countries
   b. peripheral countries
   c. semiperipheral countries
   d. industrialized countries
   e. newly industrialized countries

6. Which is NOT one of the ways in which semiperipheral countries differ from peripheral countries, according to the Brym and Lie textbook?
   a. type of colonialism
   b. geopolitical position
   c. state policy
   d. social structure
   e. number of traditional corporations

7. Neoliberal globalization resembles which theory of a generation ago?
   a. modernization theory
   b. dependency theory
   c. world system theory
   d. internal colony theory
   e. neo-Marxist theory

8. Neoliberal globalization promotes:
   a. public control of industry.
   b. moderate to strong government management in the running for the economy.
   c. the introduction of new taxes, tariffs, and regulations to check and balance the power of transnational corporations.
   d. the encouragement of foreign investment.
   e. exclusive national buying and selling of goods and services.

9. All of the following are indicators of globalization EXCEPT:
   a. tourism.
   b. international organizations and agreements.
   c. international telecommunications.
   d. international trade and investment.
   e. All of the above are indicators of globalization.

10. In leading to globalization, technological, political and economic factors:
    a. do not work independently.
    b. operate independently in the context of global competition.
    c. are interrelated and functional exclusively on a domestic level.
    d. All of the above.
    e. None of the above.

11. McDonaldization:
    a. refers to the spread of the principles of fast-food restaurants.
    b. suggests that McDonald's has turned lunch preparation into a model of rationality.
    c. has come to stand for the global spread of values associated with the United States and its business culture.
    d. All of the above.
    e. None of the above.

12. Which is an example of antiglobalization and/or anti-Americanism?
    a. *jihad*
    b. the Mexican peasant rebellion in Chiapas in the 1990s.
    c. the protest in Seattle in December 1999 when the WTO met.
    d. All of the above.
    e. None of the above.

13. Which is a current of the antiglobalization movement?
    a. violent protest.
    b. rejection of the excesses of globalization.
    c. rejection of globalization in its entirety.
    d. All of the above.
    e. None of the above.

14. South Korea, Taiwan, and Israel are examples of which type of country?
    a. core countries
    b. peripheral countries
    c. semiperipheral countries
    d. underdeveloped countries
    e. None of the above.

15. According to Table 8.1 "Indicators of Globalization, Early 1980s - Circa 2003" in the Brym and Lie textbook, which indicator showed the most change from 1980-81 to 1998-2003?
    a. foreign direct investment as percent of GDP.
    b. international tourist arrivals as a percent of the world population.
    c. Air freight and mail.
    d. number of international organizations.
    e. annual entries on globalization, *Sociological Abstracts*.

16. Michael Jordan:
    a. helps globalize Nike.
    b. is the icon of Nike, but primarily at a national level.
    c. is the primary reason why Nike exploits labor in third-world countries.
    d. All of the above.
    e. None of the above.

17. In the 1970s, the antismoking campaign:
    a. began to have an impact.
    b. led to slumping domestic sales for tobacco companies.
    c. sparked the pursuit of globalization by tobacco companies.
    d. All of the above.
    e. None of the above.

18. Figure 8.2 "The Size and Influence of the U.S. Economy, 2000" in the Brym and Lie textbook:
    a. shows how the GDP of various countries compares to that of each U.S. state.
    b. shows that the economy of each U.S. state is as big as that of a whole country.
    c. emphasizes just how large the U.S. economy is.
    d. All of the above.
    e. None of the above.

19. A half-hour's drive from the center of Manila, the capital of the Philippines, an estimated 70,000 Filipinos live on a 55-acre mountain of:
    a. rotting garbage.
    b. fertile land for agricultural production.
    c. ancient burial sites.
    d. All of the above.
    e. None of the above.

20. The gross domestic product per capita across world regions from 1975-2000, indicates that:
    a. Latin American and Caribbean countries are fast approaching high-income countries in GDP.
    b. Countries in East Asia and the Pacific are fast approaching high-income countries.
    c. although the GDP in high-income countries is significantly higher than other world regions, the GDP in high-income countries has fallen since 1975.
    d. The GDP of high-income countries has increased since 1975, and remains much higher than other world regions.
    e. None of the above.

21. From 1820 to 1992, the share of world income going to the top 10% has:
    a. increased.
    b. declined.
    c. remained consistently proportionate to diverse populations.
    d. All of the above.
    e. None of the above.

22. Which country had the greatest percentage of people living for less than $1 a day in 1999?
    a. Sub-Saharan Africa
    b. East Asia (excluding China)
    c. South Asia
    d. Latin America
    e. East Europe and Central Asia

23. Which is true in the wake of the late 1800s British takeover of what became Rhodesia, and is now Zimbabwe?
    a. Every British trooper was offered about 9 square miles of native land.
    b. The Matabele and Mashona people were subdued.
    c. Native survivors were left without a livelihood.
    d. Forced labor was introduced by the British.
    e. All of the above.

24. Based on data on national priorities collected in 2000 by the National Opinion Research Center, which priority had the highest percentage of respondents answering "Too Little" in response to the question, "I'd like you to tell me whether you think we're spending too much money on it, too little money, or about the right amount?"
    a. Improving and protecting the nation's health.
    b. Dealing with drug addiction.
    c. Highways and bridges.
    d. The military, armaments, and defense.
    e. Foreign aid.

True False

1. When we purchase a product domestically, we seldom tap into the global commodity chain, because domestic commodities tend to be produced within a country independent of the global economy.

    TRUE or FALSE

2. The new international division of labor yielded high profits for producers like *Nike*.

    TRUE or FALSE

3. McDonald's now does most of its business outside the United States.

    TRUE or FALSE

4. According to Benjamin Barber's book *Jihad vs. McWorld*, *jihad* exclusively refers to the idea of holy war against those who harm Muslims.

    TRUE or FALSE

5. September 11, 2001 was the most devastating manifestation of fundamentalist Islamic *jihad*.

    TRUE or FALSE

6. Almost all manifestations of the antiglobalization movement are extremely violent, and occur in third-world countries.

    TRUE or FALSE

7. Technology speeds globalization.

    TRUE or FALSE

8. The GDP of California is equal to that of France.

    TRUE or FALSE

Short Answer

1. Briefly explain what it means to say that people have created a "global village." (p. 201-202)

    _____

    _____

2. List five ways in which transnational corporations differ from traditional corporations. (p. 207)

    _____

    _____

3. List and explain four facts and indicators of globalization. (p. 203)

    _____

    _____

4. Explain glocalization, and provide one example of this phenomenon from the Brym and Lie textbook. (p. 210)

    _____

    _____

5. List and explain the characteristics of each of the three types of countries on the world system, according to Immanuel Wallerstein. (p. 219)

    _____

    _____

Essay Questions

1. Explain the phenomenon of McDonaldization according to George Ritzer. In your answer, be sure to mention rationalization, efficiency, predictability, and calculability. (p. 209)

2. Contrast modernization theory and dependency theory as explanations of global inequality. In your answer, be sure to provide relevant historical and contemporary support for each theory. (p. 216-218)

3. Compare and contrast neoliberal globalization and democratic globalization in terms their major assumptions and premises, their prescriptions to alleviate global inequality. (p. 221-226)

4. Explain four ways in which semiperipheral countries differ from peripheral countries. (p. 219)

Solutions

Practice Tests

Fill-In-The-Blank

1. transnational corporations
2. Glocalization
3. Imperialism
4. Dependency theory
5. global commodity chain
6. McDonaldization
7. Regionalization
8. Semiperipheral

Multiple-Choice Questions

1. B, (p. 204).
2. E, (p. 207)
3. A, (p. 211)
4. B, (p. 216)
5. B, (p. 219)
6. E, (p. 219)
7. A, (p. 221)
8. D, (p. 221)
9. E, (p. 221-226)
10. A, (p. 221-226)
11. D, (p. 209)
12. D, (p. 212)
13. D, (p. 212-226)
14. C, (p. 219)
15. E, (p. 203)
16. A, (p. 205-206)
17. D, (p. 207)
18. D, (p. 208)
19. A, (p. 214)
20. D, (p. 215)
21. A, (p. 216)
22. A, (p. 216)
23. E, (p. 217)
24. A, (p. 223)

True False

1. F, (p. 205)
2. T, (p. 206)
3. T, (p. 209)
4. F, (p. 212)
5. T, (p. 212)
6. F, (p. 212)
7. T, (p. 212)
8. T, (p. 208)

RACE AND ETHNICITY

Student Learning Objectives

After reading Chapter 9, you should be able to:

1. Engage the debate over the racial basis of athletic ability.

2. Identify social conditions involving prejudice and discrimination that lead certain racial groups into particular life chances.

3. Explain the notion of race and ethnicity as socially constructed ideas. How are these terms used to distinguish and categorize people based on perceived physical and cultural differences that have profound consequences for their lives?

4. Explain how racial and ethnic identities change over time and place in the context of insider self-conceptions and outsider labels.

5. Describe the historical experiences, demographic profiles and negotiations of racial and ethnic identity among the major Hispanic groups—Chicanos, Puerto Ricans, and Cubans.

6. Explain the notion of racial and ethnic identity as a choice versus an imposition.

7. Discuss how the identification with a racial or ethnic group can be economically, politically, and emotionally advantageous. What role does racial and ethnic identification play in ethnic community formation?

8. Identify and explain the major assumptions of ecological theory, the theory of internal colonialism, and split labor market theory.

9. Describe the historical experiences of Native Americans, Chicanos and African Americans in terms of internal colonialism—and the experiences of Irish Americans in terms of ecological theory.

10. Engage the "declining significance of race" debate, by discussing the pros and cons and the respective evidence for each position. In light of the evidence, what is the future outlook on racial and ethnic inequality in the United States?

11. Discuss recent trends and debate surrounding immigration.

12. Explain the idea of a vertical mosaic in the future of racial and ethnic relations. What can society do in terms of policy initiatives to decrease the verticality of the American ethnic mosaic?

Key Terms

(defined on the indicated pages of the textbook, and in glossary)

prejudice (229)

discrimination (229)

race (230)

scapegoats (230)

ethnic group (231)

minority group (232)

ethnic enclave (234)

symbolic ethnicity (237)

racism (237)

institutional racism (237)

ecological theory (237)

segregation (238)

assimilation (238)

internal colonialism (238)

split labor markets (238)

expulsion (240)

genocide (240)

slavery (242)

hate crimes (246)

affirmative action (249)

pluralism (238)

Detailed Chapter Outline

I. DEFINING RACE AND ETHNICITY

    A. Race, Biology, and Society

        1. Dr. Samuel George Morton, who died in 1851, claimed to show that social inequality in the United States and throughout the world had natural, biological roots, based on research on brain size of different races (indicated by skull size).

        2. Morton claimed that the people with the biggest brains were whites of European origin. Next were Asians. Then came Native Americans and African Americans.

           a. Even today archeologists cannot precisely determine race by skull shape.

        3. Although biological arguments about racial differences became more sophisticated, their scientific basis is still shaky.

        4. Examples:

           a. "Blue blood" aristocrats in medieval Europe.

           b. 1920s United States IQ scores and biology.

        5. Is there evidence to support racial differences in singing ability, athletic prowess, and crime rates?

           a. At first glance, there seems to be evidence of black athletic superiority in the NBA, NFL, and track and field.

      b. Evidence falters in light of two points.
          i. No gene connected to general athletic superiority has been identified.
          ii. Athletes of African descent do not perform unusually well in many sports, such as swimming, hockey, cycling, tennis, gymnastics, and soccer.
      c. Sociologists have identified *social conditions* that lead to high participation in sports, as well as entertainment and crime.
          i. For lack of other ways to improve their social and economic positions due to **prejudice** (an attitude that judges a person on his or her group's real or imagined characteristics) and **discrimination** (unfair treatment of people due to their group membership), people enter sports, entertainment, and crime in *disproportionate* numbers.
      d. The idea that people of African descent are genetically superior to whites in athletic ability complements the idea that they are genetically inferior to whites in intellectual ability. Both ideas reinforce black-white inequality.
          i. There are millions of professionals and probably fewer than 10,000 elite professional athletes in the United States.
          ii. Promoting the Shaquille O'Neals of the world as role models for African-American youth, the idea of black athletic superiority combined with intellectual inferiority deflects the attention of African American youth from a much safer bet—that they can achieve upward mobility through academic excellence.
6. The fact that one cannot neatly distinguish race based on genetic differences, is an additional problem with the argument that genes determine specific behaviors of different racial groups.
      a. High level of genetic mixing.
      b. Many scholars believe we all belong to one human race.
7. Although some biologists and social scientists therefore suggest we drop the term "race" from the vocabulary of science, most sociologists continue to use the term. Why?
      a. *Perceptions* of race continue to have a profound effect on the lives of most people.
      b. Race as a *sociological* concept is an invaluable analytical tool if we remember that it refers to socially significant physical differences, rather than biological differences.
8. Perceptions of racial differences are socially constructed and often arbitrary. **Race** is a social construct used to distinguish people in terms of one or more physical markers, usually with profound effect on their lives.
9. Why does race matter if it is merely a social construct?
      a. It allows social inequality to be created and maintained.
      b. Racial stereotypes embed themselves in literature, popular lore, journalism, and political debate to reinforce racial inequality.
      c. Examples of systems of racial domination.
          i. English colonization of Ireland.
          ii. American enslavement of people of Africa.
          iii. Use of Jews as **scapegoats** (a disadvantaged person or category of people who others blame for their own problems) by the Germans after World War I.

B. Ethnicity, Culture, and Social Structure

1. While race is a category of people whose perceived *physical* markers are deemed socially significant, an **ethnic group** is composed of people whose perceived *cultural* markers are deemed socially significant (i.e. language, religion, customs, values, ancestors, etc.).
2. Just as physical differences do not cause differences in the behavior of various races, ethnic values and other elements of ethnic culture have less of an effect on the way people behave than we commonly believe.
3. Social structural differences underlie cultural differences.
4. Examples:
    a. Impact of American immigration policy on social-structural conditions for Jews and Koreans on the one hand, versus descendants of Southern blacks.
5. It is misleading to claim that race and ethnicity are quite different. Both race and ethnicity are rooted in social structure, not biology and culture. Groups socially defined as races may later be redefined as ethnic.

II. RACE AND ETHNIC RELATIONS

A. Labels and Identity
1. **Minority group** refers to a group of people who are socially disadvantaged, though they may be in the numerical majority.
2. Social contexts, and in particular the nature of one's relations with members of other racial and ethnic groups, shape and continuously reshape one's *racial and ethnic identity*. Change in social context changes your *racial and ethnic self-conception.*
3. Examples:
    a. John Lie's migration experiences from South Korea to Japan, Japan to Hawaii, and from Hawaii to the American mainland.
    b. Italian immigrants in the United States around 1900.
4. The development of racial and ethnic labels and identities is a process of negotiation, as symbolic interactionists emphasize. Negotiations, between outsiders' imposition of a new label, and insiders' racial and ethnic self-conceptions and their response to the outsider labels (rejection, acceptance, or modification) results in the crystallization of a new, more or less stable ethnic identity.

B. Hispanic Americans
1. Although people scarcely used the terms "Hispanic American" and "Latino" 30 or 40 years ago, they are now common.
2. Who is Hispanic American?
    a. In 2002, 67% of Hispanic Americans were of Mexican origin, nearly 9% of Puerto Rican origin, almost 4% of Cuban origin, and 14% were from El Salvador, the Dominican Republic, and other countries in Latin America.
3. What do members of these groups have in common?
    a. Spanish language.
    b. Based on a survey, most of them do not want to called "Hispanic American," and prefer instead to be referred to by their national origin.
    c. Many want to be referred to simply as "Americans."

4. Members of the three major Hispanic groups enjoy different cultural traditions, social class positions, and vote differently.
   a. Cubans
      i. More middle-class and professional because of the large wave of middle-class Cubans who fled Castro's revolution and arrived in the Miami area in the late 1950s and early 1960s.
      ii. They formed an **ethnic enclave**, a geographical concentration of ethnic group members who establish businesses that serve and employ mainly members of the ethnic group and reinvest profits in community businesses and organizations. This benefited subsequent waves of poor Cuban immigrants.
      iii. More easily integrated into American society as result of being procapitalist and anticommunist.
      iv. More likely to vote Republican.
   b. Chicanos and Puerto Rican Americans
      i. Immigrants from Mexico and Puerto Rico tend to be working class individuals who have not completed high school.
      ii. Lower class origins, less upward mobility.
      iii. Weaker ethnic enclave formation.
      iv. More commonly vote Democrat.
5. Three reasons why the term "Hispanic American" is more widely used than it was 30 or 40 years ago, despite internal diversity:
   a. Many Hispanic Americans find it politically useful.
   b. The government finds the term useful for data collection and public policy purposes.
   c. Non-Hispanic Americans find it convenient, in light of the many ethnic divisions.

C. Ethnic and Racial Labels: Choice Versus Imposition
   1. There are wide variations over time and across societies in the degree to which people can choose their racial and ethnic identity freely.
   2. Ethnic and Racial Choice in the United States
      a. People with the most freedom to choose their ethnic or racial identity are white Americans whose ancestors came from Europe.
         i. Example—The transformation of Irish identity from imposition to choice.
         ii. Involves what Herbert Gans defines as **symbolic ethnicity**, "a nostalgic allegiance to the culture of the immigrant generation, or that of the old country; a love for and a pride in a tradition that can be felt without having to be incorporated in everyday behavior."
      b. In contrast, most African Americans lack the freedom to enjoy symbolic ethnicity.
         i. They make take pride in their cultural heritage, but their identity has been imposed on them daily by **racism**, the belief that a visible characteristic of a group, such as skin color, indicates group inferiority and justifies discrimination. **Institutional racism** is bias that is inherent in social institutions and is often not noticed by members of the majority group.

ii. Malcolm X noted that it doesn't matter to a racist whether an African American is a professor or a panhandler, a genius or a fool, a saint or a criminal. Where racism is common, racial identities are compulsory and at the forefront of one's self-identity.

III. THEORIES OF RACE AND ETHNIC RELATIONS

A. Ecological Theory
1. Robert Park's **ecological theory** focuses on the struggle for territory that involves the process by which conflict between racial and ethnic groups emerges and is resolved.
2. Five stages:
   a. *Invasion*;
   b. *Resistance*;
   c. *Competition*; and
   d. *Accommodation and Cooperation.* Eventually, groups work out an understanding of what they should segregate, divide, and share. **Segregation** involves spatial and institutional separation of racial or ethnic groups.
   e. *Assimilation.* **Assimilation** is the process by which a minority group blends into the majority population and eventually disappears as a distinct group.
3. Park's theory applies to some ethnic groups such as whites of European origin, but is too optimistic about the prospects for assimilation of African Americans, Native Americans, Hispanic Americans, and Asian Americans.

B. Internal Colonialism and the Split Labor Market
1. Robert Blauner's examination of **internal colonialism** (a condition that involves one race or ethnic group subjugating another in the same country. It prevents assimilation by segregating the subordinate group in terms of jobs, housing, and social contacts), emphasized the social-structural roots of race and ethnicity.
2. *Colonialism* involves people from one country invading another. *Internal colonialism* involves the same process but within the boundaries of a single country. Both conditions involve the following processes:
   a. Invaders change or destroy the native culture.
   b. Invaders gain virtually complete control over the native population.
   c. Invaders develop the racist belief that the natives are inherently inferior.
   d. Invaders confine the natives to work that is considered demeaning.
3. Edna Bonacich developed a second important theory that focuses on social-structural conditions hindering the assimilation of some groups. Racial identities are reinforced in **split labor markets**, where low-wage workers of one race and high-wage workers of another race compete for the same jobs. High-wage workers are likely to resent the presence of low-wage competitors, and conflict is bound to result. Consequently, racist attitudes develop or get reinforced.
4. Native Americans
   a. Expulsion and genocide best describe the treatment of Native Americans by European immigrants in the 19th century. **Expulsion** is the forcible removal of a population from a territory claimed by another population. **Genocide** is the intentional extermination of an entire population defined as a race or a people.

b. Once the British won the battle for control of North America in the late 18th century, Indian-white relations focused on land issues. Forcing the Indians to become like the European settlers and forcing them off their land became the two dominant strategies that informed American policy for centuries.

c. Indians and settlers signed treaties, whereby Indians were often forced to sign, and defined the land belonging to each group. Treaty violations on the part of settlers were common.

d. In 1830 the U.S. government passed the *Indian Removal Act*, which called for relocation of all Native Americans to land set aside for them west of the Mississippi. White European Americans fought a series of wars against various Native American tribes.

e. The end of the war against Indians came in 1890 with the slaughter of hundreds of Sioux at *Wounded Knee* in South Dakota. The remaining small bands were placed on reservations under the rule of the *Bureau of Indian Affairs*.

f. What war could not accomplish, disease and the extermination of the buffalo did.

g. In the late 19th century, the U.S. government adopted a policy of forced assimilation, through the selling of some Indian land to non-Indians, and by taking and placing Native-American children in boarding schools to be "civilized."

h. In the 1930s and 1940s, the Roosevelt administration adopted a more liberal policy, which prohibited further break up of Indian lands and encouraged Native self-rule and cultural preservation. This was only a brief deviation from traditional policy.

i. In the 1950s, the U.S. government proposed to end the reservation system, deny the sovereign status of the tribes, cut off all government services, and stop protecting Indian lands held in trust for the tribes.

j. By the 1960s a full-fledged *Red Power* movement emerged.

k. In recent decades, Native Americans have used the legal system to fight for political self-determination and the protection of their remaining lands.

l. Many Native Americans still suffer the consequences of internal colonialism.

m. Urban Indians are less impoverished than those who live on the reservations, but still fall below the national average in terms of income, education, occupation, employment, health care, and housing.

5. Chicanos
   a. In light the U.S. desire for land, the U.S. war with Mexico in 1848 led to the United States winning Arizona, California, New Mexico, Utah, and part of Colorado and Texas (formerly Northern Mexico).
   b. Due mainly to discrimination, Chicanos tend to be occupationally and residentially segregated from white European-American neighborhoods, -which has prevented upward mobility and assimilation.
      i. Until the 1970s, most Chicanos lived in *barrios*.
      ii. Still mainly agricultural and unskilled laborers.
      iii. Ironically, some Mexicans are called "illegal migrants" in places where their ancestors were expelled, such as California and Texas.
      iv. Since the 1960s, many Chicanos have participated in a movement to renew their culture and protect and advance their rights.

6. African Americans
   a. Millions of Africans were brought to America by force and enslaved. **Slavery** is the ownership and control of people.
   b. The cotton and tobacco economy of the American South depended completely on African slave labor.
   c. Slavery and later Jim Crow laws kept blacks segregated, from voting, attending white schools, and in general from participating equally in American social institutions (i.e. 1896 *Plessy v. Ferguson*).
   d. In the 19th and early 20th centuries, the opportunity to integrate the black population quickly and completely into the American mainstream was squandered in favor of policy makers choosing to encourage white European immigration.
   e. Jobs in northern and western industries that went to African Americans who migrated from the South since the 1910's, enabled them to compete with European immigrants. Here we see the operation of a *split labor market*, which fueled deep resentment, animosity, and anti-Black riots on the part of working class whites.
   f. Black migration northward and westward signaled the permanence and vitality of the new black communities, especially by the mid-1960s.
   g. Although some gains among African Americans (i.e. residential segregation in poor neighborhoods decreased, some intermarriage with the white community occurred, and many children of migrant blacks finished high school, establishment of ethnic enterprises, and employment in civil service) new and old social-structural barriers limited prosperity and assimilation.
7. Chinese Americans
   a. In 1882 Congress passed an act prohibiting the immigration of "lunatics, idiots, and Chinese" into the United States for 10 years. The act was extended for another decade in 1892, made permanent in 1907, and repealed in 1943, to grant a quota of 105 Chinese immigrants per year. The California gold rush of the 1840s and the construction of the transcontinental railroad in the 1860s had drawn in tens of thousands of Chinese immigrants, whereas the majority of them were young men who worked as unskilled laborers. They were the objects of one of the most hostile anti-ethnic movements in American history.
   b. The film and tourist industries did much to reinforce fear of the "yellow peril" in the first half of the 20th century.
   c. A *split labor market* caused anti-Chinese prejudice to boil over into periodic race riots and exclusionary laws. Where competition for jobs between Chinese and white workers was intense, trouble brewed and ethnic and racial identities were reinforced. Recent research shows that anti-Chinese activity was especially high where white workers were geographically concentrated and successful in creating anti-Chinese organizations.
   d. Chinese Americans have experienced considerable upward mobility in the past half-century. However, a social structural factor – split labor markets – did much to prevent such mobility and assimilation until the middle of the 20th century.

IV. SOME ADVANTAGES OF ETHNICITY

A. Three main factors enhance the value of ethnic group members for some white European Americans who have lived in the country for many generations.
  1. Ethnic group membership can have economic advantages.
  2. Ethnic group membership can be politically useful.
  3. *Ethnic group membership tends to persist because of the emotional support it provides*, especially for those who experience high levels of prejudice, discrimination involving expulsion and attempted genocide.

V. THE FUTURE OF ETHNICITY

A. The Declining Significance of Race?
  1. The growth of racist organizations and hate crimes are increasing problems in the United States.
     a. More than 500 racist and Neo-Nazi organizations have sprung up in the United States.
     b. The FBI recorded 9730 **hate crimes** in 2001, which are criminal acts motivated by a person's race, religion, or ethnicity. African Americans are the most frequent victims, who were the object of 31% of all offenses.
  2. While white supremacists form only a tiny fraction of the American population, many more Americans engage in *subtle* forms of racism. African Americans continue to suffer high levels of covert and overt racial prejudice and discrimination.
     a. Based on interviews with a sample of middle class blacks in 16 cities, Joe Feagin and Melvin Sykes (1994) found:
        i. Respondents often have trouble hailing a cab.
        ii. If they arrive in a store before a white customer, a clerk commonly serves them afterwards.
        iii. When they shop, store security often follows them around to make sure they don't shoplift.
        iv. Police often stop middle-class African American men in their cars without apparent reason.
     b. Blacks are less likely than whites of similar means to receive mortgages and other loans.
  3. William Julius Wilson's position that race is declining in significance as a force shaping the lives of African Americans.
     a. Argues that the civil rights movement helped to establish legal equality between blacks and whites (i.e. 1954 *Brown v. Board of Education*, 1964 Civil Rights Act, 1965 Voting Rights Act, 1968 Civil Rights Act)
     b. Reforms allowed a large black middle class to emerge. Today a third of the African-American population is middle class.
     c. Many facts support Wilson's view—increase in median family income and higher education, decrease in the number of blacks living below the poverty line, increase in white tolerance of blacks,
     d. The third of blacks living below the poverty line are not much different than other Americans in similar economic circumstances according to Wilson.

e. Calls for "color-blind" public policies intended to improve the class position of the poor; and opposes race-specific policies, such as **affirmative action** (a policy that gives preference to minority group members if equally qualified people are available for a position).

4. Wilson's critiques claim that racism remains a big barrier to black progress.
    a. Racial differences in wages and housing patterns.
    b. Many African Americans continue to live in inner-city ghettos, where they experience high rates of poverty, crime, divorce, teenage pregnancy, and unemployment.

5. Wilson argues that ghettos exist not because of racism but for three economic and class reasons.
    a. Since the 1970s, older manufacturing industries have closed down in cities where the black working class was concentrated.
    b. Many middle- and working—class African-Americans with good jobs moved out of the inner city, which deprived young people of successful role models.
    c. The exodus of successful blacks eroded the inner-city's tax base at the same time conservative federal and state governments cut budgets for public services.

6. However, Wilson's position on ghettoization does not explain the persistently high level of residential segregation among many middle-class blacks who left the ghettos for suburbs since the 1960s.

B. Immigration and the Renewal of Racial and Ethnic Groups
    1. A steady flow of immigrants gives new life to racial and ethnic groups. We can expect many vibrant racial and ethnic communities to invigorate American life for a long time.
    2. Of the broad U.S. Census Bureau's racial and ethnic categories, the fastest growing is "Asian American." Numbering nearly 12 million in the 2000 census, most in this category arrived after the mid-1960s, when legislators eliminated racial selection criteria and instead designed an immigration law emphasizing the importance of choosing newcomers who can contribute to the U.S. economy. Many Asian immigrants are middle-class professionals and business people.
    3. Some people hold up Asian Americans as models. This argument has two main problems:
        a. First, some substantial Asian-American groups, including several million Vietnamese, Cambodians, Hmong, and Laotians, do not fit the "Asian model." Members of these groups came to the United States as political refugees, and are disproportionately poor and unskilled, with a poverty rate higher than that of African Americans.
        b. Second, most economically successful Asian Americans were selected as immigrants precisely because they possessed educational credentials, skills, or capital. They arrived with advantages. Saying that unskilled Chicanos or the black descendants of slaves should follow their example ignores the social-structural brakes on mobility and assimilation.

C. A Vertical Mosaic
    1. Today, U.S. society is based on segregation, assimilation, and **pluralism**, the retention of racial and ethnic culture combined with equal access to basic social resources.
    2. The United States has come a long way over the last 200 years in terms of social tolerance, especially in comparison to other countries.
    3. The growth of tolerance is taking place in the context of increasing ethnic and racial diversity.

4. However, if current trends continue, the racial and ethnic mosaic will be vertical with some groups disproportionately clustered at the bottom.

5. Policy initiatives could decrease the verticality of the American ethnic mosaic, thus speeding up the movement from segregation to pluralism and assimilation for the country's most disadvantaged groups.

Study Activity: Applying The Sociological Compass

After reading Chapter 9 of the textbook, review the terms "race," "ethnic group," racial and ethnic "labels" and "identities." Re-read the section, "Ethnic and Racial Choice in the United States." Then, answer the following questions.

1. What is your race? Why do you self-identify racially in this manner?

2. What is your ethnicity? Why do you self-identify ethnically in this manner?

3. What is your ancestry?

4. How do you prefer to identify yourself?

5. Is your decision to self-identify a matter of choice, imposition, or both?

A. What is it about your choice of terms that indicates who you are as a person? Make a list of reasons why you chose to identify yourself as indicated in questions one, two, and four.

B. How do you think others (outside of your racial or ethnic group) perceive the labels you chose? Do their perceptions have any influence on your choices of self-identification? Make a list of reasons as to why or why not.

C. Are you choices of racial and ethnic identification consistent with your ancestry?

InfoTrac College Edition Online Exercises

For the following exercises, log on to the online library of InfoTrac College Edition at http://www.infotrac-college.com/. Make note that InfoTrac has implemented a new registration system that will allow easier access to InfoTrac through the use of a personalized username and password.

Once you've created your username and password you may proceed directly to the Log On page. To create an account, register your passcode packaged with your textbook, and create a username and password, by following the online prompt. After you are logged in, click on "Infotrac College Edition." You will arrive at a screen that enables you to search topics.

Keyword: **affirmative action**. Look for specific articles that address affirmative action for minority groups in the United States. What are the key arguments "for" and "against" affirmative action? Write a short paper addressing your findings and your own opinion on affirmative action.

Keyword: **racial profiling**. Racial profiling remains a "hot topic" in the area of race and ethnicity. What types of subjects does your racial profiling search produce? Do any articles discuss what measures can be taken to reduce racial profiling? Do you think racial profiling is justified now that the United States is at war with "terrorism?"

Keyword: **human rights violations**. Look for articles that address contemporary human rights violations. What other terms can be used interchangeably with human rights violations. Where are most human rights violations taking place?

Internet Exercises

Go to http://www.census.gov/population/www/cen2000/briefs.html. Click on "Overview of Race and Hispanic Origin." You will access a brief report that defines new terms and categories for racial and ethnic identification, and explains the reasons for the changes in race data. Make a list of the new terms and categories. Make a list of reasons for the changes. Based on the report, combined with what you learned in Chapter 9, do you think the new census enables greater choice or places more constraint on our freedom to racially and ethnically self-identify? Why?

The Federal Bureau of Investigation (FBI) publishes different types of statistics. Go to http://www.fbi.gov/ucr/hatecrime.pdf to find the UCR Hate Crimes Date Collection Guidelines. Read the short report and write a short paper about how race and ethnicity are viewed in the guidelines. Do you agree or disagree with these guidelines? Why or why not?

For information on southern women and women of color, The Center for Research on Women at the University of Memphis has the following website available: http://cas.memphis.edu/isc/crow

Write a summary paper examining what type of research projects have been conducted in recent years.

Read Thomas Sowell's essay on Race, Culture and Equality at http://www-hoover.stanford.edu/publications/he/23/23a.html

Do you agree or disagree with Sowell's ideas?

Practice Tests

Fill-In-The-Blank

Fill in the blank with the appropriate term from the above list of "key terms."

1. _____ is a social construct used to distinguish people in terms of one or more physical markers, usually with profound effects on their lives.

2. A(An) _____ is a group of people who are socially disadvantaged although they may be in the numerical majority.

3. _____ is bias that is inherent in social institutions and is often not noticed by members of the majority group.

4. In _____ , low-wage workers of one race and high-wage workers of another race compete for the same jobs.

5. _____ is the ownership and control of people.

6. _____ is the retention of racial and ethnic culture combined with equal access to basic social resources.

7. _____ is unfair treatment of people due to their group membership.

8. A(An) _____ is disadvantaged person or category of people whom others blame for their own problems.

9. A(An) _____ is a spatial concentration of ethnic group members who establish businesses that serve and employ mainly members of the ethnic group and reinvest profits in community business and organizations.

10. _____ involves the spatial and institutional separation of racial or ethnic groups.

11. _____ involves one race or ethnic groups subjugating another in the same country.

Multiple-Choice Questions

Select the response that best answers the question or completes the statement:

1. _____ is an attitude that judges a person on his or her group's real or imagined characteristics.
   a. prejudice
   b. discrimination
   c. scapegoating
   d. racism
   e. expulsion

2. According to most sociologists, minority group refers to a group of people:
   a. who are numerically smaller in population size.
   b. who tend to hold negative racial and ethnic self-conceptions
   c. who have no choice in their racial and ethnic identities.
   d. who are socially disadvantaged.
   e. None of the above.

3. John Lie's migration experience from South Korea to Japan, Japan to Hawaii, and from Hawaii to the U.S. mainland illustrates:
   a. that racial and ethnic labels change from country to country.
   b. that racial and ethnic identities are reshaped from one social context to another.
   c. that continuous negotiations take place between one's racial and ethnic self-conceptions, and outsider labels.
   d. All of the above.
   e. None of the above.

4. Which Hispanic group is more likely to be middle-class and professional?
   a. Chicanos
   b. Puerto Ricans
   c. Cubans
   d. All of the above.
   e. None of the above.

5. Which is NOT a reason why the term "Hispanic American" is more widely used that it was 30 to 40 years ago?
   a. Many Hispanic Americans find it politically useful.
   b. The term captures the internal diversity of Hispanic Americans.
   c. The government finds the term useful for data collection and public policy purposes.
   d. Non-Hispanic Americans find the term convenient.
   e. All of the above are reasons.

6. _____ is a nostalgic allegiance to the culture and traditions of the immigrant generation, or that of the old country.
   a. assimilation
   b. accommodation
   c. multiculturalism
   d. pluralism
   e. symbolic ethnicity

7. Which is NOT a stage of Robert Park's ecological theory?
   a. expulsion
   b. invasion
   c. resistance
   d. competition
   e. accommodation

8. _____ is the process by which a minority group blends into the majority population and eventually disappears as a distinct group.
   a. pluralism
   b. symbolic ethnicity formation
   c. assimilation
   d. expulsion
   e. colonialism

9. Which concept best describes the treatment of Native Americans by European immigrants in the 19th century?
   a. assimilation
   b. expulsion
   c. accommodation
   d. competition
   e. pluralism

10. Which concept best describes contemporary experiences of Irish Americans?
    a. assimilation
    b. expulsion
    c. colonialism
    d. genocide
    e. competition

11. Which government policy or historical event had an especially detrimental effect on the eviction of Native Americans from their lands?
    a. 1830 Indian Removal Act
    b. 1964 Civil Rights Act
    c. 1954 Brown v. Board of Education
    d. 1848 Treaty of Guadalupe Hidalgo
    e. None of the above.

12. Racist organizations are _____ today.
    a. declining
    b. virtually nonexistent
    c. growing
    d. made up of a large proportion of the American population
    e. None of the above.

13. The research of Joe Feagin and Melvin Sykes indicates that:
    a. African Americans continue to be most victimized by hate crime.
    b. the civil rights movement helped to establish legal equality between blacks and whites.
    c. reforms allowed the black middle-class to emerge.
    d. African Americans continue to suffer high levels of covert and overt racial prejudice and discrimination.
    e. All of the above.

14. As a solution to racial inequality in America, William Julius Wilson calls for:
    a. continued implementation of affirmative action to enhance African American representation in higher education and professional employment.
    b. an initiative to aid middle-class blacks to further their patterns of upward mobility.
    c. For "color-blind" public policies intended to improve the class position of the poor, which would likely help poor African Americans as well.
    d. All of the above.
    e. None of the above.

15. Among the major Hispanic groups in the United States, which group especially illustrates the formation of an ethnic enclave?
    a. Chicanos
    b. Puerto Ricans
    c. Cubans
    d. Costa Ricans
    e. Mexican nationals

16. Which statement is correct regarding the cultural emphasis on African-American sports heroes?
    a. Athletic heroes like Shaquile O'Neal are held up as role models for African American youth, since their chance of "making it" in professional sports is greater than their chance of going to college, due to discrimination.
    b. The cultural emphasis on African-American sports heroes dispels long-standing stereotypes of African Americans in favor of realistic images that highlight the superiority.
    c. The cultural emphasis on African-American sports heroes reinforces incorrect racial stereotypes about black athletic prowess and intellectual inferiority.
    d. All of the above.
    e. None of the above.

17. According to Figure 9.1 "The Vicious Circle of Racism," which step is the process of perceptions of behavioral differences creating racial stereotypes that get embedded in culture?
    a. first step
    b. second step
    c. third step
    d. fourth step
    e. fifth step

18. The United States is becoming a more ethnically and racially diverse society due to:
    a. a comparatively high immigration rate.
    b. a comparatively high birth rate among non-Hispanic whites.
    c. the level of out-migration of European Americans.
    d. All of the above.
    e. None of the above.

19. Which racial or ethnic group is projected to grow the fastest in terms of composition by the year 2050?
    a. White
    b. Hispanic
    c. Black
    d. Pacific Islander
    e. Native American

20. Which region of the United States had the highest percentage of Puerto Ricans in 2002?
    a. Northwest
    b. Midwest
    c. South
    d. West
    e. Pacific

21. Who suggested that "it doesn't matter to a racist whether an African American is a professional or a panhandler, a genius or a fool, a saint or a criminal. Where racism is common, racial identities are compulsory and at the forefront of one's self-identity?"
    a. Martin Luther King Jr.
    b. William Julius Wilson
    c. Robert Blauner
    d. Robert Park
    e. Malcolm X

True False

1. Researchers who were eager to prove correlations between brain size, intellectual capacity, and race in the 19th century are now widely dismissed as practitioners of racist and sexist quasi-science.

    TRUE or FALSE

2. Promoting the Shaquille O'Neal's and Kobe Bryant's as role models for African-American youth deflects the attention of African American youth from more probable avenues of upward mobility through academic excellence.

    TRUE or FALSE

3. Race as a biological concept is a useful analytical tool to explain inequality.

    TRUE or FALSE

4. The United States has long been a society where nearly all racial and ethnic groups have exercised their freedom to choose their racial and ethnic identities.

    TRUE or FALSE

5. The experience of Puerto Ricans is best captured by ecological theory.

    TRUE or FALSE

6. African Americans lack the freedom to enjoy symbolic ethnicity.

    TRUE or FALSE

7. Because the United States has come a long way in social tolerance over the past 200 years, assimilation is for the most part equally accessible for all racial and ethnic groups.

    TRUE or FALSE

8. Asian Americans are the most frequent victims of hate crimes today.

    TRUE or FALSE

9. Puerto Ricans and Chicanos have similar experiences as minority groups in the United States.

    TRUE or FALSE

10. Like most Americans, Collin Powell fits neatly into an ethnic category.

    TRUE or FALSE

Short Answer

1. If race is merely a social construct and not a useful biological term, explain why race continues to matter in the United States today? (p. 230)

    _____

    _____

2. Compare and contrast the terms "race" and "ethnic group." Why are these two terms often used interchangeably, and is it misleading to claim that race and ethnicity are quite different? Why? (p. 230-231)

   _____

   _____

3. Explain the difference between and ethnic enclave and residential segregation. (p. 234-238)

   _____

   _____

4. Briefly explain the similarities among and difference between Chicanos, Puerto Ricans, and Cubans in terms of immigration experiences, economic status, and community formation. (p. 233-235)

   _____

   _____

Essay Questions

1. Contrast ecological theory and the theory of internal colonialism as explanations of racial and ethnic relations. In doing so, be sure to mention the major assumptions, conditions, and critiques of each theory. (p. 237-244).

2. Explain the pros and cons for the "declining significance of race" debate. Take a stance on the issue by providing research, statistical, and/or historical support for your position cited in the textbook. (p. 247-254)

3. Explain the contradictory relationship between the notion of black athletic superiority and the idea of black intellectual inferiority, in their perpetuation of racial inequality. (p. 227-231)

Solutions

Practice Tests

Fill-In-The-Blank

1. Race
2. minority group
3. Institutional racism
4. split labor markets
5. Slavery
6. Pluralism
7. Discrimination
8. scapegoat
9. ethnic enclave
10. Segregation
11. Internal colonialism

Multiple-Choice Questions

1. A, (p. 229)
2. D, (p. 232)
3. D, (p. 232)
4. C, (p. 233)
5. B, (p. 233)
6. E, (p. 237)
7. A, (p. 237)
8. C, (p. 238)
9. B, (p. 240)
10. A, (p. 238)
11. A, (p. 240)
12. C, (p. 246)
13. D, (p. 247)
14. C, (p. 247)
15. C, (p. 234)
16. C, (p. 229)
17. C, (p. 230)
18. A, (p. 234)
19. B, (p. 235)
20. A, (p. 234)
21. E, (p. 237)

True False

1. T, (p. 227)
2. T, (p. 228)
3. F, (p. 228)
4. F, (p. 235)
5. F, (p. 237)
6. T, (p. 237)
7. F, (p. 238)
8. F, (p. 246)
9. T, (p. 233)
10. F, (p. 230)

CHAPTER **10**

SEXUALITY AND GENDER

Student Learning Objectives

After reading Chapter 10, you should be able to:

1. Explain the differences and connections between sex and gender.

2. Contrast essentialist and social constructionist theories of gender differences.

3. Explain the role of gender socialization and the mass media in constructing our ideas of masculinity and femininity.

4. Discuss the patterns of male-female interaction in terms of gender socialization, especially in the family, schools, and the workplace.

5. Discuss social reactions to people who resist traditional gender roles (transgendered, transsexuals, homosexuals, and bisexuals).

6. Identify and describe the main factors that account for the earnings gap between men and women in the United States.

7. Explain the social forces and sources of rape and sexual harassment of women by men.

8. Describe current trends regarding equality between men and women in a comparative perspective.

9. Discuss the future prospects and obstacles for nontraditional socialization of children, affirmative action, child-care reform, and comparable worth laws, as avenues toward gender equality.

10. Describe the historical emergence of the women's movement.

Key Terms

(defined on the indicated pages of the textbook, and in glossary)

intersexed (259)

sex (260)

gender (260)

gender identity (260)

gender role (260)

heterosexuality (261)

essentialism (261)

social constructionism (262)

gender ideologies (267)

glass ceiling (271)

comparable worth (282)

transgendered (271)

transsexuals (271)

homosexuals (271)

bisexuals (271)

gender discrimination (275)

female-male earning ratio (275)

quid pro quo harassment (279)

hostile environment harassment (279)

affirmative action (281)

Detailed Chapter Outline

I. SEX VERSUS GENDER

   A. Is It a Boy or a Girl?
      1. The case of Bruce/Brenda raises several issues and questions about sex and gender.
         a. Whether hormonal and surgical measures combined with socialization can alter the sex and gender identity of **intersexed** infants (babies born with ambiguous genitals due to a hormone imbalance in the womb), and other ambiguous children, as Dr. John Money suggested and attempted.
         b. That being male or female partly involves biology, but also certain "masculine" and "feminine" feelings, attitudes, and behaviors. Unlike sex, gender is not determined just by biology.
         c. Biology is not destiny, but that the *social learning* of gender begins early in life.
      2. **Sex** depends on whether you were born with distinct male or female genitals and a genetic program that released either male or female hormones to stimulate the development of your reproductive system. **Gender** is your sense of being male or female and your playing masculine and feminine roles in ways defined as appropriate by your culture and society.
      3. **Gender identity** is your identification with, or sense of belonging to a particular sex—biologically, psychologically, and socially.
      4. **Gender role** is the set of behaviors associated with widely shared expectations about how males and females are supposed to act.

   B. Chapter Plan
      1. The first half of this chapter:

a. Helps you better understand what makes us male or female, by outlining competing theories of gender differences.

b. Examines how people learn gender roles during socialization in the family and at school.

c. Discusses how members of society enforce **heterosexuality**, the preference for members of the opposite sex as sexual partners.

2. The second half of Chapter 11 examines gender inequality.

II. THEORIES OF GENDER

A. Essentialism

1. **Essentialism** is a school of thought that sees gender differences as a reflection of biological differences between women and men. In contrast, **social constructionism** is a school of thought that sees gender differences as a reflection of the different social positions occupied by women and men.

2. Sociobiology and Evolutionary Psychology

a. All humans are assumed to instinctively attempt to ensure their genes get passed generationally, however men and women develop different strategies. "Universal features of our evolved selves" contribute to the survival of the human species.

b. Because women produce a small number of eggs, they have a bigger investment in ensuring the survival of their offspring. It is thus in the best interest of a woman to locate the best mate to intermix her genes.

c. Men can develop hundreds of millions of sperm every 24–48 hours, thus a man increases the chance of his and only his genes will get passed on. Because men compete with other men for sexual access to women, men evolve competitive, aggressive and violent dispositions.

3. A Critique of Essentialism

a. *Essentialists ignore the historical and cultural variability of gender and sexuality.*

i. Notions of the male "good provider," and domestic skills for females, decrease in societies with low levels of gender inequality.

ii. Social situations involving competition and threat stimulate production of testosterone in women, causing more aggressive behavior.

iii. Gender differences are declining rapidly.

b. *Essentialism tends to generalize from the average, ignoring variations within gender groups.*

c. *No evidence directly supports the essentialists' major claims.*

d. *Essentialists' explanations for gender differences ignore the role of power.*

B. Social Constructionism

1. The main alternative to essentialism.

2. Gender Socialization

a. Toys

i. When they play with Barbie, girls learn the ideal woman and body image.

ii. G I Joe teaches boys stereotypical male roles.

      b.   Research shows that from birth, infant boys and girls are treated differently by parents, especially by fathers.
          i.   Girls are: perceived as delicate, cute, weak and beautiful; encouraged in cooperative and role-playing games; and praised for compliance.
          ii. Boys are: treated as strong, alert, and well coordinated; encouraged in boisterous and competitive play; and praised for assertiveness.
      c.   Teachers and other authority figures impose their ideas of appropriate gender behavior on children.
      d.   Barrie Thorne's research indicates that children are actively engaged in the process of constructing gender roles, and the content of children's gendered activities is not fixed.
      e.   By adolescence, **gender ideologies** (sets of interrelated ideas about what constitutes appropriate masculine and feminine roles and behavior) are well formed.
   3.   The Mass Media and Body Image
      a.   Children, adolescents, and adults continue to negotiate gender roles as they interact with the mass media.
      b.   Women are more frequently seen cleaning house, caring for children, modeling clothes, and acting as objects of male desire, while men are more frequently seen in aggressive, action-oriented, and authoritative roles. This reinforces the normality of traditional gender roles.
      c.   Survey data show how widespread dissatisfaction with our bodies is and how important a role the mass media plays in generating our discomfort. North Americans' anxiety about their bodies increased substantially between 1972 and 1997.
      d.   Body ideals are influenced by gender.
          i.   Women are more concerned about their stomachs.
          ii. By 1997 men were more concerned about their chests than women were about their breasts.
      e.   Body dissatisfaction motivates many women to diet, and even prompts some people to take dangerous and life threatening measures to lose weight (i.e. anorexia and bulimia).
   4.   Male-Female Interaction
      a.   Early gender role socialization is the basis of children's social interactions as adults. Examples
          i.   Boys learn competition, conflict, self-sufficiency, hierarchical relationships, taking center-stage, and boasting, by playing sports.
          ii. Girls learn to maintain cordial relationships, avoid conflict, and resolve differences through negotiation, give advice, and not be bossy, by playing with dolls.
      b.   Misunderstandings between men and women are thus common.
      c.   Gender-specific interaction styles have implications for who gets heard and who gets credit at work, which sometimes leads to complaints about a **glass ceiling**, a social barrier that makes it difficult for female managers to rise to the top level of management. Example: Deborah Tannen's research.
C. Homosexuality
   1.   A minority of people resist traditional gender roles.

    a. **Transgendered** people are individuals who want to alter their gender by changing their appearance or resorting to medical intervention.

    b. Some transgendered people are **transsexuals**, who believe they were born with the "wrong" body, and therefore identify with and want to live fully as members of the "opposite" sex. They often undergo a sex change operation.

    c. **Homosexuals** are people who prefer sexual partners of the same sex.

    d. **Bisexuals** prefer sexual partners of both sexes.

2. Homosexuality has existed in every society, was identified as a distinct category in the 1860s, and has become less stigmatized over the past century.

3. Sociologists are more interested in the way homosexuality is socially constructed, that is the ways it is expressed and repressed.

4. In the 1940s, American sexologist Alfred Kinsey and others concluded that homosexual practices were so widespread that homosexuality could hardly be considered an illness affecting a tiny minority.

5. Since the middle of the 20th century, gays and lesbians have gone public with their lives and built large communities and subcultures.

6. Opposition to people who do not conform to conventional gender roles remains strong at all stages of the life cycle. Some people are prepared to back up their beliefs with force and violence.

7. Due to widespread animosity toward homosexuals, many people who have wanted or who had sex with members of the same sex do not consider themselves gay, lesbian or bisexual.

8. Antigay violence
    a. Recent research suggests some antigay crimes may result from repressed homosexual urges on the part of the aggressor.
    b. Aggressors may be "homophobic" or afraid of homosexuals because of their inability to cope with their own homosexual impulses.
    c. Some assaults occurred to prove toughness, heterosexuality, alleviate boredom and have fun.
    d. Antigay violence is not just a question of abnormal psychology, but a broad cultural problem, and seems to be growing in America. Example: the 1998 murder of Matthew Shepard.

III. GENDER INEQUALITY

A. The Earnings Gap Today

1. In the first quarter of 2000, women over the age of 15 working full-time in the paid labor force earned only 78.3% of what men earned. Four main factors account for the earnings gap.
    a. *Gender discrimination.*
        i. 1985 Microsoft example
        ii. **Gender discrimination** is the rewarding of women and men differently for the same work.
        iii. Antidiscrimination laws have helped increase the **female-male earnings ratio** (women's earnings as a percentage of men's earnings), which has increased 17.3% between 1960 and 2000.

    b. *Heavy domestic responsibilities reduce women's earnings.*
- i. Women do more housework, child rearing and elderly care than men, which substantially decreases the time women spend training, and doing paid work.
- ii. Women who work full-time in the paid labor force continue to shoulder a disproportionate share of domestic responsibilities.

    c. *Women tend to be concentrated in low-wage occupations and industries.*
- i. High school and college courses tend to limit women to jobs in low-wage occupations.

    d. *Work done by women is commonly considered less valuable than work done by men because it is viewed as involving fewer skills.*

B. Male Aggression Against Women
1. Why do men commit more frequent (and more harmful) acts of aggression against women than women commit against men? Greater physical power is more likely to be used to commit acts of aggression when norms justify male domination and men have much more *social* power than women.
2. Rape
   - a. Although some rapists suffer from psychological disorders, and others misinterpret signals in what they regard as sexually ambiguous situations, such cases account for only a small proportion of total rapists.
   - b. Rape is sometimes not about sexual gratification, but all rape involves domination and humiliation as principal motives.
   - c. Social situations increase the rate of rape.
     - i. In war, conquering male soldiers often use rape to humiliate the vanquished.
     - ii. Spousal abuse is common among police officers, in which aggressiveness is an important part of their work.
     - iii. The relationship between male dominance and rape is evident in research on college fraternities.
     - iv. There are proportionately more rapists among men who participate in athletics than among nonathletes, although the overwhelming majority of athletes are not rapists.
     - v. The incidence of rape is highest in situations where early socialization experiences predispose men to want to control women, where norms justify the domination of women, and where a big power imbalance between men and women exists.
3. Sexual Harassment
   - a. Two types of sexual harassment:
     - i. **Quid pro quo harassment** takes place when sexual threats or bribery are made a condition of employment decisions.
     - ii. **Hostile environment harassment** involves sexual jokes, comments, and touching that interferes with work or creates an unfriendly work setting.
   - b. Research suggests that:
     - i. relatively powerless women are most likely to be sexually harassed.
     - ii. sexual harassment is most common in work settings that exhibit high levels of gender inequality and a culture of male domination of women.

      iii. women who are young, unmarried, and employed in nonprofessional occupations are the most likely targets.

  c. Many aspects of our culture legitimize male dominance.

  d. Gender inequality is the foundation of aggression against women.

C. Toward 2050

  1. Equality between men and women in many countries grew in the 20th century. Why?

    a. Women started having fewer children because children became more costly to raise and less economically useful.

    b. The growth of the service sector increased the demand for women in the paid labor force.

    c. The legalization and availability of contraception enabled women to control their bodies.

    d. The women's movement.

  2. The "Gender Empowerment Measure" (GEM) indicates that:

    a. Scandinavian countries were the most gender-egalitarian.

    b. The United States ranked 11th in the world.

    c. There is more gender equality in rich than in poor countries.

    d. Gender equality is a function of government policy.

    e. American women still have a long way to go before they achieve equality with men.

  3. Socializing children at home and in school to understand that women and men are equally adept at all jobs is important to motivate girls to excel in nontraditional fields. **Affirmative action**, which involves hiring more qualified women to diversify organizations, is important in helping to compensate for past discrimination in hiring.

  4. Child Care

    a. High quality, government -subsidized, affordable child-care is widely available in most Western European countries, but not in the United States. Consequently, many American women with small children are unable to work outside the home or able to work only on a part-time basis.

    b. Child-care options and the quality of child-care vary by social class for women who have small children and work outside the home.

    c. A third of all day-care facilities in the United States do not meet children's basic health and safety needs, due to lack of government regulation and low wages for child care workers.

    d. Many companies, schools, and religious organizations in the United States provide high-quality day care.

  5. Comparable Worth

    a. Researchers attempted to establish gender-neutral standards to judge the dollar value of work to identify pay inequities between men and women to promote equal pay for jobs of **comparable worth**, even if men and women did different jobs.

    b. A number of U.S. states adopted laws requiring equal pay for work of comparable worth. Minnesota leads the country. Obstacles:

      i. The Laws do not apply to most employers.

      ii. Comparable worth assessments have been challenged in the courts.

      iii. No federal legislation on comparable worth is in development.

IV. THE WOMEN'S MOVEMENT

    A. Progress has always depended in part on the strength of the organized women's movement, not just on the sympathy of government and business leaders.

    B. In the 1840s, the chief demand of the "first wave" of the women's movement was the right to vote (paralleled the oppression of black slaves).

    C. In the mid-1960s, the "second wave" was inspired by the successes of the civil rights movement, and advocated equal rights with men in education and employment, the elimination of sexual violence, and women's control over reproduction (i.e. Equal Rights Amendment ERA).

    D. *Antiracist* and *postmodernist* feminists have extended the relevance of feminism to previously marginalized groups.

    E. Some feminist ideas have gained widespread acceptance in American society over the last three decades, partly due to the political and intellectual vigor of the women's movement. (i.e. 1998 General Social Survey).

    F. Traditional patterns of gender socialization weigh heavily on men,—"But socialization is not destiny."

Study Activity: Applying the Sociological Compass

After reading Chapter 10, review essentialism and social constructionism. Consider this scenario. You are at your neighborhood park playing with your five-year old son and seven-year old daughter (or your five-year old brother, nephew, or male cousin and your seven-year old sister, niece, or female cousin). Your "son" falls off the swing and scrapes his knee. What is a likely masculine response to this incident? How might you react to the situation? Five minutes later, your "daughter" falls off the monkey bars and bruises her elbow. In both cases, injuries are minor. What is a likely feminine response? Are there any differences in the way you might react to your son's versus daughter's injury? Based on your personal experiences, make a list of masculine reactions to the injury of male five-year old boy, and a list of feminine reactions to the injury of the seven-year old girl. Then, make a list of your first impressions when pondering the questions of how you would respond. Finally, consider whether the responses to each situation are guided by essentialist or social constructionist assumptions about gender differences by writing the letter 'E' for essentialist or 'SC' for social constructionist next to each response. Briefly explain why you consider the responses as examples of essentialism and social constructionism, respectively.

Traditional Masculine Reactions

1.

2.

3.

Traditional Feminine Reactions

1.

2.

3.

4.

Your Reactions

1.

2.

3.

4.

Essentialist and Social Constructionist Explanations:

InfoTrac College Edition Online Exercises

For the following exercises, log on to the online library of InfoTrac College Edition at http://www.infotrac-college.com/. Make note that InfoTrac has implemented a new registration system that will allow easier access to InfoTrac through the use of a personalized username and password.

Once you've created your username and password you may proceed directly to the Log On page. To create an account, register your passcode packaged with your textbook, and create a username and password, by following the online prompt. After you are logged in, click on "Infotrac College Edition." You will arrive at a screen that enables you to search topics.

Keyword: **glass ceiling**. Identify and read the latest article/periodical that discusses women and the glass ceiling. Read the article, identify its major contribution, and make a list of major findings.

Keyword: **fatherhood**. Is the role of fatherhood changing? Is so, how, and in what ways?

Keyword: **women's movement**. Examine the women's movement in third world countries. Are the issues and concerns the same as those involved in the women's movement in westernized countries?

Keyword: **masculinity**. Examine the different ways that masculinity is defined. Is there a masculine men's movement? Is it credible? What evidence can you provide for your responses?

Keyword: **date rape**. The relationship between date rape and drugs has increasingly become an issue of concern. Research the recourse victims have to this gender-based problem. Make a list of your findings.

Internet Exercises

Look up the Web site: http://www.fordham.edu/halsall/mod/Senecafalls.html to see a Declaration of Sentiments written in 1848 by Elizabeth Cady Stanton. How have things changed for women in the last 155 years? Write a short paper discussing your findings.

The media is always portraying images of the *ideal* body type. For more information on this subject link http://www.intergrouprelations.uiuc.edu/dim2000/page3.html

This is an article written on body image by DeNeishia Manual. What do you think is the ideal body type? Compare your ideal body type with Manual's.

To learn about the men's movement, link to the National Organization for Men's homepage at: http://www.tnom.com/

You can also link to the National Organization for Women's homepage at http://www.now.org/

Compare and contrast the purposes of the National Organization for Men with the National Organization for Women.

The National Council for Research on Women has put out a Report on Girls and IQ in Science. Go to http://www.ncrw.org/ to investigate their research report. What does it say about the relationship between gender and science IQ? Be sure to click on Research for Action.

Practice Tests

Fill-In-The-Blank

Fill in the blank with the appropriate term from the above list of "key terms."

1. _____ refers to the equal dollar value of different jobs, which is established in gender-neutral terms by comparing jobs in terms of the education and experience needed to do them.

2. Your _____ depends on whether you were born with distinct male or female genitals and a genetic program that released either male or female hormones to stimulate the development of your reproductive system.

3. _____ is one's identification with, or sense of belonging to, a particular sex.

4. _____ are sets of ideas about what constitutes appropriate masculine and feminine roles and behavior.

5. The _____ is a social barrier that makes it difficult for women to rise to the top level of management.

6. The _____ is women's earnings expressed as a percentage of men's earnings.

7. _____ involves sexual jokes, comments, and touching that interfere with work or creates an unfriendly work setting.

8. A(An) _____ is the set of behaviors associated with widely shared expectations about how males or females are supposed to act.

9. _____ is a school of thought that sees gender differences as a reflection of biological differences between women and men.

10. _____ are people who prefer sexual partners of both sexes.

Multiple-Choice Questions

Select the response that best answers the question or completes the statement:

1. _____ is the set of behaviors associated with widely shared expectations about how males and females are supposed to act.
   a. Sex
   b. Sex type
   c. Gender role
   d. Gender prescription
   e. None of the above.

2. Which school of thought sees gender differences as a reflection of biological differences between men and women?
   a. essentialism
   b. social constructionism
   c. functionalism
   d. feminism
   e. None of the above.

3. _____ and _____ suggest that "universal features of our evolved selves" contribute to the survival of the human species.
   a. Essentialists; social constructionists
   b. Sociobiologists; evolutionary psychologists
   c. Evolutionary psychologists; social constructionists
   d. Sociobiologists; feminists
   e. None of the above.

4. Which is a critique of essentialism?
   a. Essentialists ignore the historical and cultural variability of gender and sexuality.
   b. Essentialism tends to generalize from the average, ignoring variations within gender groups.
   c. Essentialists' explanations for gender differences ignore the role of power.
   d. All of the above.
   e. None of the above.

5. Barry Thorne's research indicates that:
   a. children are actively engaged in the process of constructing gender roles.
   b. because men compete with other men for sexual access to women, men evolve competitive, aggressive and violent dispositions.
   c. the very idea of gender needs to be changed to bring an end to male domination.
   d. All of the above.
   e. None of the above.

6. Based on social constructionism, children, adolescence, and adults continue to negotiate gender roles as they _____ the mass media.
   a. ignore
   b. reject
   c. interact with
   d. All of the above.
   e. None of the above.

7. Research on gender socialization shows that:
   a. girls are perceived as delicate and weak.
   b. girls are perceived as cute and beautiful.
   c. girls are encouraged in cooperative and role-playing games.
   d. All of the above.
   e. None of the above.

8. _____ believe they were born with the "wrong" body, and therefore identify with and want to live fully as members of the "opposite" sex.
   a. Homosexuals
   b. Bisexuals
   c. Transsexuals
   d. All of the above.
   e. None of the above.

9. Homosexuality:
   a. has existed in every society.
   b. was identified as a distinct category in the 1860s.
   c. has become less stigmatized over the past century.
   d. All of the above.
   e. None of the above.

10. Regarding homosexuality, sociologists are interested in:
    a. the way homosexuality is socially constructed.
    b. the ways homosexuality is expressed.
    c. the ways homosexuality is repressed.
    d. All of the above.
    e. None of the above.

11. Which is a main factor for the earning gap between men and women?
    a. gender discrimination
    b. Heavy domestic responsibilities reduce women's earnings.
    c. Women tend to be concentrated in low-wage occupations and industries.
    d. Work done by women is commonly considered less valuable than work done by men.
    e. All of the above.

12. In 2001, women over the age of 15 working full-time in the paid labor force earned what percentage of men's earnings?
    a. 96%
    b. 88%
    c. 76%
    d. 47%
    e. 29%

13. Which is UNTRUE about rape?
    a. There is a relationship between male dominance and rape according to research on college fraternities.
    b. In war, conquering male soldiers often use rape to humiliate the vanquished.
    c. The majority of rapes are committed by strangers.
    d. All rape involves domination and humiliation.
    e. Rape is sometimes not about sexual gratification.

14. Sexual jokes, comments, and touching that creates an unfriendly work setting are examples of:
    a. quid pro quo harassment
    b. sexist labor exploitation
    c. hostile environment harassment
    d. sexist ideologies
    e. All of the above.

15. The "Gender Empowerment Measure" (GEM) indicates that:
    a. The United States ranked 11th in gender-egalitarianism in the world.
    b. Scandinavian countries were the most gender-egalitarian.
    c. There is more gender equality in rich than in poor countries.
    d. American women still have a long way to go to achieve equality with men.
    e. All of the above.

16. By conventional North American standards, the ceremonial dress of male Wodaabe nomads in Niger may appear:
    a. masculine
    b. feminine
    c. transgendered
    d. hyper masculine
    e. bisexual

17. A movement to market more gender-neutral toys emerged in the:
    a. 1940s and 1950s
    b. 1960s and 1970s
    c. 1980s and 1990s
    d. 2000s
    e. None of the above.

18. In 2001, the percentage of women among employed people in administrative support occupations was around:
    a. 45%
    b. 78%
    c. 68%
    d. 87%
    e. 98%

19. Which part of the body were men and women most dissatisfied with in 1997?
    a. stomachs
    b. thighs
    c. buttocks
    d. All of the above.
    e. None of the above.

20. Which country recognized full and equal marriage rights for homosexual couples in April 2001?
    a. Mexico
    b. The United States
    c. The Netherlands
    d. Guatemala
    e. Canada

21. Which statement is an accurate description of the movie *Boys Don't Cry*, as discussed in Box 10.2 of the textbook?
    a. Although her only transgression was that she wanted to be a man, the character "Teena Brandon" was murdered.
    b. Although wanting a sex change, "Teena Brandon" took the inexpensive route by stuffing a sock down the front of her jeans to pose as a man.
    c. "Brandon" develops a romantic relationship with a woman named "Lana Tisdel," who despite later discovering that "Brandon" is female, continues to love her anyhow.
    d. All of the above.
    e. None of the above.

True False

1. Gender depends on whether you were born with distinct male or female genitals.

   TRUE or FALSE

2. Social constructionism is a main alternative to essentialism.

   TRUE or FALSE

3. Research shows that toys have an influence on gender socialization.

   TRUE or FALSE

4. With the changes influenced by the women's movement, the mass media portrays far less gender stereotypes.

   TRUE or FALSE

5. Body dissatisfaction motivates many women to diet, and even prompts some people to take dangerous and life-threatening measures to lose weight.

   TRUE or FALSE

6. The female-male earnings ratio indicates that women's earnings as a percentage to men's earnings have decreased slightly since 1960.

   TRUE or FALSE

7. Because traditional patterns of gender socialization weigh so heavily on men in the context of a male-dominant world, changing socialization patterns is virtually impossible.

   TRUE or FALSE

8. The chief demand of the "first wave" of the women's movement was the right to vote.

   TRUE or FALSE

9. Federal legislation on comparable worth is on the books in a number of U.S. states.

   TRUE or FALSE

Short Answer

1. Define and briefly explain the connection between the terms transgendered and transsexual. (p. 271)

   _____

   _____

2. Explain the idea of the "glass ceiling" for women in managerial professions. (p. 271)

   _____

   _____

3. What is the difference between sex and gender as categories of distinction between men and women? How are the two terms related? (p. 260)

   _____

   _____

4. List four reasons why equality between men and women grew in the 20th century in many countries. (p. 274)

   _____

   _____

Essay Questions

1. Contrast the major assumptions of essentialist and social constructionist perspectives on gender differences. In doing so, identify the major critiques of essentialism in terms of one of the essentialist theories discussed in the textbook. (p. 261-271)

2. Think about the intersection of gender roles and gender ideologies and describe how these ideas compare and contrast, and most importantly, how they work with both internal and external forces in the construction of gender identity. (p. 260-267)

Solutions

Practice Tests

Fill-In-The-Blank

1. Comparable worth
2. sex
3. Gender identity
4. Gender ideologies

5. glass ceiling
6. female-male earnings ratio
7. Hostile environment sexual harassment

8. gender role
9. Essentialism
10. Bisexuals

Multiple-Choice Questions

1. C, (p. 260)
2. A, (p. 261)
3. B, (p. 262)
4. D, (p. 262-263)
5. A, (p. 266-267)
6. C, (p. 261-267)
7. D, (p. 265-266)

8. C, (p. 271)
9. D, (p. 271)
10. D, (p. 271)
11. E, (p. 274)
12. C, (p. 274)
13. C, (p. 277)
14. C, (p. 279)

15. E, (p. 280)
16. B, (p. 263)
17. B, (p. 265)
18. B, (p. 277)
19. A, (p. 268)
20. C, (p. 272)
21. D, (p. 275)

True False

1. F, (p. 260)
2. T, (p. 262)
3. T, (p. 265)

4. F, (p. 267)
5. T, (p. 269)
6. F, (p. 275)

7. F, (p. 264-267)
8. T, (p. 282)
9. F, (p. 282)

FAMILIES

Student Learning Objectives

After reading Chapter 11, you should be able to:

1. Identify and describe prevailing forms of families in the United States.

2. Discuss the historical trends of the traditional nuclear family in the United States since the 1940's.

3. Compare and contrast functionalist, conflict and feminist perspectives on families.

4. Identify the main functions of marriage and the nuclear family.

5. Describe the trends of the nuclear family since the second half of the 19th century in terms of divorce, marriage, and fertility rates.

6. Discuss the relationship between love and marriage in a historical perspective.

7. Identify and explain the forces underlying marital satisfaction.

8. Explain the economic and emotional effects of divorce on women and children.

9. Discuss the gender, political and ethical issues surrounding reproductive choice and reproductive technologies.

10. Describe the prevailing patterns of housework, child-care, and wife abuse in the context of gender inequality.

11. Discuss the prevailing patterns and controversies of family diversity in terms of cohabitation, same-sex marriage, single-motherhood and race.

12. Compare and contrast family policy in the United States and Sweden.

Key Terms

(defined on the indicated pages of the textbook, and in glossary)

nuclear family (290)

traditional nuclear family (290)

polygamy (293)

extended family (293)

marriage (293)

divorce rate (295)

marriage rate (295)

total fertility rate (295)

Detailed Chapter Outline

I. INTRODUCTION

    A. Our most intense emotional experiences are bound up with our families.

        1. Seemingly trivial issues hold deep meaning and significance for family members.

        2. Family issues are central to political debate in the United States.

    B. As a subject of sociological inquiry, family issues generate much debate, which centers on the question, "Is the family in decline, and if so, what should be done about it?"

        1. Whenever the family changes rapidly, and when the divorce rate increases, this crisis alarm is sounded.

    C. Two forms of families when people speak of "the decline of the family."

        1. The **nuclear family** is composed of a cohabiting man and woman who maintain a socially approved sexual relationship and have at least one child.

        2. The **traditional nuclear family** is a nuclear family in which the wife works in the home without pay while the husband works outside the home for money, making him the "primary provider and ultimate authority."

    D. Trends of the traditional nuclear family.

        1. In the 1940s and 1950s, much of the American public and many sociologists considered the traditional nuclear family the most widespread and ideal family form.

        2. Between 1950 and 1999, the percentage of women over the age of 16 in the paid labor force increased from approximately 34% to 60%.

    E. Functionalist sociologists view the decreasing prevalence of the married-couple family and the rise of the "working mother" as sources of various social problems (i.e. crime rates, illegal drug use, poverty, and welfare dependency)—and call for legal and cultural reforms to shore up the traditional nuclear family.

    F. Conflict and feminist sociologists disagree with functionalists. They argue that:

        1. It is inaccurate to talk about *the* family as this assumes one single form.

        2. Changing family forms do not necessarily represent deterioration, but often represent improvement in the way people live.

        3. Various economic and political reforms, such as an affordable nationwide day-care system, would eliminate most of the negative effects of single-parent households.

II. FUNCTIONALISM AND THE NUCLEAR IDEAL

A. Functional Theory
   1. Since the 1940s, functionalists have argued that the nuclear family is ideally suited to meet the challenges of reproducing and raising offspring in an emotionally supportive environment so that they may operate as productive adults.
   2. Other family forms.
      a. **Polygamy** expands the nuclear unit "horizontally" by adding one or more spouses (almost always wives) to the household. The overwhelming majority of families are *monogamous*.
      b. The **extended family** expands the nuclear family "vertically" by adding another generation (one or more of the spouse's parents) to the household. This family form was common throughout the world, and still is in some places.
   3. **Marriage** is a socially approved, presumably long-term, sexual and economic union between a man and a woman, and involves rights and obligations.
   4. Five main functions of marriage and the nuclear family:
      a. *Sexual regulation*;
      b. *Economic cooperation*;
      c. *Reproduction*;
      d. *Socialization*; and
      e. *Emotional support*.

B. The American Middle Class in the 1950s
   1. Functionalism had its merits in the 15 years after World War II, a time when Americans wanted to enjoy the security of family life in the wake of the Great Depression.
      a. Conditions were ideal for these family goals.
         i.   Unparalleled optimism and prosperity.
         ii. Real per capita income rose.
         iii. Home-ownership jumped.
         iv. Government assistance supported and promoted the nuclear family.
      b. Thus people married younger, had more children, got divorced less —and middle-class women engaged in an "orgy of domesticity."
   2. However, the immediate postwar period was in many respects atypical as Andrew J. Cherlin shows.
      a. Divorce, marriage, and childbearing trends show a gradual weakening of the nuclear family from the second half of the 19th century until the mid-1940s, and after the 1950s. Throughout the 19th century:
         i.   The **divorce rate** rose.
         ii. The **marriage rate** fell.
         iii. The **total fertility rate** fell.

III. CONFLICT AND FEMINIST THEORIES

    A. Karl Marx and Friedrick Engels argued that the control of wives sexually and economically exists in the context of the emergence of the traditional nuclear family along side inequalities of wealth.

        1. Sexual control ensured that a man's property would be transmitted only to his offspring, particularly his sons.

    B. Although Engels was correct to highlight the long history of male economic and sexual domination in the traditional nuclear family, he was incorrect in terms of other assumptions.

        1. He was wrong to think communism would eliminate gender inequality in the family.

        2. Gender inequality exists in non-capitalist and pre-capitalist societies.

    C. Feminists

        1. Feminists view *patriarchy* (male dominance and norms justifying that dominance) as more deeply rooted in the economic, military, and cultural history of humankind than classical Marxists.

        2. Only a "genuine gender revolution" can alter gender inequality.

IV. POWER AND FAMILIES

    A. Love and Mate Selection

        1. Although most Americans take for granted that marriage ought to be based on love, love has little to do with marriage in most societies throughout human history.

            a. Marriage:

                i. Was typically arranged by a third party.

                ii. Was based mainly on maximizing prestige, economic benefits, and political advantages for families from which the bride and groom came from.

        2. The origins of love and marriage:

            a. The idea of love in the choice of marriage first gained currency in 18th-century England with the rise of liberalism and individualism.

            b. The intimate linkage between love and marriage that we are familiar with emerged in the early 20th century, when Hollywood and the advertising industry began to promote self-gratification and heterosexual romance on a grand scale.

        3. Love alone still does not determine mate selection. Three sets of social forces that influence falling in love and mate selection:

            a. *Marriage resources*

            b. *Third parties*

            c. *Demographic and compositional factors*

    B. Marital Satisfaction

        1. As women became autonomous and free, marital stability came to depend more on marital satisfaction, than its mere usefulness.

        2. Factors that contributed to women's autonomy.

            a. The birth control pill allowed women to delay childbirth and to have fewer children.

        b.   The entry of millions of women into higher education and the paid labor force made it easier for women to leave unhappy marriages. In the 1960s divorce laws were changed to make divorce easier and divide property more equitably.

   3.   Five forces underlying marital satisfaction:

        a.   *Economic forces*;

        b.   *Divorce laws*;

        c.   *The family cycle*

        d.   *Housework and child care*; *and*

        e.   *Sex*

   4.   Religion has little effect on the level of marital satisfaction, but influences the divorce rate.

C. Divorce

   1.   Economic Effects

        a.   After divorce, the most common pattern is a rise in the husband's income and a decline in the wife's, because husbands usually earn more, and children typically live with their mother, and support payments are often inadequate if paid at all. Consequently, while child support payments declined in the 1970s and 1980s, they rose in the 1990s.

   2.   Emotional Effects

        a.   Children of divorced parents:

            i.   Tend to develop behavioral problems and do less well in school.

           ii.   Are more likely to engage in delinquent acts and abuse drugs and alcohol.

          iii.   Often experience an emotional crisis, particularly in the first 2 years after divorce.

        b.   Adults of divorced parents are:

            i.   Less likely to be happy than people of nondivorced parents.

           ii.   More likely to suffer health problems.

          iii.   More likely to depend on welfare.

          iv.   More likely to earn low incomes.

           v.   More likely to experience divorce themselves.

        c.   Much of this research is based on families who seek psychological counseling. Researchers who utilize representative samples and control for the separate effects of many factors on children's well being show otherwise. Amato and Keith showed that the overall effect of divorce on children's well being is not strong and declining over time. Three factors account for much of the distress among children of divorce.

            i.   *A high level of parental conflict.*

           ii.   *A decline in living standards.*

          iii.   *The absence of a parent.*

D. Reproductive Choice

   1.   As a result of the gender revolution, women now have more voice over having children, when they will have them, and how many they will have.

   2.   Most women want to work in the paid labor force, many to pursue a career.

   3.   Women's reproductive decisions are carried out by means of contraception and abortion.

   4.   Americans have been sharply divided on the abortion issue since the 1970s.

       a. "Right-to-life" activists:
-     i.   Want to repeal laws legalizing abortion.
-    ii.   Tend to be homemakers in religious, middle-income families.
-   iii.   Argue that life begins at conception, thus abortion destroys human life.
-    iv.   Advocate adoption over abortion.

       b. "Pro-choice" activists:
-     i.   Want laws legalizing abortion preserved.
-    ii.   Tend be women in pursuit of careers.
-   iii.   Are more highly educated, less religious, and better off financially.
-    iv.   Argue that every woman has a right to make choices about her body.

       c. Randall Collins and Scott Coltrane note, it seems likely that a repeal of abortion laws would return us to conditions of the 1960s. Abortions would be expensive, hard to obtain, pose more dangers to women's health, and poor women and their unwanted children would suffer most.

E. Reproductive Technologies
1. Reproductive technologies facilitate pregnancy, as well as prevent pregnancy.
2. Demand is strong for techniques to help infertile couples, some lesbian couples, and some single women have babies.
3. Four main reproductive technologies:
   - a. *Artificial insemination*;
   - b. *Surrogate motherhood*;
   - c. *In vitro fertilization*; and
   - d. Various *screening techniques*
4. Sociological and ethical issues:
   - a. Discrimination
   - b. Social and legal problems of rendering the terms "mother" and "father" obsolete.

F. Housework and Child Care
1. Despite the gender revolution, the domain of housework, child-care, and senior care remains resistant to change.
2. Arlie Hochschild showed that even women who work full-time in the paid labor force begin a "second shift" when they return home.
3. Although some change has occurred as men have taken a more active role in household work, the change is modest.
4. Men tend to do low-stress chores that have less pressing deadlines (i.e. mowing the lawn, repairing the car, and preparing income tax forms). Women tend to do higher stressed tasks that cannot wait (i.e. dressing children, preparing dinner, and washing clothes).
5. Two main factors that shrink the gender gap in housework:
   - a. The smaller the difference in income between husband and wife, the more equal the division of household labor.
   - b. The more husband and wife agree there should be equality in the household, the more equality there is (attitude), which is linked to both spouses' having a college education.

G. Equality and Wife Abuse
   1. Wife abuse is widespread in America.
   2. Murray A. Straus has established that severe forms of wife assault occur in all categories of the population, but is most common in lower class, less highly educated families, where men are more likely to believe that male domination is justified, and among couples who witnessed the abuse of their mothers as children.
   3. Straus also showed that high levels of wife assault are associated with gender inequality in the larger society. As gender equality increases, wife abuse declines.

V. FAMILY DIVERSITY

   A. Cohabitation
      1. In the last three decades, the number of American couples who are unmarried and cohabiting increased more than 500%. Once considered a disgrace, cohabitation has gone mainstream.
      2. Disapproval of cohabitation has decreased due to cultural and economic factors. In recent decades, the force of religious sanction has weakened, hence affecting opposition to premarital sex. The sexual revolution and growing individualism have allowed people to pursue intimate relationships outside of marriage. Because women have pursued higher education and entered the paid labor force in increasing numbers, their gender roles are not tied so closely to marriage as they once were.
      3. Cohabitation is a relatively unstable relationship. Marriages that begin with cohabitation are associated with a higher divorce rate than marriages that begin without cohabitation.
      4. The most often cited and best supported explanation for the association between cohabitation and marital instability is that people who cohabit before marriage differ from those who do not, and these differences increase the likelihood of divorce. People who cohabit tend to be less religious and religious people are less likely to divorce. Those who cohabit are more likely to be African American, occupy a lower class position, hold more liberal political and sexual views, and have parents who divorced.
      5. Sociologists have debated the meaning and significance of cohabitation for two decades. Some view it as a prelude to marriage or a new form of marriage. Others think cohabitation is more like being single.

   B. Sexual Orientation
      1. Same-sex marriage
         a. In 2001 the Netherlands became the first county in the world to legalize same-sex marriage. By 2003 Belgium and Canada had followed suit. Eight other countries allow homosexuals to register their partnerships under the law, recognizing these partnerships as having some or all of the legal rights of marriage; which include Denmark, Greenland, Hungary, Norway, Sweden, France, Iceland, Spain, and Germany. In the United States, there is more opposition to registered partnerships and same-sex marriages than in these other countries. Nevertheless, the direction of change is clear. The legal and social definition of "family" is being broadened to include cohabiting, same-sex partners in long-term relationships.

2. Research shows that most homosexuals want a long-term, intimate relationship with one other adult, like most heterosexuals. More than 1 million same-sex partners cohabit in the United States today, where there is more opposition to same-sex marriages.

3. Most people believe that children raised in homosexual families will develop a confused sexual identity, exhibit tendencies toward homosexuality themselves, and suffer discrimination.
   a. There is little research in this area.
   b. Much of the research is based on small, unrepresentative samples.
   c. Nevertheless, the research findings consistently suggest that children from homosexual families are much like children from heterosexual families.

4. Differences between homosexual and heterosexual families:
   a. Lesbian couples with children report higher satisfaction with their partnerships than lesbian couples without children; while childless heterosexual couples report higher marital satisfaction.
   b. The partners of lesbian mothers spend more time than husbands of heterosexual mothers caring for children.
   c. Homosexual couples tend to be more egalitarian.

C. Race and Adaptations to Poverty
   1. Single-Mother Families
      a. Whites have the lowest incidence of single-mother families. African-Americans have the highest. Although the last few years of the 20th century witnessed a reversal in the trend toward more single-mother families in the African-American community.
      b. Single-mother families outnumber two-parent families.
      c. Some sources of single-parent families:
         i. Separation, divorce, or death.
         ii. People not getting married in the first place.
      d. What accounts for a decline of the two-parent family among African Americans?
         i. Some scholars trace the decline of the African-American family back to slavery.
         ii. Since about 1925, proportionately fewer black men have been able to help support a family, as a result of discrimination, unemployment, and the decline of manufacturing industries in the Northeast and the movement of blue-collar jobs to the suburbs in the 1970s and 1980s.
         iii. The declining ratio of eligible black men to black women due to the disadvantaged economic and social position of the African-American community, and the disproportionate number of black men imprisoned, murdered, and addicted to drugs; the disproportionately large number of black men in the armed forces; and the fact that a black man is nearly twice as likely as a black woman to marry a nonblack, and intermarriage has increased to nearly 10% of all marriages involving at least one black person.
         iv. The relative earnings of black women and men. In recent decades, the average income of African-American women has increased, while the earning power of African-American men has fallen.

VI. FAMILY POLICY

 A. Is the decline of the nuclear family a bad thing for society?

  1. As suggested by the research, the answer is yes and no.

 B. A comparison of the United States and Sweden

  1. The United States is a good example of how social problems can emerge from nuclear family decline. Sweden is a good example of how such problems can be averted.

  2. *Sweden leads the United States on most indicators of nuclear family decline.*

   a. In Sweden:

    i. There is a smaller percentage of people.

    ii. People marry at a later age.

    iii. The proportion of births outside of marriage is twice as high.

    iv. A much larger proportion of Swedish women with children under age three work in the paid labor force.

  3. *Sweden leads the United States on most measures of children's well being.*

   a. In Sweden:

    i. Children enjoy higher average reading test scores.

    ii. The poverty rate is only one twelfth as high.

    iii. The rate of infant abuse is one-eleventh the U.S. rate.

    iv. The rate of juvenile drug offenses is less than half as high.

    v. There is a slightly higher rate of juvenile delinquency for minor offenses.

  4. Sweden has a substantial family support policy, which the United States does not. In Sweden:

   a. Parental leave.

    i. When a child is born, a parent is entitled to 360 days of parental leave at 80% of his or her salary, and an additional 90 days at a flat rate.

    ii. Fathers can take an additional 10 days of leave with pay when the baby is born.

   b. Health *care*.

    i. Parents are entitled to free "well baby clinics."

    ii. All Swedish citizens receive free health care from the state-run system.

   c. Child-care.

    i. Temporary parental benefits are available for parents with a sick child under the age of 12.

    ii. One parent can take up to 60 days off per sick child per year at 80% salary.

    iii. Government subsidized high-quality day care is available for all parents.

    iv. Direct cash payments based on the number of children in each family.

   d. The United States is at the other extreme among industrialized countries.

    i. Since 1993, a parent is entitled to 12 weeks of unpaid parental leave.

    ii. About 44 million citizens have no health care coverage. Millions more experience a low standard of health care.

    iii. No system of state day care, and no direct cash payments based on the number children.

    iv. The value of the dependent deduction on income tax has fallen by nearly 50% since the 1940s.

5. Three criticisms commonly raised in the United States against generous family support policies.
   a. Some say it encourages long-term dependence on welfare, illegitimate births, and the breakup of two-parent families. Research shows that:
      i. The divorce rate and the rate of births to unmarried mothers are not higher when welfare payments are higher.
      ii. Welfare dependency is not widespread in general, even among African-American teen mothers, who are thought of a particularly susceptible.
   b. Some say nonfamily child-care is bad for children under age 3. Research shows that:
      i. When comparing family care with high quality day care (as opposed to the comparison of upper-middle class family care with child care in existing facilities in the United States), studies find no negative consequences for children over age 1.
      ii. Negative effects of day care usually disappear by the time a child reaches age 5.
      iii. Day care has some benefits, like making friends, and is generally beneficial to low-income families.
   c. They are expensive and have to be paid by high taxes.
      i. This is true. It is a trade-off. Swedes have made the political decisions to pay higher taxes partly to avoid the social problems and costs that emerge when the traditional nuclear family is replaced with other family forms and no institutional support.

Study Activity: Applying the Sociological Compass

After reading Chapter 11, review the abortion debate in the section "Reproductive Choice." Make a list of the "right-to-life" and "pro-choice" positions and social characteristics as described in the text. Consider the debate from the functionalist and feminist perspectives. Make a list of possible arguments for or against abortion from each perspective. Which perspective makes most sense to you, with respect to your own personal views, and why? As Brym and Lie ask, "Do you think your opinions are influenced by your social characteristics?" In what ways do your social characteristics influence your preference for either the functionalist or feminist perspective?

Right-To-Life

Positions and Arguments:

1.

2.

3.

Social Characteristics:

1.

2.

3.

Pro-Choice

Positions and Arguments:

1.

2.

3.

Social Characteristics:

1.

2.

3.

Functionalist Arguments

1.

2.

3.

Feminist Arguments

1.

2.

3.

InfoTrac College Edition Online Exercises

For the following exercises, log on to the online library of InfoTrac College Edition at http://www.infotrac-college.com/. Make note that InfoTrac has implemented a new registration system that will allow easier access to InfoTrac through the use of a personalized username and password.

Once you've created your username and password you may proceed directly to the Log On page. To create an account, register your passcode packaged with your textbook, and create a username and password, by following the online prompt. After you are logged in, click on "Infotrac College Edition." You will arrive at a screen that enables you to search topics.

Keyword: **Extended family**. Choose an article that discusses the prevalence of extended families in contemporary society. Make a list of reasons why the extended family still exists.

Keyword: **Family policy**. Search for the key words "family policy." Identify two specific policies from at least two articles, and explain its advantages and disadvantages based on what you learned in Chapter 11.

Keyword: **divorce**. What are recent divorce trends in the United States based on any relevant article(s)? Are the trends described consistent with the information in Chapter 11?

Keyword: **Stepfamily, blended family, reconstituted family**. Look up each of these key words separately. These terms really mean the same thing. Assess the similarities and differences between these three terms. What conclusions can you draw?

Keyword: **Daddy stress, second shift**. Look up each of these keywords separately. Many people assume these two terms are equivalent for men and women. Investigate daddy stress and distinguish it from the second shift. What are your thoughts? Support your answer with research findings from the articles.

Keyword: **Polygamous families**. Learn about family life in polygamous families. See the article on Bedouin - Arab families in The Journal of Social Psychology. Compare your life with life in polygamous families. How is it similar? Different?

Keyword: **Cohabitation**. Assess the legal consequences of cohabitation. Do you think that cohabitating couples should be recognized the same under the law as legally married couples? Do you think that same-sex couples should be recognized the same under the law as legally married couples? Write a short opinion paper stating your answers.

Internet Exercises

Go to: http://www.trinity.edu/mkearl/family.html.

There is a lot of information about marriage and family processes. Read over the different definitions of the family that are presented. How do these definitions compare with the definition of family found in Chapter 11? Come up with your own definition of the family. Compare and contrast all of the definitions. Are there similar patterns?

There are many ways to define the family. Look at the way the U.S. government defined family during the 2000 Census. Go to: http://www.census.gov/ and click on Asearch@ and then type in family. This will give you the top 100 documents. Look at two or three different documents and see how the government defines the family.

What are the consequences for families on welfare when they leave welfare? To learn more about these success stories, go to: http://newfederalism.urban.org/html/discussion99-02.html

Where do individuals go for advice when they are thinking of divorce? To learn more about issues of concern, go to: http://www.divorce-online.com/

What advice would you give to one of your friends who is thinking of divorce?

Everyone wants to know what the keys to successful relationships are. Make your own list of what you think are the keys to successful relationship. Then go to:

http://www.smartmarriage.com/ and compare your list with those listed here.

Practice Tests

Fill-In-The-Blank

Fill in the blank with the appropriate term from the above list of "key terms."

1. A(An) _____ is a nuclear family in which the husband works outside the home for money and the wife works for free in the home.

2. _____ expands the nuclear family horizontally by adding one or more spouses to the household.

3. The _____ is the number of marriages that occur in a year for every 1,000 people in the population.

4. The _____ expands the nuclear family vertically by adding another generation to the household.

5. The _____ is the number of divorces that occur in a year for every 1,000 people in the population.

Multiple-Choice Questions

Select the response that best answers the question or completes the statement:

1. A family unit made up of parents, children and grandparents living in one household is:
    a. a nuclear family.
    b. a traditional nuclear family.
    c. an extended family.
    d. a blended family.
    e. None of the above.

2. Which form of the family was considered the most widespread and ideal in the 1940s and 1950s?
    a. the extended family
    b. the blended family
    c. the traditional nuclear family
    d. All of the above.
    e. None of the above.

3. Which is NOT a main function of the family?
    a. egalitarian division of labor
    b. sexual regulation
    c. economic cooperation
    d. reproduction
    e. socialization

4. The extended family expands the nuclear family _____ by adding another generation to the household.
    a. horizontally
    b. vertically
    c. laterally
    d. All of the above.
    e. None of the above.

5. What trends indicate a gradual weakening of the nuclear family from the second half of the 19th century until the mid-1940s, according to Andrew J. Cherlin?
    a. divorce rate
    b. marriage rate
    c. total fertility rate
    d. All of the above.
    e. None of the above.

6. Which is true of love and marriage?
    a. The idea of love in the choice of marriage originated in the early 20th century, when Hollywood began promoting self-gratification and heterosexual romance.
    b. Love was always a prerequisite for marriage in most societies.
    c. In industrial societies, love alone determines mate selection.
    d. All of the above.
    e. None of the above.

7. Which is NOT one of the forces underlying marital satisfaction as highlighted in the textbook?
    a. the entry of women into the paid labor force
    b. economic factors
    c. divorce laws
    d. housework and child care
    e. sex

8. Children of divorced parents:
    a. tend to develop behavioral problems and do less well in school.
    b. are more likely to engage in delinquent acts.
    c. often experience an emotional crisis, especially in the first 2 years following divorce.
    d. All of the above.
    e. None of the above.

9. According to Amato and Keith, the overall effect of divorce on children's well-being is not strong and is declining over time. Which factor does NOT account for the distress among children of divorce, according to Amato and Keith?
    a. a high level of parental conflict
    b. a decline in living standards
    c. the absence of a parent
    d. the divorce itself
    e. All of the above are factors according to Amato and Keith.

10. "Right-to-life" activists tend to be:
    a. homemakers in religious families.
    b. upper class.
    c. highly educated.
    d. All of the above.
    e. None of the above.

11. The sociological and ethical issues surrounding reproductive technologies include:
    a. discrimination
    b. legal issues.
    c. social problems rendering the terms "mother" and "father" obsolete.
    d. All of the above.
    e. None of the above.

12. Arlie Hochschild showed that:
    a. as women's participation in the paid labor force increased, equality in the home became more common.
    b. even though income difference remain between men and women, the division of household labor becomes more equal as long as the wife strongly agrees there should be equality in the household.
    c. Even women who work full-time in the paid labor force remain primarily responsible for taking care of the household and children.
    d. All of the above.
    e. None of the above.

13. According the Murray Straus, severe forms of wife abuse:
    a. occur in all categories of the population.
    b. is most common in lower classes, less highly education families.
    c. is most common where men are more likely to believe that male domination is justified.
    d. All of the above.
    e. None of the above.

14. Which is NOT true of homosexuality based on the research cited in the textbook?
    a. Most homosexuals a want long-term, intimate relationship with one other adult.
    b. Children raised in homosexual families develop confused sexual identities and exhibit homosexual tendencies themselves.
    c. Partners of lesbian mothers spend more time than husbands of heterosexual mothers caring for children.
    d. Lesbian couples with children report higher satisfaction with their partners than lesbian couples without children.
    e. All of the above are true.

15. From the 1940s to the 1950s in the United States, the percentage of women age 20-24 who never married:
    a. fell.
    b. increased.
    c. remained constant.
    d. All of the above.
    e. None of the above.

16. What does the character played by Kevin Spacey in American Beauty do to make so many people so angry?
    a. He forgoes the pretenses of a middle-class, suburban husband.
    b. He returns in spirit to his teenage self.
    c. He gets fired from his professional job as a magazine writer, and gets a new one as a cook at a fast-food restaurant.
    d. He lusts after his teenage daughters best friend.
    e. All of the above.

17. Which type of household has emerged since the 1980s?
    a. women living alone.
    b. men living alone.
    c. other types of families without children.
    d. All of the above.
    e. None of the above.

18. In the last three decades, the number of American couples who are unmarried and cohabiting increased:
    a. approximately 50%.
    b. between 100% and 150%.
    c. approximately 200%.
    d. more than 500%.
    e. None of the above.

True False

1. The TV portrayals of the family as a happy, smooth functioning, mother-householder, father-breadwinner in the 1950s were quite accurate depictions of postwar families.

    TRUE or FALSE

2. The entry of millions of women into higher education and the paid labor force made it easier for women to leave unhappy marriages.

    TRUE or FALSE

3. As a result of the gender revolution, the domain of housework, childcare, and senior care has changed dramatically.

    TRUE or FALSE

4. Following divorce, men often experience upward mobility, while women often experience a decline in their standard of living.

    TRUE or FALSE

5. High levels of wife assault are associated with gender inequality in the larger society.

    TRUE or FALSE

6. Two-parent families outnumber single-mother families.

    TRUE or FALSE

7. The tendency to rely on the extended kin network declines with migration status and upward mobility.

    TRUE or FALSE

8. Cohabitation is a relatively unstable relationship.

    TRUE or FALSE

Short Answer

1. List and define the five main functions of the family. (p. 293)

    _____

    _____

2. List and define the four main reproductive technologies. Explain the two major sociological and ethical issues concerning reproductive technologies in general. (p. 304)

    _____

    _____

3. What does Arlie Hochschild mean by "the second shift"? (p. 305)

    _____

    _____

4. Briefly explain why those who cohabit before marriage are at greater risk for marital instability and divorce than married couples who did not cohabit, based on information from the Brym and Lie textbook. (p. 307)

    _____

    _____

5. What are three main differences between homosexual and heterosexual families based on research cited in the textbook? (p. 310)

    _____

    _____

Essay Questions

1. Americans have been sharply divided on the abortion issue especially since the 1970s. Provide an overview of the "right-to-life" versus the "pro-choice" arguments. What are the social characteristics of each group of activists? Explain the position of Randall Collins and Scott Coltrane on abortion. (p. 303-304)

2. Describe the sources and explain the reasons for the decline of the two-parent family among African Americans. (p. 312-313)

3. Sweden and the United States are described as opposite extremes on a continuum of family policy. Compare and contrast family policy in Sweden and the United States. What are the relative advantages and disadvantages of family support policies in each country? (p. 313-316)

Solutions

Practice Tests

Fill-In-The-Blank

1. traditional nuclear family
2. Polygamy
3. marriage rate
4. extended family
5. divorce rate

Multiple-Choice Questions

1. C, (p. 293)
2. C, (p. 290)
3. A, (p. 293)
4. B, (p. 293)
5. D, (p. 295)
6. E, (p. 297)
7. A, (p. 300)
8. D, (p. 303)
9. D, (p. 303).
10. A, (p. 304)
11. D, (p. 304)
12. C, (p. 305)
13. D, (p. 306-307)
14. B, (p. 310)
15. A, (p. 295)
16. E, (p. 291)
17. D, (p. 292)
18. D, (p. 308)

True False

1. F, (p. 295)
2. T, (p. 300)
3. F, (p. 301-306)
4. T, (p. 301-303)
5. T, (p. 306)
6. F, (p. 311)
7. T, (p. 311-313)
8. T, (p. 307)

CHAPTER **12**

RELIGION AND EDUCATION

Student Learning Objectives

After reading Chapter 12, you should be able to:

1. Compare and contrast Durkheimian, Marxist, and Weberian approaches to religion.

2. Identify and explain the general components of "religious" experiences with respect of "collective effervescence" and social solidarity.

3. Explain the role of religion in justifying inequality and promoting conflict.

4. Explain the connection between the rise of Protestantism and capitalist development.

5. Describe the historical patterns of religious rise, decline and revival.

6. Identify and define the types of religious groups.

7. Discuss the major trends and indicators of religiosity, and the future of religion.

8. Engage the debate and controversy over affirmative action.

9. Identify and describe the manifest and latent functions of schools.

10. Explain how education reproduces the existing social stratification system in terms of standardized tests, tracking, self-fulfilling prophecies, and cultural capital.

11. Critically discuss pressing educational issues in terms of schools standards, educational attainment, and inequality.

12. Discuss proposed solutions to school crisis and their limitations.

Key Terms

(defined on the indicated pages of the textbook, and in glossary)

collective conscience (319)

profane (319)

sacred (319)

totems (319)

rituals (319)

civil religion (321)

secularization thesis (325)

fundamentalists (327)

revised secularization (331)

church (331)

ecclesia (331)

denominations (332)

sects (332)

cults (332)

routinization of charisma (321)

religiosity (334)

meritocracy (337)

educational attainment (338)

educational achievement (338)

tracking (340)

stereotype threat (345)

cultural capital (345)

Detailed Chapter Outline

I. INTRODUCTION

    A. Psychologically, religion is a common human response and coping device to the fact that we must all die. It provides meaning and purpose.

    B. Religious response takes thousands of forms. Sociologists of religion study this variation.

        1. Why does one religion predominate here, another there?

        2. Why is religious belief more fervent at one time than another?

        3. Under what circumstances does religion act as a source of social stability and under what circumstances does it act as a source of social change?

        4. Are we becoming more or less religious?

    C. Although God is still very much alive in America, the scope of religious authority has declined in the United States and many other parts of the world. Consequently, other institutions have grown in importance as the scope of religious authority has declined.

II. CLASSICAL APPROACHES IN THE SOCIOLOGY OF RELIGION

    A. Durkheim and the Problem of Order

        1. Super Bowl Sunday is second only to Christmas as a religious holiday in the United States." Although there is no god of the Super Bowl, the Super Bowl meets Durkheim's definition of a religious experience.

        2. The Super Bowl generates a sense of "collective effervescence" and **collective conscience**, which is composed of common sentiments and values that people share as a result of living together.

3. We distinguish everyday world of the **profane** from the religious transcendent world of the **sacred**. **Totems** are objects that symbolize the sacred.
    a. The game is a sacred event.
    b. The Super Bowl trophy and team logos would be considered totems.
4. **Rituals** are public practices that connect us to the sacred.
    a. The football game itself is a public ritual.
5. Rituals and religion reinforce *social solidarity*.

B. Religion, Conflict, and Inequality
    1. Two criticisms of Durkheim's account of religion:
        a. It overemphasizes religion's role in maintaining social cohesion, when in reality religion often incites conflict.
        b. When religion does increase social cohesion, it often reinforces social inequality.
    2. Over time, the charismatic leadership of the world religions became routinized. The **routinization of charisma** is Weber's term for the transformation of divine enlightenment into a permanent feature of everyday life. It involves turning religious inspiration into a stable social institution with defined roles, such as interpreters of the divine message, teachers, dues-paying lay people, and so forth.
    3. Marx called religion "the opium of the people,"—that is how religion often tranquilizes the underprivileged into accepting their lot in life.
    4. We can draw evidence for Marx's interpretation from many time, places, and institutions. For example, all the major world religions have traditionally placed women in a subordinate position.
    5. Religion has traditionally supported gender inequality and class inequality.
    6. According to Robert Bellah, **civil religion** is a set of quasi-religious beliefs and practices that binds the population together and justifies our way of life.
        a. Example—The celebration of social equality and the American Dream diverts our attention from social inequalities in the United States.
    7. Examples of religion promoting conflict:
        a. Discrimination in white churches and the separation of black and white churches in the South in the 1940s.
        b. Black churches and the Civil Rights movement in the 1950s and 1960s.

C. Weber and the Problem of Social Change
    1. Weber stressed the way religion can contribute to social change—*The Protestant Ethic and the Spirit of Capitalism*.
        a. According to Weber, what prompted vigorous capitalist development in Catholic Europe and North America was a combination of:
            i. Favorable economic conditions.

      b.   The *Protestant Ethic*
          i.   Followers of John Calvin stressed the need to engage in intense worldly activity, to display industry, punctuality, and frugality in everyday life.
         ii.   The idea that people could assure a state of grace by working diligently and living simply.
    2. Problem of Weber's argument:
      a.   The correlation between the Protestant work ethic and the strength of capitalist development is weaker than Weber thought.

III. THE RISE, DECLINE, AND PARTIAL REVIVAL OF RELIGION

  A. Secularization
    1. In medieval and early modern Europe, Christianity replaced magic as the popular source of answers to mysterious, painful, and capricious events—and became a powerful presence in religious affairs, music, art, architecture, literature, philosophy, marriage, education, morality, economic affairs, politics, etc.
    2. The Church was the center of both spiritual and worldly life. European countries proclaimed official state religions, and persecuted members of religious minorities.
    3. A few hundred years later, Weber's observations of the replacement of religious authority with forms of rationalism by the turn of the 20th century became known as the **secularization thesis**, which says that religious institutions, actions, and consciousness are on the decline worldwide.

  B. Religious Revival
    1. Many sociologists revised their judgments about secularization in the 1990s, because accumulated survey evidence showed that religion was not in a state of decay in many places including the United States.
    2. Fundamentalism
      a.   The second reason many sociologists have modified their views about secularization is that an intensification of religious belief and practice has taken place among some people in recent decades. Fundamentalist religious organizations have rapidly increased their membership since the 1960s, especially among Protestants. **Fundamentalists** interpret their scriptures literally, seek to establish a direct, personal relationship with their higher being(s), are relatively intolerant of nonfundamentalists, and often support conservative social issues. For example, in 2000 only 23% of Americans who identified themselves as fundamentalist agreed with the statement that abortion is acceptable if "the women want it for any reason."
      b.   Such social issues often spill over into political struggles, which is why religion in American politics is resurgent.
      c.   Fundamentalism has spread throughout the world since the 1970s, and is typically driven by politics.
          i.   Hindu nationalists in India.
         ii.   Jewish fundamentalists in Israeli political life.
        iii.   Muslim fundamentalism in the Middle East, Africa, and parts of Asia.
      d.   Fundamentalism and Extremist Politics in the Arab World

      i.   Personal Anecdote. Robert Brym at the Hebrew University of Jerusalem in 1972.

     ii.   Religious fundamentalism often provides a convenient vehicle for framing political extremism, enhancing its appeal, legitimizing it, and providing a foundation of solidarity of political groups.

   iii.   Many people fail to see the religious underpinnings of religious fundamentalism. They regard religious fundamentalism as an independent variable, and extremist politics as a dependent variable. In this view, some people happen to become religious fanatics, which commands them to kill their opponents – for example, George W. Bush's presidential address to Congress on September 20, 2001.

    iv.   What President Bush ignored are the political sources of this fringe from of Islamic extremism. Fundamentalism, like other forms of religion, is powerfully influenced by the social context in which it emerges.

C. The Revised Secularization Thesis

   1. According to the **revised secularization** thesis, in most countries, worldly institutions have broken off or "differentiated" from the institution of religion over time.

   2. Education is an example of a worldly institution. Religious institutions used to run schools.

IV. RELIGION IN THE UNITED STATES

A. Church, Sect, and Cult

   1. Three types of religious groups:

     a. A **Church** is any bureaucratic religious organization that has accommodated itself to mainstream society and culture.

       i.   Two main forms of churches:

       ii.   (a) **Ecclesia** are state-supported churches

      iii.   (b) **Denominations** are the various streams of belief and practice that some churches allow to coexist under their overarching authority.

     b. **Sects** often form by breaking away from churches due to disagreement about church doctrine.

       i.   Sects are less integrated into society and less bureaucratized than churches.

     c. **Cults** are small groups of people deeply committed to a religious vision that rejects mainstream culture and society.

       i.   Cults are often led by charismatic leaders, men and women claim to be inspired by supernatural power and whose followers believe them to be so inspired.

B. Religiosity

   1. **Religiosity** refers to how important religion is to people.

   2. Indicators of religiosity include:

     a. Strength of belief;

     b. Emotional attachment to religion;

     c. Knowledge about a religion;

     d. Frequency of performing rituals; and

     e. Frequency of applying religious principles in daily life.

3. How often do people attend religious services?
   a. Based on GSS data:
      i. Older people attend religious services more frequently than younger people. Older people have more time and more need for religion and are closer to death.
      ii. Frequent church attendance is more common among African Americans than whites, because the central political role the church historically played in helping African Americans combat oppression.
      iii. Respondents whose mothers attended religious services frequently are more likely to do so themselves. Religiosity is a *learned* behavior.

C. The Future of Religion
   1. Secularization is one of the two dominant trends influencing religion throughout the world.
      a. Even as secularization absorbs many people, many others in the United States, and throughout the world, have been caught up by a religious revival of vast proportions.
      b. The contradictory social processes of secularization and revival are likely to persist for some time, resulting in a world that is neither more religious nor more secular, but that is certainly more polarized.

V. AFFIRMATIVE ACTION AND MERITOCRACY

A. Legacy considerations affect acceptance rates.
   1. President George W. Bush was accepted at Yale with an SAT score of 1206, which was below average at Yale for his admission year.

B. Affirmative Action
   1. Much controversy surrounds the awarding of admission points based on cash gifts, family ties, and minority status. Consider the arguments for and against special treatment:
      a. *Advocates of affirmative action.*
      b. *Opponents of affirmative action.*
      c. *Advocates of special treatment for the well to do.*
      d. *Advocates of meritocracy.* **Meritocracy** is a stratification system in which equality of opportunity allows people to rise or fall to a position that matches their talent and effort.

VI. MACRO-SOCIOLOGICAL PROCESSES

A. Manifest and Latent Functions
   1. Many Americans believe that there is equal access to basic schooling, and think schools identify and sort students based on merit and effort. The school system is the American Dream in action. **Educational attainment** is seen as largely an outcome of individual talent and hard work. Educational attainment, which refers to the number of years of school completed, should not be confused with **educational achievement**, which refers to how much students actually learn.
   2. The view that the American educational system *sorts* students based on talent and effort is central to the *functional theory* of education, which also stresses the *training* role of schools. A third function involves the *socialization* of the young. Finally, schools *transmit culture* generationally, fostering a common identity and social cohesion in the process.

3. Sorting, training, socializing and transmitting culture are *manifest* functions or positive goals that schools accomplish intentionally. Schools also perform *latent* or unintentional functions, such as encouraging the development of a separate youth culture, serving the "marriage market," custodial service, and encouraging critical thinking and dissent.

B. The Effect of Economic Inequality
   1. From the *conflict perspective*, the problem with the functionalist view is that it exaggerates the degree to which schools sort students by ability to ensure that the most talented students get the most rewarding jobs. Conflict theorists argue that schools distribute the benefits of education unequally, thus reproducing social stratification generation after generation, rather than functioning as meritocracy.
   2. Schools reproduce stratification partly because they vary in quality.
   3. In the 1950s and 1960s, U.S. schools were homogeneous in resources and educational outcomes. Since the 1970s, big gaps have opened up the quality of education.
   4. For example, Jonathan Kozol's (1991) research in Chicago city schools compared average spending in an upper-middle-class, suburban school.
   5. Wide variations in the wealth of communities and a system of school funding based mainly on local property taxes ensure that most children from poor families learn inadequately in ill-equipped schools, and most well-to-do children learn well in better-equipped schools.
   6. Some schools, mainly those in poor neighborhoods, have a lot of students from disadvantaged homes, dropouts, and disciplinary problems. They pay less well and thus tend to have weaker teachers.

C. Standardized Tests
   1. Standardized tests are a second feature of schools that perpetuates stratification. In a society supposedly based on equality of opportunity, one's ability must be judged by objective standardized testing.
   2. Schools sort students into high-ability, middle-ability, and low-ability classes based on IQ and other tests (i.e. ACT and SAT), which is called **tracking**.
   3. How Do IQ and Social Status Influence Academic and Economic Success?
      a. IQ by itself contributes to academic success and to economic success later in life, which is what *functionalists* would predict.
      b. However, home environment background factors such as family income, parents' education, encouragement of creativity and studying, number of siblings, and so forth, influence success. This is in accordance with *conflict* predictions.
      c. Home environment, community environment, and schooling experience affect IQ test results. IQ is partly genetic and partly social in origin.
      d. Two cases where changed social circumstances resulted in improved IQ scores.
      e. The example of 300 black and Latino students at the Hostos-Lincoln Academy of Science in the South Bronx.

4. Are SAT and ACT Tests Biased?
   a. SAT and ACT tests sort students for college entrance.
   b. Culturally biased items can be found in the SAT and ACT tests, in which equally skilled member of different groups have significantly different rates of correct response to test items.
   c. More affluent students can afford coaching that boosts scores.
   d. According to Brym and Lie, the biggest problem with the SAT and ACT tests lies in the background factors that determine who gets to take the test in the first place and how well prepared different groups of test-takers are.

VII. MICRO-SOCIOLOGICAL PROCESSES
   A. The Self Fulfilling Prophecy
      1. Low expectations often encourage low achievement. A minority student is often under suspicion of intellectual inferiority and feels rejected. This **stereotype threat** has a negative impact on the school performance of disadvantaged groups.
      2. Minority students often cluster together because they feel alienated from dominant groups in their school or college or perhaps even from school or college itself.
      3. As a result of resentment and defiance of authority, many minority students reject academic achievement as a goal, because they see it as a goal of the dominant culture, hence can lead to discipline problems, apathy, and disruptive and illegal behavior.
      4. Challenging minority students, giving them emotional support and encouragement, giving greater recognition in the curriculum to the accomplishments of their group, creating an environment where they can relax and achieve- can explode self-fulfilling prophecies and improve academic performance.

   B. Cultural Capital
      1. **Cultural capital** accounts for some differences in school performance.
      2. Although the independent effect of cultural capital is sometimes exaggerated, the most often cited American study on the subject suggests that cultural capital may be as important as measured ability in determining grades.
      3. The original research on cultural capital was conducted in France, and it showed that possession of cultural capital is linked to being born in high-status families. American research shows a weaker and fluid link between one's family status and acquiring cultural capital. Having parents with or without education does not guarantee the acquisition of cultural capital, or lack there of.

VIII. CONTESTED TERRAIN: CRISIS AND REFORM IN U.S. SCHOOLS
   A. Solutions to the School Crisis
      1. Much research underscores the crisis in the American school system.
      2. Statistics on completion and dropout rates suggest that the crisis of the American school system is strongly related to minority status, which is strongly related to social class.
         a. In 2002, more than 21% of non-Hispanic whites older than 24 had a B.A., while only 17% of African Americans and 11% of Hispanic Americans older than 24 had a B.A.
         b. Eighty nine percent of non-Hispanic whites over age 25 had a high school diploma, compared to 79% of African Americans and 57% of Hispanic Americans.

c. The high school dropout rate for white non-Hispanics was less than 7%, compared to 13% for black students and 28% for Latinos.

3. For 40 years, the main strategy to improve educational attainment of disadvantage minorities has been school desegregation by busing to make schools more racially and ethnically integrated. Things did not work out as hoped.

    a. Many whites moved to all-white suburbs or enrolled their children in private schools.
    b. In integrated public schools, gains among minority students were limited by racial tensions, competition among academically mismatched students with different family backgrounds, and related factors.
    c. Many think a wiser course of action to improve the quality of under-financed minority schools is needed, while many educators fear that ignoring integration will deny American students of different races and ethnic groups the opportunity to learn to work and live together.

4. Local Initiatives

    a. In light of self-fulfilling prophecies, challenge minority students, give them emotional support and encouragement, prepare a curriculum that gives more recognition to the accomplishments of their group, and create a relaxing and achievement oriented environment.
    b. The mentoring movement involving community members volunteering to work with disadvantaged students in schools, church basements, community centers, and housing projects (i.e. "computer clubhouses").

5. Redistributing and Increasing School Budgets

    a. It would be helpful if the federal and state governments collected school taxes and tied them in part to people's ability to pay.

6. Economic Reform and Comprehensive Preschools

    a. Limitations with the first two proposed solutions.
        i.   With James Coleman's survey of American schools, sociologists discovered in the 1960s that schools were limited in what they could do on their own to encourage upward mobility and end poverty. Coleman found that differences in the quality of schools accounted for at the most a third of the variation in student's academic performance, while two thirds was due to inequalities imposed on children by their homes, neighborhoods, and peers.
        ii. Little research contradicts his findings today. Follow-up studies of Head Start found gains in cognitive and socio-emotional functioning displayed by Head Start graduates within 2 years of leaving the program. A 1997 Department of Education study of Title I of the Elementary and Secondary Education Act found no academic differences between students who received assistance and those who did not.
    b. Programs aimed at increasing school budgets and encouraging local reform initiatives need to be augmented by policies that improve the social environment of young, disadvantaged children *before and outside* school.

     i.   Children from disadvantaged homes do better when their parents create a healthy, supportive, and academically enriching environment at home and if peers do not lead children to a life of drugs, crime, and disdain for academic achievement.

    ii.   Policies aimed at creating these conditions would be far-reaching (i.e. job training for parents, comprehensive child and family assistance programs that start when a child is born).

  B. Realistically, many people are likely to oppose such reforms because they are costly in an era of school budget cuts in the inner cities, and an era when many parents prefer private schools or move to neighborhoods in suburbs with excellent public schools. On the other hand, 70% of Americans said too little money is being spent on the nation's schools based on 1998 GSS data.

Study Activity: Applying the Sociological Compass

Consider the various functions and problems at the high school you graduated from. Did your high school efficiently perform the functions as described in Chapter 12? If so, in what ways were these functions performed efficiently? Make a list of these functions and provide specific examples of their efficiency or lack thereof. Are the problems you remember consistent with the school problems discussed in Chapter 12? Make a list of common problems you recall from your high school. Attempt to explain the sources of these problems from the functionalist and conflict perspective. Make a list of possible solutions.

Functions of Your High School:

1.

2.

3.

4.

Examples of Each Function:

1.

2.

3.

4.

School Problems:

1.

2.

3.

4.

Sources of School Problems

Functionalist explanations:

Conflict explanations:

Possible Solutions:

1.

2.

3.

4.

InfoTrac College Edition Online Exercises

For the following exercises, log on to the online library of InfoTrac College Edition at http://www.infotrac-college.com/. Make note that InfoTrac has implemented a new registration system that will allow easier access to InfoTrac through the use of a personalized username and password.

Once you've created your username and password you may proceed directly to the Log On page. To create an account, register your passcode packaged with your textbook, and create a username and password, by following the online prompt. After you are logged in, click on "Infotrac College Edition." You will arrive at a screen that enables you to search topics.

Keyword: **religiosity**. Read at least two articles that reveal patterns of religiosity across at least two denominations under the same religious authority (i.e. Catholicism and Protestantism) or two religions (i.e. Christianity and Hinduism). What are the major findings? What are the differences and/or similarities in levels of religiosity?

Keyword: **liberation theology**. Determine the key issues according to one article.

Keyword: **prayer and school**. Search this term and see how the two ideas intersect. What are the major areas of focus in the literature on prayer and school? Do you think this debate will ever end? Write a short paper stating your findings.

Keyword: **Supreme Court and religion**. What is the emphasis of the Supreme Court cases dealing with religion and the state? Is there a specific pattern? Is so, how long has the pattern existed? Write a short paper stating your findings.

Keyword: **school vouchers**. Examine the different viewpoints on school vouchers from two articles. What are the arguments for and against the use of school vouchers?

Keyword: **distance education**. Distance education, through the use of telecourses and online courses, is increasing in popularity. What are the arguments for and against the use of distance education in higher education? What sociological issues lie behind this debate?

Keyword: **education** and **child poverty**. Look for three articles that address educational concerns and children who live in poverty. What suggestions does the research give to help children from poverty homes get an "equal" education?

Internet Exercises

The Church of Jesus Christ of Latter-day Saints is one of the fastest growing global churches. Go to this Web site and see how this religion places an emphasis on education. Go to: http://www.lds.org/

The official website of the American Atheists is located at http://www.atheists.org/schoolhouse/faqs. prayer.html

They present much information about prayer in schools. Write a short paper about the interplay between the major social institutions of education and religion.

Look at the homepage of the National Education Association (NEA) at http://www.nea.org/

Click on *issues*. This list provides a good basis for contemporary education issues. Write a "pro" and "con" paper on a specific issue facing the American education system.

Distance education has become a hot topic in the area of education. Recently, people being home-schooled have increasingly been using distance education as another medium of learning. Go to this site and see what this method of learning and teaching has to offer our society: http://www.internethomeschool.com/

Do you agree with the use of distance education in grades 1-12? Why or why not? What are the strengths and weakness of such an approach to education?

Search for "education" using the search engine of the General Social Survey (GSS) found at: http://www.icpsr.umich.edu/GSS99/search.htm.

Choose one research report and read it. List the major conclusions from the report you chose.

Practice Tests

Fill-In-The-Blank

Fill in the blank with the appropriate term from the above list of "key terms."

1. The _____ is composed of the common sentiments and values that people share as a result of living together.

2. The _____ says that religious institutions, actions, and consciousness are on the decline worldwide.

3. _____ are state-supported churches.

4. _____ usually form by breaking away from churches due to disagreement about church doctrine.

5. _____ refers to how important religion is to people.

6. _____ interpret their scriptures literally, and seek to establish a direct, personal relationship with the higher being(s) they worship.

7. The _____ holds that worldly institutions break off from the institution of religion over time.

8. _____ involves sorting students into high-ability, middle-ability, and low-ability classes based on the results of IQ and other tests.

9. _____ refers to how much students actually learn.

10. A(An) _____ is a stratification system in which equality of opportunity allows people to rise or fall to a position that matches their talent and effort.

11. _____ refers to widely shared, high-status cultural signals used for social and cultural exclusion.

Multiple-Choice Questions

Select the response that best answers the question or completes the statement:

1. What is a collective conscience?
    a. Common sentiments and values that people share as a result of living together.
    b. A feeling of guilt that emerges in the presence of a collective.
    c. A transcendence of social influences in order to be closer to one's religion.
    d. The shaming of an individual by a social group in an attempt to sanction.
    e. None of the above.

2. _____ are public practices that connect us to the sacred.
    a. Routines
    b. Public patterns
    c. Rituals
    d. Secularization
    e. None of the above.

3. We distinguish the everyday world of the _____, from the religious transcendent world of the _____.
    a. sacred; profane
    b. profane; sacred
    c. profane; secular
    d. sacred; secular
    e. None of the above.

4. Which theorist equated religion with a drug based on the argument that religion often tranquilizes the underprivileged into accepting their lot in life?
    a. Emile Durkheim
    b. Max Weber
    c. Thomas Hobbes
    d. John Calvin
    e. Karl Marx

5. In Durkheim's terms, the Super Bowl trophy is a(n) _____.
    a. positive reinforcement.
    b. secular object.
    c. example of material culture.
    d. totem.
    e. None of the above.

6. Weber made a historical connection between _____ and capitalism.
   a. the opium of the masses
   b. social solidarity
   c. secularization
   d. the Protestant ethic
   e. None of the above.

7. Which type of religious organizations interpret their scriptures literally, and seek to establish a direct personal relationship with their higher beings?
   a. orthodox religious organizations
   b. liberation organizations
   c. fundamentalists
   d. All of the above.
   e. None of the above.

8. Frequent church attendance is more common among _____ than _____.
   a. African Americans; whites.
   b. whites; African Americans.
   c. whites; racial minorities.
   d. All of the above.
   e. None of the above.

9. Which type of religious groups tends to be high on social integration, bureaucratization and longevity?
   a. sect
   b. church
   c. cult
   d. All of the above.
   e. None of the above.

10. What percentage of Americans who identified themselves as fundamentalist, agree with the statement that abortion is acceptable if "the woman wants it for any reason?"
    a. 72%
    b. 56%
    c. 44%
    d. 38%
    e. 23%

11. Which statement provides evidence that American experience in terms of fundamentalism is by no means unique?
    a. Fundamentalism has spread throughout the world since the 1970s.
    b. Fundamentalism is typically driven by politics.
    c. A revival of Muslim fundamentalism began in Iran in the 1970s.
    d. All of the above.
    e. None of the above.

12. Even in urban settings, strictly enforced rules concerning dress, diet, prayer, and intimate contact with outsiders can separate members from the larger society. This is an example of a(an):
    a. cult
    b. sect
    c. charismatic
    d. ecclesia
    e. fundamentalist

13. In the 1950s and 1960s, black churches formed the breeding ground of:
    a. fundamentalism.
    b. secularization.
    c. revival.
    d. the Civil Rights movement.
    e. None of the above.

14. _____ refers to the number of years of school completed.
    a. educational attainment
    b. educational achievement
    c. educational potential
    d. educational tracking
    e. educational enhancement

15. Which is a social mechanism that plays out in the school system to reproduce inequality based on the conflict perspective?
    a. unequal funding
    b. testing
    c. tracking
    d. the self-fulfilling prophecy
    e. All of the above

16. Schools commonly teach students to view their nation with pride. This is considered a _____ function of schools.
    a. manifest
    b. latent
    c. unintended
    d. hidden
    e. None of the above.

17. As a result of 40 years of school desegregation, educational attainment between racial minorities and whites:
    a. have approached equity.
    b. remain sharply different.
    c. have improved dramatically.
    d. All of the above.
    e. None of the above.

18. A historically patterned response to school desegregation by whites has been:
    a. an overwhelming acceptance as indicated by the number of integrated neighborhoods throughout metropolitan U.S. cities.
    b. a practically formal return to Jim Crow legislation.
    c. the movement of whites to all-white suburbs or enrollment of their children in private schools.
    d. All of the above.
    e. None of the above.

19. About what fraction of schools are in need of immediate repair in New York City?
    a. three-fourths
    b. one-half
    c. one-fifth
    d. one-eighth
    e. one-sixteenth

20. Schools sort students into high, middle, and low-ability classes based on the results of intelligence quotient (IQ) and other tests. This is called:
    a. tracking
    b. level-placement
    c. directed study
    d. learner style sorting
    e. re-directation

21. Which of the following is NOT a manifest function of educational institutions?
    a. transmission of culture
    b. bringing potential mates together
    c. custodial service
    d. encouragement of critical thinking and dissent
    e. serving the marriage market

22. The negative impact of negative stereotypes on school performance of disadvantaged groups is referred to as:
    a. tracking
    b. stereotype threat
    c. cultural capital
    d. stereotyped inflation
    e. meritocracy

23. What is the biggest problem with the SAT and ACT scored tests according to Brym and Lie?
    a. More affluent students can afford to be coached, hence raise their scores.
    b. These tests are culturally biased.
    c. Background factors determine who gets to take the test in the first place and how well prepared different groups of test-takers are.
    d. IQ tests are used to track students.
    e. None of the above.

24. Minority students often cluster together because:
    a. they would rather stick together in a pluralistic pattern to maintain their ethnic identities.
    b. they often feel alienated from dominant groups in their school or college or perhaps even from school or college itself.
    c. they often refuse to assimilate to achieve upward educational mobility.
    d. All of the above.
    e. None of the above.

True False

1. Durkheim would argue that the "psyche-up" ritual football players engage in to prepare for a game has a religious quality.

   TRUE or FALSE

2. Marx called religion the "opium of the people."

   TRUE or FALSE

3. Religiosity refers to one level of spirituality, despite the strength of belief in a particular religion.

   TRUE or FALSE

4. Religiosity is a learned behavior.

   TRUE or FALSE

5. In light of the fact that a religious revival is taking place, secularization is likely to decline in the future according the Brym and Lie.

   TRUE or FALSE

6. Religion in American politics is resurgent in part because social issues regarding religion often spill over into political struggles.

   TRUE or FALSE

7. Religious fundamentalism has become a worldwide political phenomenon.

   TRUE or FALSE

8. From a Durkheimian point of view, Super Bowl Sunday can be considered an example of the routinization of charisma.

   TRUE or FALSE

9. Educational attainment and educational achievement are synonymous.

   TRUE or FALSE

10. The function of schools in providing custodial care is a latent function.

    TRUE or FALSE

11. The majority of Americans believe that the public school system has increased the level of school standards to prepare ever more students for college.

    TRUE or FALSE

12. While other countries siphon off poor academic performers to trade schools before they graduate, the United States tries to graduate as many students as possible because it enhances democracy and social cohesion in the context of U.S. diversity.

    TRUE or FALSE

Short Answer

1. Briefly explain the impact of the Protestant ethic on capitalist development according to Weber. Briefly explain two problems with Weber's argument. (p. 324)

   _____

   _____

2. What is the "secularization thesis"? Provide one historical example of it. (p. 325)

   _____

   _____

3. Define fundamentalism and provide an example of America fundamentalist attitudes toward abortion. (p. 326-327)

   _____

   _____

4. Describe the characteristics of a charismatic leader and give examples of some charismatic figures. Why do people follow them so willingly? (p. 332)

   _____

   _____

5. Explain the difference between a church, sect, and cult, and provide an example for each. (p. 331-332)

   _____

   _____

6. Explain the difference between educational attainment and educational achievement. Why is it important to make a distinction in the context of inequality in education? (p. 338)

   _____

   _____

7. Provide a conflict criticism of the functionalist view on education. Be sure to provide one concrete example from the textbook to support the criticism. (p. 338-340)

_____

_____

Essay Questions

1. Explain how Super Bowl Sunday is like a religious holiday according to Durkheim. (p. 31-319).

2. Compare and contrast perspectives of Marx and Weber on religion and capitalism. (p. 321-324).

3. Many argue that the public school system in the United States is in crisis. What is the evidence for this argument? Provide an overview of the three main solutions to school crisis. Be sure to explain their merits, drawbacks and likelihood of implementation. (p. 346-350)

4. Explain the functions of education from a functionalist perspective. Also, explain educational inequality from a conflict perspective. In your answer, be sure to discuss manifest functions, latent functions, and standardized tests. (p. 337-340)

Solutions

Practice Tests

Fill-In-The-Blank

1. collective conscience
2. secularization thesis
3. Ecclesia
4. Sects
5. Religiosity
6. Fundamentalists
7. revised secularization thesis
8. Tracking
9. Educational achievement
10. meritocracy
11. Cultural capital

Multiple-Choice Questions

1. A, (p. 319)
2. C, (p. 319)
3. B, (p. 319)
4. E, (p. 321)
5. D, (p. 319)
6. D, (p. 324)
7. C, (p. 326)
8. A, (p. 334)
9. B, (p. 331)
10. E, (p. 327)
11. D, (p. 329)
12. B, (p. 332)
13. D, (p. 322-323)
14. A, (p. 338)
15. E, (p. 338-340)
16. A, (p. 338)
17. B, (p. 346)
18. C, (p. 339)
19. C, (p. 339)
20. A, (p. 340)
21. A, (p. 338)
22. B, (p. 345)
23. C, (p. 342)
24. B, (p. 345)

True False

1. T, (p. 318)
2. T, (p. 321)
3. F, (p. 334)
4. T, (p. 334)
5. F, (p. 330)
6. T, (p. 326-331)
7. T, (p. 329)
8. F, (p. 321)
9. F, (p. 338)
10. T, (p. 338)
11. F, (p. 345-349)
12. T, (p. 344-349)

CHAPTER **13**

POLITICS, WORK AND THE ECONOMY

Student Learning Objectives

After reading Chapter 13, you should be able to:

1. Identify and define the three bases of authority according to Max Weber.

2. Compare and contrast competing theories of democracy.

3. Understand and apply theories of democracy to discuss the future of democracy.

4. Explain the role of elites in the decision-making processes that govern society according to C. Wright Mills' elite theory.

5. Describe the philosophies of liberal and conservative policy groups.

6. Discuss the patterns of party support in terms of social class, religion, race, and gender.

7. Discuss democracy as an ideal versus a reality.

8. Define the core concepts of politics.

9. Explain the role of organization as a source of the distribution of political power.

10. Describe how the state can structure political life, regardless of how power is distributed.

11. Explain why the U.S. political system is ironically less responsive to the needs of the disadvantaged, in spite of its promotion of democracy.

12. Describe the development of the three sectors of the economy.

13. Discuss the current and future prospects for "good" and "bad" jobs in terms of competing perspectives on work and labor.

14. Explain the difficulty of moving from the primary to secondary labor market, and describe the demographic characteristics of the barriers in regards to gender, race, ethnicity, and union membership.

15. Describe and explain the problem of social inequality in the labor market in general, and in relation to corporate control and globalization, in particular.

16. Contrast capitalism and communism as ideal-types of economic systems in a comparative context.

17. Describe the working conditions of workers in multinational corporations in less developed countries.

18. Discuss future trends of work and the economy based on prevailing patterns involving the implementation of new technologies and the organization of work.

Key Terms

(defined on the indicated pages of the textbook, and in glossary)

power (355)

authority (356)

legitimate (356)

traditional authority (356)

legal-rational authority (356)

charismatic authority (356)

political revolution (356)

state (356)

civil society (356)

authoritarian state (356)

democracy (359)

political parties (359)

lobbies (359)

mass media (360)

social movements (360)

pluralists (360)

elite theory (361)

elites (361)

power resource theory (363)

state-centered theorists (366)

economy (372)

productivity (372)

markets (372)

division of labor (373)

deskilled (374)

scientific management (374)

labor market segmentation (377)

primary labor market (377)

secondary labor market (377)

free market (379)

regulated market (379)

capitalism (380)

corporations (380)

communism (380)

democratic socialist (381)

conglomerates (382)

interlocking directorates (382)

Detailed Chapter Outline

I.   INTRODUCTION

    A.   The Tobacco War

       1.   In the spring of 1998, Congress was ready to pass an anti-tobacco bill that would be very costly for tobacco companies.

       2.   The public seemed eager to support the legislation, due to compelling health concerns, and the targeting of teenagers by the tobacco industry.

3. Representatives of the tobacco industry mobilized enormous resources against the bill (i.e. lobbyists and ad campaigns), and wined, dined, and cajoled members of Congress to vote against the bill.
4. Ads swayed public opinion, and influenced the belief that the bill's real aim was to raise revenue.
5. The bill was defeated in June 1998.
6. The defeat of the federal bill raises important political questions.
    a. Does the outcome of the tobacco war illustrate the operation of "government of the people, by the people, for the people" as Abraham Lincoln defined democracy?
    b. Does big business's access to economic and political resources lead one to doubt Lincoln's definition of democracy?
7. The tobacco war raises the core question of political sociology.
    a. What accounts for the degree to which a political system responds to the demands of all its citizens?
    b. Political sociologists examine the effects of social structures, especially class structures, on politics.
    c. An adequate theory of democracy requires that we also examine how state institutions and laws affect political processes.

B. What is Politics? Core Concepts
    1. Politics is a machine that determines "who gets what, when, and how." **Power**, the ability to control others against their will, fuels the machine.
    2. Power:
        a. May involve force.
        b. Becomes **authority** when it is legitimate and institutionalized to the point that people basically agree or accept how the political machine is run, even if grudgingly.
        c. Is **legitimate** when regarded as valid or justified.
        d. Is institutionalized when the norms and statuses of social organizations govern its use.
    3. Three bases of authority according to Max Weber:
        a. **Traditional authority** is the norm in tribal and feudal societies, involves the inheritance of authority by rulers through family or clan ties. The right of a family or clan to monopolize leadership is deemed justified by religion.
        b. **Legal-rational authority** is typical of modern societies, and is derived from respect for law. Laws are generally believed to be rational. And if someone achieves office by following laws, their authority is respected.
        c. **Charismatic authority** is based on belief in the claims of extraordinary individuals to be inspired by God of some higher principle. Charismatic figures sometimes emerge during a **political revolution**, an attempt by many people to overthrow existing political institutions and establish new ones.
    4. Political sociology is concerned with institutions that *specialize* in the exercise of power and authority, which form the **state**, institutions that formulate and carry out a country's laws and public policies.
    5. **Civil society** is the private sphere of social life, where the state regulates citizens.

6. Types of states:
   a. **Authoritarian state** is characterized by sharp restrictions on citizen control.
   b. **Democracy** involves citizens exerting a relatively high degree of control over the state, partly by choosing representatives in regular, competitive elections.
7. Citizens control the state indirectly through several organizations in modern democracies.
   a. **Political parties** compete for control of government in regular elections. They give voice to policy alternatives and rally adult citizens to vote.
   b. **Lobbies** are formed by special interest groups to advise and influence politicians.
   c. The **mass media** help to keep the public informed about the quality of government by keeping a critical eye on the state.
   d. Public opinion refers to values and attitudes of the adult population as a whole, and is expressed in polls and letters to lawmakers.
   e. **Social movements** are collective attempts to change all or part of the political and social order.

II. THEORIES OF DEMOCRACY

   A. Pluralist Theory
      1. Pluralists believe:
         a. Politics operate democratically in the United States as a whole.
         b. America is a heterogeneous society with many competing interests and centers of power, none of which can consistently dominate.
         c. Politics involves negotiation and compromise between competing groups.
         d. Democracy is guaranteed.

   B. Elite Theory
      1. **Elite theorists** sharply disagreed with pluralists.
      2. C. Wright Mills is a chief elite theorist.
         a. **Elites** are small groups that occupy the command posts of America's most influential institutions, including the two or three biggest corporations, the executive branch of government, and the military.
         b. Elites make decisions that profoundly affect all members of society, yet without regard for elections or public opinion.

   C. A Critique of Pluralism
      1. In light of the well-established existence of wealth-based inequalities in political influence and participation, most political sociologists today question the pluralist perspective.
      2. Examples.
         a. "Citizen Participation Study" found that people with higher incomes are more politically active.
         b. Dan Clawson's research on PACs found a split between a unified business-Republican group and a labor-women-environmentalist-Democratic group.

   D. Power Resource Theory
      1. While elite theorists believe it makes little difference whether Republicans or Democrats are in power, and the victory of one party doesn't deserve much sociological attention, **power**

resource theory focuses on how *variations* in the distribution of power affect the fortunes of parties and policies.

2. American voters cluster in two policy groups.
    a. *Liberal* or left-wing voters promote extensive government involvement in the economy, a strong "social safety net" of health and welfare benefits to help less fortunate members of society, and equal rights for women, racial and sexual minorities.
    b. *Conservative,* or right-wing, voters favor a reduced role for government in the economy, a smaller welfare state, individual initiative in promoting economic growth, and traditional social and moral values.
3. There are different patterns of support for one party over another by social class, religious groups, races, and other groups.
4. Class and Other Political Cleavages
    a. In most Western societies, *class* support is a main factor, but varies by country. The strength of this class tendency depends on how socially organized or cohesive classes are.
    b. The main insight of power resource theory—*Organization* is a source of power. Change in the distribution of power between major classes partly accounts for the fortunes of different political parties and different law and policies.
    c. *Religion*, *race*, and *gender* are also important factors that distinguish parties.

E. State-Centered Theory
1. Theda Skocpol and other **state-centered theorists** show how the state itself can structure political life, regardless of how power is distributed.
2. Example—American voter registration law and nonvoting in the United States.
    a. The United States has a proportionately smaller pool of eligible voters than other democracies.
    b. Only in the United States do individual citizens have to take the initiative to register themselves in voter registration centers, however many Americans are unable or unwilling to register.
    c. The poor, less educated, and members of racial minority groups are less likely to vote.
    d. American voter registration law is a pathway to democracy for some, and a barrier for others.
3. Two reasons why the American political system is less responsive than other rich democracies to the needs of the disadvantaged.
    a. The working class is nonunionized and weak.
    b. The law requires citizen-initiated voter registration.
4. Summing Up
    a. Political sociology has made good progress since the 1950s.

III. Politics by Other Means

A. War
1. A **war** is a violent armed conflict between politically distinct groups who fight to protect or increase their control of territory.
    a. Humanity has spent much of its history preparing for, fighting, and recovering from war.

     b. Wars have become more destructive over time with "improvements" in the technology of human destruction. The 20th century represents 2.6% of the time since the beginning of recorded war history but accounts for roughly 3.3% of the world's war deaths, military and civilian.

  2. War is an expensive business, and the United States spends far more than any other country financing it.

     a. With 4.5% of the world's population, the United States accounts for about a third of total military expenditures in the world. The United States is by far the largest exporter of arms, accounting for nearly 60% of world arms exports. Nearly all the big arms importers are U.S. allies, such as our best customers Saudi Arabia and Taiwan.

  3. Wars may take place between countries (interstate wars) and within countries (civil or societal wars).

     a. A special type of interstate war is the colonial war, which involves a colony engaging in armed conflict with an imperial power to gain independence.

     b. Since the mid-1950s, most armed conflict in the world has been societal rather than interstate.

     c. Wars like the 2003 U.S.-Iraq war account for little of the total magnitude of armed conflict although loom large in the mass media. Wars like the ongoing conflict in the Democratic Republic of the Congo account for most of the total magnitude of armed conflict yet are rarely mentioned in the mass media.

  4. War risk varies from one country to the next, but what factors determine the risk of war on the territory of a given country?

     a. Type of government affects risk of war. Government types include democracy, autocracy, and "intermediate" forms. Intermediate-type countries are at highest risk of war, especially civil war, because these types of countries have neither "high legitimacy", as in democratic countries, nor "iron rule", as in autocratic countries.

     b. Level of prosperity affects risk of war. A country's gross domestic product per capita (GDPpc) indicates level of prosperity. Democracy is more common and autocracy is less common in prosperous countries.

B. Terrorism and Related Forms of Political Violence

  1. Why has societal war largely replaced interstate warfare since World War II. A historical perspective is useful.

  2. From the rise of the modern state in the 17th century until World War II, states increasingly monopolized the means of coercion in society. This had three important consequences.

     a. As various regional, ethnic, and religious groups came under the control of powerful central states, regional, ethnic, and religious wars declined and interstate warfare became the norm.

     b. Because states were powerful and monopolized the means of coercion, conflict became more deadly.

     c. Civilian life was pacified because the job of killing for political reasons was largely restricted to state-controlled armed forces.

  3. All this changed after World War II (1939-1945). Since then, there have been fewer interstate wars and more civil wars, guerrilla wars, massacres, terrorist attacks, and instances of

attempted ethnic cleansing and genocide perpetrated by militias, mercenaries, paramilitaries, suicide bombers, and the like. Large-scale violence has increasingly been visited on civilian rather than military populations.

4. This change in the form of collective action came about for three main reasons.
    a. Decolonization and separatist movements roughly doubled the number of independent states in the world, and many of these new states, especially in Africa and Asia, were too weak to control their territories effectively.
    b. Especially during the Cold War (1946-1991), the United States, the Soviet Union, Cuba, and China often subsidized and sent arms to domestic opponents of regimes that were aligned against them.
    c. The expansion of international trade contraband provided rebels with new means of support.

5. From this perspective, al Qaeda is a typical creature of contemporary warfare.
    a. Al Qaeda originated in Afghanistan, a weak and dependent state.
    b. The United States supported al Qaeda's founders militarily in their struggle against the Soviet occupation of Afghanistan in the 1980s.
    c. Al Qaeda organized international heroin, diamond, and money laundering operations.
    d. It established a network of operatives around the world.

6. International terrorists of the type the U.S. Department of State collects data on, typically demand autonomy or independence from some country, population, or region.
    a. For example, among al Qaeda's chief demands are Palestinian statehood and the end of U.S. support for the wealthy regimes in Saudi Arabia, Kuwait, and the Gulf States. Al Qaeda has turned to terror as a means of achieving these goals because other ways are largely closed off.
    b. The United States considers support for the oil-rich Arab countries to be of national interest. It has so far done little to further the cause of Palestinian statehood, although this may change with President Bush's Roadmap to Peace, which envisages Palestinian statehood by 2005.

7. Staunch opponents of American policy cannot engage in interstate warfare with the United States because they lack states of their own. Because the existing structure of world power closes off other possibilities for achieving political goals, terror emerges as a viable alternative for some desperate people.

IV. THE PROMISE AND HISTORY OF WORK

A. Three Revolutions
    1. The **economy** is the institution that organizes the production, distribution, and exchange of goods and services. Three sectors of the economy:
        a. *Primary* or "agricultural" sector, which includes farming, fishing, logging, and mining.
        b. *Secondary* or "manufacturing" sector, which turns raw materials into finished goods, and manufacturing takes place.
        c. *Tertiary* or "service" sector, where services are bought and sold.
    2. Each sector rose to dominance respectively within three revolutionary events—the agricultural revolution, the industrial revolution, and the revolution in services.

3. The Development of Agriculture
   a. With the invention of the plow, cultivation of land and **productivity** (the amount produced for every hour worked) increased.
4. The Development of Modern Industry
   a. Since the 15th century, international exploration, trade, and commerce stimulated the growth of **markets**, social relations that regulate the exchange of goods and services.
   b. About 225 years ago, the steam engine, railroads, and other technological innovations increased the ability of producers to supply markets, which marked the era of the Industrial Revolution that began in Western Europe and spread to other parts of Europe, North America, Russia, and Japan within a century.
5. The Development of the Service Sector
   a. By 1960, over half the labor force of the highly industrialized countries was providing services. Forty years later, the figure was nearly 75%.
   b. The computer is responsible for the rapid change in the composition of the labor force during the final decades of the 20th century.
6. These three revolutions increased the **division of labor**, or specialized work tasks, which consequently created new skills. Social relations among workers became more hierarchical.

V. "GOOD" VERSUS "BAD" JOBS

A. What can we say about the overall mix of jobs in the United States? Are there more good jobs than bad jobs? What does the future hold? Are good or bad jobs likely to become more plentiful? What are your job prospects?

B. The Deskilling Thesis
   1. Thirty years ago, Harry Braverman argued that because capitalists are eager to organize work to maximize profits, and break complex tasks into simple routines (replacing labor with machines and managerial control over workers), work tends to become **deskilled** overtime.
      a. In the early 1900s, Henry Ford introduced the assembly line.
      b. In the 1900s, Frederick W. Taylor developed the principles of **scientific management**, a system of improving productivity and efficiency by eliminating unnecessary actions.
   2. Criticisms of Braverman's deskilling thesis:
      a. Although his characterization of factory work was in some respects accurate, factory workers represent only a small proportion of the labor force.
      b. The manufacturing sector is declining, and the service sector is expanding, which accounts for three quarters of U.S. jobs today.
   3. In the 1980s and 1990s, some analysts feared that good jobs in manufacturing were being replaced by bad jobs in services.

C. A Critique of the Deskilling Thesis
   1. Braverman and Zuboff exaggerated the downward slide of the U.S. labor force because they underestimated the continuing importance of skilled labor in the economy. So rather than involving a downward shift in the entire labor force, a polarization between good jobs and bad jobs seems more accurate.

    a.   The top of the service sector is growing, the bottom is growing more rapidly, and the middle is growing more slowly.

D. Worker Resistance and Management Response

    1.   An additional criticism of Braverman's analysis is that he inaccurately portrays workers as passive victims of management control. Workers often resist the imposition of task specialization and mechanization by managers.

    2.   Worker resistance has often forced management to modify its organizational plans (i.e. Henry Ford). In the 1920s, some employers started to treat their employees more humanely in hopes of improving the work environment and make employees more loyal and productive.

    3.   Over the next 80 years, owners and managers in all rich industrialized countries realized they had to make concessions to labor, such as higher wages, more decision-making authority, promotion policies, job design, product innovation, and company investments.

    4.   The biggest concessions to labor were made in countries with the most powerful trade union movements such as Sweden. A large proportion of workers are members of unions (over 80% in Sweden).

    5.   In contrast, in the United States less than 14% of eligible workers are union members. In comparison to other rich industrialized countries, Americans work more hours per week, have fewer paid vacation days per year, and lag behind Western Europe and Japan in industry-level decision making among workers.

        a.   Job polarization is taking place. Work is found and experienced in different ways, in two labor markets. Social barriers make it difficult to move from one setting to another.

        b.   The labor market has been divided into two distinct parts:

            i.   The **primary labor market** is composed mainly of highly skilled or well-educated white males, employed in large corporations that enjoy high levels of capital investment. Employment is secure, earnings are high, and fringe benefits are generous.

           ii.   The **secondary labor market** contains a disproportionately large number of women and members of racial minorities, particularly African and Hispanic Americans. Employees tend to be unskilled and lack higher education. They work in small firms with low levels of capital investment. Employment is insecure, earnings are low, and fringe benefits are meager.

E. Barriers Between the Primary and Secondary Labor Markets

    1.   Three social barriers that make the primary labor market difficult to penetrate:

        a.   Often, there are few entry-level positions in the primary labor market.

        b.   A second barrier preventing people in the secondary labor market from penetrating the primary labor market is their lack of informal networks linking them to good job openings.

        c.   Finally, mobility out of the secondary labor market is difficult because workers usually lack the required training and certification for jobs in the primary labor market.

    2.   Men, non-Hispanic whites, and unionized workers tend to be concentrated in the primary labor market, while women, African and Hispanic Americans, and nonunion members tend to be concentrated in the secondary labor market.

VI. THE PROBLEM OF MARKETS

A. The secondary labor market is a relatively **free market**, which means that the supply of and demand for labor regulates wage levels and other benefits. The primary labor market is a more **regulated market**, whereby wage levels and other benefits are not just by supply and demand, but also by the power of workers and professionals, who exercise their influence to their advantage.

B. The freer the labor market, the higher the level of social inequality, which is why the secondary labor market cannot be entirely free.

   1. The federal government had to establish a legal minimum wage to prevent the price of unskilled labor from dropping below the point at which people are able to make a living.

C. Although the question of whether free or regulated markets are better lies at the center of economic and political debates, many economic sociologists find the question too abstract.

   1. The structure of markets varies widely across cultures and historical periods.

   2. The degree and type of regulation depend on how power, norms, and values are distributed among various social groups.

D. Capitalism, Communism, and Democratic Socialism

   1. Capitalism

      a. **Capitalism** is the world's dominant economic system today, and has two distinct features.

         i. *Private ownership of property.* Individuals and **corporations** (legal entities) own nearly all the means of producing goods and services, and are free to buy and sell. Corporate ownership has the advantages of lower tax rates, and liability in the event of consumer harm or bankruptcy.

         ii. *Competition is the pursuit of profit.* A purely capitalist economy is often called a *laissez-faire* system, whereby the government does not interfere with the operation of the economy.

      b. In reality, no economy is purely laissez-faire.

         i. The state had to intervene to create markets in the first place (European conquest and land acquisition from native peoples in what is now North America, to transform the land into a marketable commodity).

         ii. Today, governments must intervene in the economy to keep the market working effectively (economic infrastructure involving roads and ports, laws governing minimum wage, occupational health and safety, child labor, and industrial pollution).

         iii. Governments play an influential role in establishing and promoting many leading industries, especially those that require large outlays on research and development.

   2. Communism

      a. Like laissez-faire capitalism, **communism** is an ideal, and the term Karl Marx gave to the classless society that, according to him, is bound to develop out of capitalism. *Socialism* is the name Marx gave to the transitional phase between capitalism and communism.

      b. While no country is pure communist, about two dozen in Asia, South America, and Africa consider themselves socialist, including China, North Korea, Vietnam, and Cuba.

      c. As an ideal, communism is an economic system with two distinct features.

         i. *Public ownership of property.*

    ii. *Government planning.*

  d. In perhaps the most surprising and sudden change in modern history, the countries of Central and Eastern Europe (formerly single-party, socialist societies) namely the Soviet Union introduced capitalism and started holding multiparty elections in the late 1980s and 1990s. Factors for the collapse socialism in Central and Eastern Europe:

    i. The citizens of the region enjoyed few civil rights.

    ii. Their standard of living was only about half as high as that of people in the rich industrialized countries of the West.

    iii. Dissatisfaction was widespread and expressed in many ways including strikes and political demonstrations.

  e. In the 1990s, some Central and East European countries were more successful in introducing elements of capitalism and raising the standard of living. Example—the Czech Republic versus Russia.

    i. The most important factor for the different success rates lies in the way different countries introduced reforms.

    ii. The Czechs introduced private property and competition, while Russia introduced private property without competition.

    iii. Russia's level of socioeconomic inequality became among the highest in the world.

    iv. Russia is full of oligopolies, giant corporations that control a part of an economy, are few in number, compete against one another, and set prices at levels that are most profitable for them, which constrains innovation.

3. Democratic Socialism

  a. Several prosperous and highly industrialized countries are **democratic socialist societies**, including Sweden, Denmark, Norway, and to a lesser degree France and Germany.

  b. Such societies have two distinctive features:

    i. *Public ownership of certain basic industries.* These industries include telecommunications, electricity, railways, airlines, and steel. The level of public ownership is still not high. The great bulk of property is privately owned, and competition in pursuit of profit is the main motive of business.

    ii. *Government Intervention in the market.* These countries enjoy regular, free, multiparty elections, like the United States. Unlike the United States, political parties backed by a strong trade union movement have formed governments in democratic socialist countries for much of the post − World War II period. The governments that these unions back intervene strongly in the operation of markets for the benefit of ordinary workers. Taxes are considerably higher than in capitalist countries. Social services are much more generous. The gap between the rich and the poor is much narrower than in capitalist countries. On average, workers earn more, work fewer hours, and enjoy more paid vacation days.

  c. Since the 1980s, the democratic socialist countries have moved in a somewhat more capitalist direction, but still retain their distinctive approach to governments and markets, which is why democratic socialism is sometimes called a "Third Way" between capitalism and socialism.

E. The Corporation
   1. In the United States and other Western countries, "antitrust" laws limit the growth of oligopolies (i.e. 1890 Sherman Antitrust Act and the 1914 Clayton Act in the United States).
   2. The law has been only partly effective in stabilizing its growth, especially when the four largest corporations in an industry make up 4 out of every 10 dollars in sales—and when the top 500 corporations control over two thirds of business resources and profit.
   3. United States antitrust law encourages companies to diversify; that is, move into new industries. Big companies that operate in a number of industries simultaneously are referred to as **conglomerates**. Conglomerates are growing rapidly in the United States.
   4. **Interlocking directorates** is a way corporations may be linked, and are formed when an individual sits on the board of directors of two or more non-competing companies (1997 Board of Directors of IBM).
   5. Smaller businesses continue to exist, and are especially important in the service sector.
   6. Most of the United States labor force works in large corporations.

F. The Future of Work and the Economy
   1. In the future, it is likely that businesses will continue to introduce new technologies and organize the workplace in more efficient ways, to cut costs and maximize profits.
   2. It is less predictable how these practices will be implemented.
      a. Possibilities
         i. Complement the abilities of skilled workers.
         ii. Replacement of workers, deskilling of jobs, and employment of low-cost labor (mainly women and minority group members) on a large scale.
   3. Polarization of good jobs and bad jobs in the secondary sector is likely to continue—however, workplace struggles have a significant impact on how technologies are implemented and work is organized.

Study Activity: Applying the Sociological Compass

Interview a handful of family members, friends, and associates. Ask them to identify their political party preferences in general, and the reasons for their preferences. Make a list of responses by party preference and reasons. Analyze the list by applying power resource theory. In other words, explain your findings according to power resource theory.

Party Preferences and Reasons

Power Resource Theory

InfoTrac College Edition Online Exercises

For the following exercises, log on to the online library of InfoTrac College Edition at http://www.infotrac-college.com/. Make note that InfoTrac has implemented a new registration system that will allow easier access to InfoTrac through the use of a personalized username and password.

Once you've created your username and password you may proceed directly to the Log On page. To create an account, register your passcode packaged with your textbook, and create a username and password, by following the online prompt. After you are logged in, click on "Infotrac College Edition." You will arrive at a screen that enables you to search topics.

Keyword: **Voting**. Identify and read an article that discusses patterns of voting. Read the article. Are voting patterns discussed in the article consistent with what you learned in Chapter 13? Why or why not? Are there any implications for electronic democracy that you can draw from the article? If so, what are they?

Keyword: **Osama bin Laden**. Search for articles that discuss the political philosophy of bin Laden's involvement with politics. What key political ideas do they support and reject?

Keyword: **Political Action Committees (PACs)**. Political Action Committees work with special interest groups to support specific political ideas. Search for articles that discuss what type of political ideas PACs support. Make a list of the ideas.

Keyword: **National Rifle Association (NRA)**. The National Rifle Association has a lot of political influence. Search for articles that discuss how the NRA is involved with politics. Do you think that the NRA should be involved with politics? Write a short paper stating your opinion.

Keyword: **voter apathy**. Not very many eligible voters vote in American elections. Search for articles that discuss why people are indifferent about voting? What reasons are there for voter apathy?

Keyword: **Age discrimination**. Search for articles that deal with age discrimination in the labor force. How common is this problem. Is there any evidence that employers are willing to hire older persons?

Keyword: **sweatshops**. Look for articles dealing with the sweatshop industry. How widespread is the sweatshop industry?

Keyword: **absenteeism**. Search for articles that discuss the causes of absenteeism. How much of absenteeism can be explained by lack of day care or worker alienation?

Internet Exercises

Go to: http://www.theatlantic.com/issues/96jul/gender/gender.htm

for a discussion on the growing gap in politics in American society. There is a growing trend for women to move to the Democratic party and men to move to the Republican party. Read this short article. Make a list of the reasons why there appears to be this gender polarization in politics. Do you agree or disagree with this phenomenon?

A good site for research about politics can be found at The Center for Responsible Politics homepage http://www.opensecrets.org/

You can access political profiles, political participation, voter perceptions and subjects along these lines.

With the 2000 presidential election so close in history, students may want to look at The Federal Election Commission website at http://www.fec.gov/ and look over the process of voting and the elections in general.

Compare and contrast one major issue of concern (for example, tax reform) on all of the following four political party websites.

http://www.democrats.org/index.html

http://www.greenparty.org/

http://rnc.org/

http://www.reformparty.org/

Go to http://www.panix.com/~dhenwood/Work.html and read about work in the future. Write a short about your feelings concerning this provocative analysis of the future of work. Compare this analysis of future work with some key concepts in Chapter 13.

For information about the stock market, go to http://library.thinkquest.org/3088/

Research stocks and learn about stocks. Complete the online tutorial. Write a short paper discussing your experience.

The United for a Fair Economy website deals with different aspects of our economy. Visit the site at: http://www.ufenet.org/

Write a short comparison paper comparing what was presented in class lecture with the information found at this Website.

Practice Tests

Fill-In-The-Blank

Fill in the blank with the appropriate term from the above list of "key terms."

1. A(An) _____ is the overthrow of political institutions by an opposition movement and replacement by new institutions.

2. _____ is composed of the values and attitudes of the adult population as a whole.

3. In a(an) _____ , citizens exercise high degree of control over the state, mainly by choosing representatives in regular, competitive elections.

4. _____ is the private sphere of social life.

5. _____ are organizations formed by special interest groups to advise and influence politicians.

6. _____ is defined by American law as premeditated, politically motivated violence against noncombatant targets including unarmed or off-duty military personnel by subnational groups.

7. The _____ is the institution that organizes the production, distribution, and exchange of goods and services.

8. The _____ refers to specialization of works tasks.

9. _____ is a system of improving productivity developed in the 1910s by Frederick W. Taylor.

10. The _____ contains a disproportionately large number of women and members of racial minorities, who tend to be unskilled and lack higher education.

11. In a(an) _____ , prices are only by supply and demand.

12. _____ are legal entities that can enter into contracts and own property.

13. In _____ countries, democratically elected governments own certain basic industries entirely or in part and intervene vigorously in the market to redistribute income.

14. _____ are large corporations that operate in several industries at the same time.

Multiple-Choice Questions

Select the response that best answers the question or completes the statement:

1. Which is a question of political sociology?
   a. What accounts for the degree to which a political system responds to the demands of all its citizens?
   b. What are the effects of social structures, especially class structures, on politics?
   c. How do state institutions and laws affect political processes?
   d. All of the above.
   e. None of the above.

2. According to Max Weber, which type of authority is derived from respect for law, and is typical of modern societies?
   a. traditional authority
   b. legal-rational authority
   c. charismatic authority
   d. totalitarian authority
   e. formal democracy

3. In _____ states, citizen control is sharply restricted.
   a. authoritarian
   b. totalitarian
   c. democratic
   d. egalitarian
   e. traditional

4. Political organizations are utilized by citizens to control the state in modern democracies. Which organization is formed by special interest groups to advise and influence politicians?
   a. political parties
   b. lobbies
   c. mass media
   d. All of the above.
   e. None of the above.

5. Sometimes _____ leaders emerge when the historical conditions are ripe for extraordinary leadership such as a political revolution.
   a. traditional
   b. totalitarian
   c. charismatic
   d. All of the above.
   e. None of the above.

6. Which policy group tends to support a smaller welfare state?
   a. liberals
   b. radicals
   c. conservatives
   d. revolutionaries
   e. None of the above.

7. Staunch opponents of American policy who engage in terrorism:
   a. can engage in interstate warfare with the United States.
   b. use terror because the existing structure of world power closes off other possibilities for achieving political goals.
   c. have states of their own, but suffer from insufficient infrastructure.
   d. All of the above.
   e. None of the above.

8. With 4.5% of the world's population, the United States accounts for about how much total military expenditures in the world?
   a. one-eighth
   b. one-fourth
   c. one-third
   d. three-fourths
   e. nearly all of military expenditures in the world.

9. Vladmir Lenin, the Bolshevik leader of the Russian Revolution of 1917, represents an example of which type of authority according to Max Weber?
   a. traditional authority
   b. charismatic authority
   c. legal-rational authority
   d. All of the above.
   e. None of the above.

10. In a nationally televised address on January 17, 1961, President Eisenhower sounded much like _____ when he warned of the "undue influence" of the military-industrial complex" in American society.
   a. Theda Skocpol
   b. Richard Lee
   c. Max Weber
   d. Emile Durkheim
   e. C. Wright Mills

11. In the 2000, presidential election, which social group tended to support George W. Bush?
    a. low-income earners
    b. African Americans
    c. Hispanic Americans
    d. male voters
    e. supporters of reproductive choice

12. Which sociological theory of democracy views power as being dispersed as opposed to concentrated?
    a. pluralist theory
    b. elitist theory
    c. power resource theory
    d. state-centered theory
    e. All of the above.

13. In which sector of the economy are services bought and sold?
    a. primary sector
    b. secondary sector
    c. tertiary sector
    d. manufacturing sector
    e. None of the above.

14. With the development of the three sectors of the economy, and as social relations among workers became more hierarchical, specialized work tasks increased and became more complex. The increase in specialized work tasks and its complexity is referred to as:
    a. the division of labor
    b. labor market segmentation
    c. internal labor markets
    d. the deskilling of the workforce
    e. scientific management

15. Which is NOT a criticism of the deskilling thesis?
    a. It is too narrowly focused on jobs toward the top of the occupational hierarchy.
    b. Lacks explanation of the processes of the occupational structure as a whole.
    c. Exaggerates the downward slide of the U.S. labor force.
    d. It overlooks the polarization between "good" and "bad" jobs.
    e. All of the above are critiques.

16. Which part of the labor market contains disproportionately large numbers of women and members of racial minorities?
    a. the primary labor market
    b. the secondary labor market
    c. the tertiary labor market
    d. All of the above.
    e. None of the above.

17. Which is a decision-making innovation that has improved communication between workers and managers, and the quality of goods?
    a. The emergence of interlocking directorates.
    b. The growth of socialist revolutions.
    c. Reforms that give workers more authority on the shop floor.
    d. All of the above.
    e. None of the above.

18. Which economic system is dominant in the world?
    a. communism
    b. socialism
    c. communalism
    d. oligopolies
    e. capitalism

19. Marx gave the name _____ to the transitional phase between capitalism and communism.
    a. communalism
    b. socialism
    c. bourgeoisie
    d. proletariat
    e. petite bourgeoisie

20. Which is a characteristic of communism in its ideal form?
    a. private ownership of property
    b. public ownership of property
    c. laissez-faire
    d. competition in the pursuit of profit
    e. free market

21. Which is NOT a negative consequence of multinationals to less developed countries?
    a. Fewer jobs are available than the number of workers.
    b. Governments in developing countries lack pollution controls.
    c. Branch plants create few jobs involving design and technical expertise.
    d. Exploitation of children and women.
    e. Workers of multinationals rarely resist exploitation.

22. Although the future of work and the economy is difficult to predict, which is a likely pattern in the future?
    a. Polarization of good jobs and bad jobs in the secondary sector is likely to continue.
    b. Businesses will likely continue to introduce new technologies.
    c. Businesses will likely continue to attempt to cut costs and maximize profits.
    d. Businesses will likely attempt to organize the workplace in more efficient ways.
    e. All of the above.

23. Interlocking directorates is a way _____ may be linked.
    a. workers
    b. workers and managers
    c. unions and workers
    d. corporations
    e. multinationals and workers in developing countries

24. What is the occupation with the second highest estimated number of new jobs, from 1998-2008, according to table 13.3 on p. 376?
    a. computer engineer
    b. teachers, secondary schools
    c. retail salespersons
    d. truck drivers
    e. sociologists

True False

1. Civil society is the private sphere of social life, where the state regulates citizens.

   TRUE or FALSE

2. The mass media help to keep the public informed by keeping a critical eye on the state.

   TRUE or FALSE

3. The strength of social classes to influence political processes depends on how socially organized and cohesive they are.

   TRUE or FALSE

4. Humanity has spent much of its history preparing for, fighting, and recovering from war.

   TRUE or FALSE

5. Wars have become less destructive with the improvements in the technology to aid humanity.

   TRUE or FALSE

6. Pluralist theory portrays politics as a neatly ordered game of negotiation and compromise in which all players are equal.

   TRUE or FALSE

7. New opportunities make it relatively easy to move from the secondary labor market to the primary labor market.

   TRUE or FALSE

8. The freer the labor market, the higher the level of social inequality.

   TRUE or FALSE

9. The structure of markets varies widely across cultures and historical periods.

   TRUE or FALSE

10. The central assumption of most economic sociologists is that free markets maximize economic growth, which is beneficial to society at large.

    TRUE or FALSE

11. The number of conglomerates is declining in the United States.

    TRUE or FALSE

12. The primary labor market is more regulated than the secondary labor market.

    TRUE or FALSE

Short Answer

1. Define and describe the types of political systems. (p. 356)

2. Briefly describe the differences between elite theory and power-resource theory. (p. 361-363)

3. List and define three bases of authority according to Max Weber. (p. 356)

4. List and define the three sectors of the economy. (p. 372)

5. Define the term "laissez-faire." Are there any purely laissez-faire economies? Why or why not? (p. 380)

6. Identify the three stages of labor market development in the United States. (p. 377)

7. What are the two distinct features of capitalism? (p. 380?)

_____

_____

8. What are the two distinct features of communism? (p. 380?)

_____

_____

Essay Questions

1. Compare and contrast pluralist theory and elite theory. (p. 360-363)

2. Consider the 2000 presidential election to compare and contrast power resource theory and state-centered theory. (p. 363-366)

3. Explain the necessary conditions for a country to become fully democratic based on what you learned in Chapter 13. (p. 363–368)

4. Describe and explain the historical development of the agricultural, manufacturing and service sectors. (p. 372-373)

5. Contrast the deskilling thesis and the labor segmentation perspective. (p. 374-380)

6. Define the terms capitalism, communism, and democratic socialism. Explain the differences between the three economic systems in their ideal and real forms. (p. 380-382)

7. Discuss the positive and negative consequences of having governments constrained by large corporations. In what respects is this relationship symbiotic or parasitic, and how are checks on relative powers maintained or created, and are they effective? How do you see this relationship changing over the next 25 years? 50 years? (p. 382-384)

Solutions

Practice Tests

Fill-In-The-Blank

1. political revolution
2. Public opinion
3. democracy
4. Civil society
5. Lobbies

6. Terrorism
7. economy
8. division of labor
9. Scientific management
10. secondary labor market

11. free market
12. Corporations
13. democratic socialist
14. Conglomerates

Multiple-Choice Questions

1. D, (p. 355)
2. B, (p. 356)
3. A, (p. 356)
4. B, (359)
5. C, (p. 356)
6. C, (p.363)
7. B, (p. 368-372)
8. C, (p. 369)

9. B, (p. 356)
10. E, (p. 361)
11. D, (p. 364)
12. A, (p. 360)
13. C, (p. 372
14. A, (p. 373)
15. A, (p. 375)
16. B, (p. 377)

17. C, (p. 376-377)
18. E, (p. 380)
19. B, (p. 380)
20. B, (p. 380)
21. E, (p. 382-384)
22. E, (p. 382-384)
23. D, (p. 382)
24. C, (p. 376)

True False

1. T, (p. 356)
2. T, (p. 360)
3. T, (p. 363)
4. T, (p. 368)

5. F, (p. 368-372)
6. T, (p. 360)
7. F, (p. 377)
8. T, (p. 378)

9. T, (p. 377)
10. F, (p. 378)
11. F, (p. 382)
12. T, (p. 377)

HEALTH, MEDICINE, DISABILITY, AND AGING

Student Learning Objectives

After reading Chapter 14, you should be able to:

1. Describe how and explain why health problems change over time.

2. Explain the contradiction of medical advances and new problems.

3. Describe how health is measured.

4. Discuss the social causes of illness and health in terms of public health and health care systems.

5. Describe variations in health risk, public health, and health care systems in the context of global inequality.

6. Identify indicators of health care inequality.

7. Explain the American anomaly of health in terms of social class, race, and gender.

8. Explain the connections among health, politics, inequality, and privatization from a conflict perspective.

9. Describe the emergent dominance of scientific medicine and professionalization.

10. Discuss patient activism, alternative medicine, and holistic medicine as challenges to traditional scientific medicine within the larger social, political, and cultural contexts.

11. Explain the social construction of disability across different times and places, and the normality of disability.

12. Discuss ablism in terms of active prejudice, discrimination, and unintended neglect, which results in the social disadvantage of disabled people.

13. Explain age as yet another dimension of social stratification and inequality, and specific social problems of the elderly.

14. Discuss the increased power and wealth of the elderly in recent decades.

15. Discuss attitudes toward death and dying, as a reflection of the nature of society and culture.

Key Terms

(defined on the indicated pages of the textbook, and in glossary)

life expectancy (394)   impaired (408)

maximum human life span (394)   disabled (393)

maximum average human life span (394)   rehabilitation (408)

public health system (395)   ablism (409)

health-care system (395)   age cohort (412)

infant mortality (396)   age stratification (412)

sick role (405)   gerontocracy (412)

placebo effect (406)   ageism (417)

holistic medicine (407)   euthanasia (419)

Detailed Chapter Outline

I. THE BLACK DEATH

    A. In the 1300s, the Black Death killed a third of Europe's population, and ranks as the most devastating catastrophe in human history. Today we know the cause was a bacillus that spread from lice to rats to people, that spread so efficiently because people lived close together in unsanitary conditions.

    B. The only people who had luck avoiding the plague were the well to do, who could afford to flee densely populated cities for the countryside, and the Jews, whose religion required that they wash their hands before meals, bathe once a week, and conduct burials soon after death.

    C. The sociology of health, aging, and medicine are embedded or implied in the story of the Black Death.

        1. Health risks are unevenly distributed across gender, social class, race, and ethnicity.

        2. Health problems change over time.

            a. Today we know that sanitation and hygiene prevent the spread of disease.

            b. We are able to treat many infectious diseases.

            c. People live longer; that is, there is greater **life expectancy** (the average age of death of the members of a population).

        3. In contrast, we cannot help but to be struck by the superstition and ignorance surrounding the treatment of the ill in medieval times.

        4. However, medieval doctors stressed the importance of prevention, exercise, a balanced diet, and a congenial environment in maintaining good health. One of the great shortcomings of modern medicine is its emphasis on high-tech cures rather than preventive and environmental measures.

II. HEALTH AND INEQUALITY

    A. Defining and Measuring Health

1. Sociologists typically examine negative aspects such as rates of illness and death, when *measuring* the health of the population.
2. The **maximum human life span** is the longest an individual can live under current conditions (currently about 122 years), which may well increase in the 21st century.
3. The **maximum average human life span**, the average age of death for a population under *ideal* conditions (currently at about 85 years), is also likely to increase in the 21st century.
4. Conditions are nowhere ideal, and vary across countries. Life expectancy tends to be lower in poor countries.
5. Sociologists of health account for the difference between the maximum average human life span and life expectancy, and the impact of social causes on illness and death.

B. The Social Causes of Illness and Death
   1. Three types of social causes of illness and death
      a. Human-environmental factors.
      b. Lifestyle factors.
      c. Factors related to the public health and health care systems.
         i. The **public health system** is composed of government-run programs that ensure access to clean drinking water, basic sewage and sanitation services, and inoculation against infectious diseases.
         ii. The **health care system** is composed of a nation's clinics, hospitals, and other facilities for ensuring health and treating illness. The absence of a public health system and minimum standard health care is associated with high rates of disease and low life expectancy.
   2. Country of Residence
      a. AIDS is the leading cause of death in urban Haiti and in the poverty-stricken part of Africa south of the Sahara desert. The absence of adequate health care and medical facilities makes the epidemic's impact more devastating.
      b. AIDS/HIV is nearly 15 times more common in sub-Saharan Africa than in North America and 40 times more common than in Western Europe. However, spending on research and treatment is concentrated in the rich countries of North America and Western Europe.
      c. Global inequality influences the exposure of people to different health risks.
      d. Biomedical advances that increase with prosperity partly increases life expectancy.
      e. A sound public health system is more important.
      f. While industrialized countries were able to develop their public health systems to help create a healthier labor force and citizenry in the 19th century, it is not possible for many developing countries to do so today.
      g. Indicators of health inequality.
         i. Access to sanitary water supply
         ii. **Infant mortality** (the annual number of deaths before the age of one for every 1,000 live births)
         iii. Health expenditures
         iv. Malnutrition
         v. Number of Physicians

vi. Number of nurses and midwives

vii. Immunization of children against measles

3. Class, Race, and Gender

a. An "American anomaly." Why does the United States spend far more health care than any other country in the world yet on average, is less healthy than the population of other rich countries, such as Japan, Sweden, Canada, and France?

b. The higher the level of inequality in a country, the more unhealthy its population tends to be.

i. The gap between the rich and the poor is greater in the United States.

ii. The United States contains a higher percentage of poor people than other countries contain.

c. Manifestations of health inequality.

i. Infant mortality rates.

ii. Life expectancy.

d. Reasons for disparities in health inequality.

i. The poor are more likely to be exposed to violence, high-risk behavior, and environmental hazards.

ii. Because poverty is more common among African Americans, they have higher mortality rates than whites.

iii. The poor cannot afford adequate, and in some cases even minimal, health care, and often live in areas where medical treatment facilities are inadequate.

iv. The poor tend to have less knowledge about healthy lifestyles as a result of less access to doctors and hospitals.

v. *Racism.* The health status of African Americans is somewhat lower than the health status of European Americans even within the same income group. Three ways racism affects health: Income and other rewards do not have the same value across racial groups. For instance, due to discrimination, each year of education completed by African Americans results in smaller income gains than for white Americans, which consequently affects health. Also, racism affects access to health services, because African Americans at all income levels tend to live in racially segregated neighborhoods with fewer health-related facilities. Finally, the experience of racism induces psychological distress that negatively affects health.

e. Health inequalities based on gender.

i. Gender bias exists in medical research.

ii. Gender bias exists in medical treatment (i.e. fewer kidney transplants and various cardiac procedures).

iii. Although women experience greater lifetime risk of functional disability and chronic illness, and greater need for long-term care because they live longer, more is spent on men's health care in the United States.

iv. There are 40% more poor women than poor men in the United States.

C. Health and Politics: The United States in Comparative Perspectives

1. Another reason for the American anomaly lies in the nature of the American health care system.

2. From a conflict perspective, the United States health care system is seen as a system of privilege for some and disadvantage for others.
    a. About 80% of medical costs are paid by governments or taxes in other rich postindustrial countries, while about 44 million Americans have no health insurance, and another 40 million are inadequately covered. Only the elderly, the poor, and veterans receive Medicaid and Medicare.
3. Private insurance programs run by employers and unions cover the vast majority of Americans.
    a. About 85% of employees buy their health coverage from HMO's.
    b. HMOs are private organizations that collect regular payments from employers and employees, and administer medical treatment.
    c. HMOs are corporations that pursue profit.
4. Four main strategies employed by HMOs to keep shareholders happy.
    a. Some HMOs avoid covering sick people and people who are likely to get sick. An HMO can show you had a preexisting medical condition.
    b. HMOs try to minimize the cost of treating sick people they can't avoid covering. Doctor-compensation formulas for withholding unprofitable treatments exist.
    c. Allegations that HMOs routinely inflate diagnoses to maximize reimbursements.
    d. HMOs keep overhead charges high.
5. From a functionalist point of view, one big advantage of running for-profit organizations is that they can invest enormous sums in research, development, latest diagnostic equipment, and high salaries to attract the best medical researchers and practitioners. Thus the United States has the best health-care system in the world for those who can afford it.
6. Although HMOs and the American Medical Association attempt to convince Americans that the private-system serves the public better than a state-run system, they have been only partly successful.
    a. Based on GSS data, 41% of Americans disagree or strongly disagree that HMOs improve the quality of medical care.
7. Attempts to create a national system of health care in which everyone is covered have failed. Congress rejected President Clinton's 1993–94 Health Security proposal, because media campaigns were largely funded by health insurance companies.

D. The Professionalization of Medicine
1. In 1850, the practice of medicine was chaotic, which involved competition among herbalists, faith healers, midwives, druggists, and medical doctors. A century later, medical science was victorious following its first series of breakthroughs involving the identification of bacteria and viruses, and effective procedures and vaccines to combat them.
2. Sociologically, scientific medicine also became dominant because doctors were able to professionalize—that is, the process by which people gain control and authority over their occupation and their clients.
3. The American Medical Association (AMA)
    a. Founded in 1847, the AMA quickly broadcasted the successes of medical science, and criticized alternative approaches to health.

      b. By the early years of the 20th century, the AMA convinced state licensing boards to certify only doctors who had been trained in programs recognized by the AMA.

      c. Historically, doctors did not earn much until it was possible to lay virtually exclusive claim to health.

  4. The modern hospital is the institutional manifestation of the medical doctor's professional dominance.

E. Recent Challenges to Traditional Medical Science

  1. Patient Activism

      a. According to Talcott Parsons, playing the **sick role** involves the nondeliberate suspension of routine responsibilities, wanting to be well, seeking competent help, and cooperating with health care practitioners at all times. By definition, a patient cannot reasonably question doctor's orders, no matter how well educated the patient and how debatable the effect of the prescribed treatment.

      b. The sick role probably sounds authoritarian and foreign to most young people because things have changed. Patients want to play a more active role in their own care.

          i.   The American public is more highly educated.

          ii. Patients are taught to perform simple, routine medical procedures themselves.

          iii. People now seek the Internet for medical advice.

          iv. Patients are increasingly uncomfortable with doctors that act like patriarchal fathers.

          v.   Doctors seek patient's informed consent.

          vi. Most hospitals have established ethics committees.

      c. Organized and political challenges to the authority of medical science.

          i.   The challenge of AIDS as a "gay disease" by AIDS activists.

          ii. Feminist support of reintroducing midwifery, and raised attention to women's bodies and diseases.

          iii. Movements that empower people with disabilities, who have been traditionally treated like incompetent children.

  2. Alternative Medicine

      a. Alternative medicine is a less organized and less political challenge to the authority of medical science.

      b. The most frequent types of alternative medicine include chiropractic, acupuncture, massage therapy, and various relaxation techniques.

      c. Alternative medicine is most frequently use by highly educated, upper-income white Americans in the 25- to 49-year age group, and has grown in popularity.

      d. Many medical doctors were hostile to alternative medicine, and dismissed them as unscientific, until recently.

      e. By the 1990s, a more tolerant attitude was evident.

          i.   For instance, a 1998 editorial in *New England Journal of Medicine* admitted that beneficial effect of chiropractic on low back pain is "no longer in dispute." This was due in part to new scientific evidence.

      f. The uneasy relationship between scientific and alternative medicine is likely to continue in the coming decades.

3. Holistic Medicine
   a. Research shows that strong belief in the effectiveness of a cure can by itself improve the condition of about a third of people suffering from chronic pain or fatigue, which is known as the **placebo effect**.
   b. Traditional scientific medicine often responds to illness by treating disease symptoms as physical and individual problems, with drugs and high-tech machinery.
   c. In contrast, traditional Indian medicine sees individuals in terms of the flow of vital fluids or "humors" and their health in the context of their environment. Traditional Chinese medicine seeks to restore individuals' internal balance, as well as their relationship to the outside world.
   d. The third challenge to traditional scientific medicine is contemporary **holistic medicine**, which is like these "ethnomedical" traditions, and argues that good health requires maintaining a balance between mind and body, and between individual and the environment.
   e. Most holistic practitioners:
      i. Do not reject scientific medicine, but emphasize disease prevention;
      ii. Seek to establish close ties with their patients and treat them in their homes or other relaxed settings;
      iii. Expect patients to take an active role in maintaining their good health; and
      iv. Recognize that industrial pollution, poverty, racial and gender inequality, and other social factors contribute heavily to disease.

III. DISABILITY

A. The Social Construction of Disability
   1. Historical cases of the treatment of left-handed people. Almost universally, people have considered left-handedness a handicap.
   2. We don't think of left-handed people, who make up roughly 10% of the population, as **impaired** or deficient in physical or mental capacity. Nor do we think of them as **disabled** or incapable of performing with a range of "normal" human activity. The fact that so many people once thought otherwise suggests that definitions of disability vary socially, historically, and even in any one time and place when people disagree.

B. Rehabilitation and Elimination
   1. Modern Western approaches to disability emerged in the 19th century. All scientists and reformers of the time viewed disability as a biological reality, and some sought **rehabilitation**.
   2. Other scientists and reformers sought to eliminate disability altogether by killing the disabled or sterilizing them.
   3. One of the ugliest chapters in American history involves the federally funded, forced sterilization of native North American women from the 1920s to the 1970s, in which the "disability" of these women was being native North Americans.

C. Ablism
   1. Because society is structured around norms of the able-bodied, disabled people are disadvantaged, especially if they are elderly, women, lower class, or racial or ethnic minorities.

2. People routinely stigmatize and stereotype the disabled. The resulting prejudice and discrimination against the disabled is called **ablism**.
3. In addition to active prejudice and discrimination, ablism also involves unintended *neglect* of the conditions of disabled people.

D. Challenging Ablism: The Normality of Disability
1. H.G. Wells' 1927 short story, "The Country of the Blind."
2. Wells' tale makes blindness seem normal, which comes close to the way disabled people today think of their disabilities – not as a form of deviance but as a different form of normality.
3. The idea of normality of disability partly supplanted the rehabilitation ideal that originated in the 19ᵗʰ century. Disabled people participated little in efforts to improve the conditions of their existence, which began to change when they organized in the 1960s. Since the 1980s, disabled people have begun to assert their autonomy and the "dignity of difference." Rather than see disability as a personal tragedy, they see is as a social problem, and rather than see themselves as deviant, they think of themselves as inhabiting a different but normal world.
4. The deaf community typifies the new challenge to ablism.

IV. AGING

A. Sociology of Aging
1. Sociologists see aging in a complex light. Aging is a process of socialization, and its significance varies from one society to the next.
2. Age Cohort
   a. An **age cohort** is a category of people born in the same range of years, and have learned common patterns of behavior.

B. Aging and Inequality
1. Age Stratification
   a. **Age stratification** refers to social inequality between age cohorts, which exists in all societies but varies across social contexts.
   b. The very young are often at the bottom of the stratification system.
   c. Even in rich countries, poverty is more widespread among children than adults. Childhood poverty exceeds poverty among adults by 71%. The United States has the highest child poverty rate among the world's two- dozen richest countries.
2. Gerontocracy
   a. **Gerontocracies** are societies in which elderly men ruled, earned the highest incomes, and enjoyed the most prestige, such as ancient China. People in some industrialized countries pay more attention to age than Americans do.
   b. Powerful, wealthy, and prestigious leaders are often mature, but not the oldest people in society. The United States, past and present, is typical in this regard.
   c. True gerontocracy in generally rare.
   d. The rule by youth is also uncommon.
3. Theories of Age Stratification
   a. *Functionalists* suggest that it came about when age cohorts were differentiated in the course of industrialization, and the cohort of retired elderly people grew.

      i.   Age stratification grew and developed because different age cohorts performed functions of differing value to society. In preindustrial societies, the elderly were important as a storehouse of knowledge and wisdom. With industrialization, their function became less important and their status declined.

      ii.   Systems of age stratification "converge" under the force of industrialization.

   b. *Conflict theorists* agree with functionalists regarding the needs of industrialization generating age categories. However, they disagree on two points:

      i.   They dispute that age stratification reflects the functional importance of different age cohorts. Instead, age stratification stems from competition and conflict. Power and wealth do not necessarily correlate with functional roles; competition and conflict may redistribute power and wealth between age cohorts.

      ii.   Regarding convergence, conflict theorists suggest that political struggle can make a big difference in how much age stratification exists in a society.

   c. *Symbolic interactionists* focus on the meanings people attach to age-based groups and age stratification. They stress the way people understand aging as a matter of interpretation. They have helped us understand the degree and nature of prejudice and discrimination against the elderly.

C. Social Problems and the Elderly

   1. The growth of the elderly population.

     a. In 1900, 4% of the U.S. population was 65 and over.

     b. Today, the figure is around 13%.

     c. By 2040, nearly 21% will be elderly.

     d. After 2040, the proportion of Americans 65 years and over will start to decline.

   2. Many sociologists of aging categorize elderly people as those who enjoy relatively good health, usually between 65 and 74 years, as the "young old"; 85 and older as the "old old."

   3. The reasons for the rising proportion of elderly people are clear. On the one hand, fertility rates have been declining in virtually all industrial societies. On the other hand, life expectancy has been increasing because of medical advances, better welfare provisions, and other factors.

   4. Aging and Poverty

     a. The proportion of "young old" is expected to decline, and the "old old" are expected to continue increasing, which raises many health concerns such as physiological decline, life-threatening diseases, social isolation, and poverty.

     b. Because the sex ratio imbalance (greater number of women than men) is most marked in the oldest age cohorts, poverty and related problems among the elderly is a gender issue.

     c. Economic inequality between elderly women and men is largely the result of women's lower earning power when they are younger. Women's employer pensions tend to be inferior to men's.

     d. In addition to the "old old" and women, the categories of elderly people most likely to be poor include African Americans, people living alone, and in rural areas. The elderly are sometimes socially segregated.

     e. Another problem is the shortage of caregivers.

  f. Among rich countries, the United States is a relatively young society. The proportion of the old to the total population is comparatively low.

 5. Ageism

  a. Especially in a society like the United States that highly values vitality and youth, being elderly is a *social stigma*. **Ageism** is prejudice about, and discrimination against, people based on their age.

  b. Elderly people often do not conform to the negative stereotypes. Retirees are seldom a tangle of health problems and a burden on society.

  c. Their housing arrangements are not usually desolate and depressing.

 6. The Power and Wealth of the Elderly

  a. Many elderly people own assets.

  b. The elderly are well organized politically, which partly accounts for their relative economic security.

D. Death and Dying

 1. The ultimate social problem the elderly face is their own demise. Why are death and dying *social* problems, rather than just religious, philosophical, and medical issues?

 2. Attitude toward death and dying vary widely across time and place. In most traditional societies, most people accepted death, partly because dying was not isolated from other people, and was emotionally supported.

 3. In contrast, in the United States today, dying and death are separated from everyday life. Our culture celebrates youth and denies death, which makes us less prepared for death than our ancestors were.

 4. Our reluctance to accept death is evident in our many euphemisms.

 5. Psychiatrist Elisabeth Kubler-Ross's analysis of the stages of dying suggests how reluctant we are to accept death.

  a. *Denial*

  b. *Anger*

  c. *Negotiation*

  d. *Acceptance*

 6. Euthanasia

  a. The debate of euthanasia reveals the reluctance of many Americans to accept death.

  b. **Euthanasia**, also known as mercy killing or assisted suicide, involves a doctor prescribing or administering medication or treatment that is intended to end a terminally ill patient's life.

  c. The American Medical Association's Council on Ethical and Judicial Affairs (AMA-CEJA) says it is the duty of doctors to withhold life-sustaining treatment if that is the wish of a mentally competent patient.

  d. Public opinion polls show that about two thirds of Americans favor physician-assisted suicide euthanasia, and between 33% and 60% of American doctors say they would be willing to perform euthanasia if it were legal.

  e. The AMA-CEJA, the Catholic Church, some disabled people, and other groups oppose euthanasia.

     f.   Euthanasia is legal in the Netherlands, is likely to become legal in some other countries in the next few years, and in Oregon, a physician-assisted suicide law took effect in October 1997. However, in a June 1997 ruling, the United States Supreme Court upheld constitutional state laws that bar assisted suicide.

     g.   What is clear is that, "throughout the nation, Americans are engaged in an earnest and profound debate about the morality, legality and practicality of physician assisted suicide."

7.   The Business of Dying

     a.   The way we die reflects the nature of our society and culture. In the United States, a capitalist, business-oriented society, funerals are big business – a $20 billion a year industry in 1999. The average undertaker's bill in the late 1990s was $4700, and adding other expenses the bill grew to $7800.

     b.   Two main reasons why funerals are so expensive:

         i.   Big corporations and supplanting small family operations in the funeral industry, in which the undisputed giant is Services Corp. International (SCI).

         ii.   The funeral industry takes full advantage of the vulnerability of people who lost their loved ones.

Study Activity: Applying the Sociological Compass

After reading Chapter 14, re-read Box 14.1 "Social Policy: What Do You Think? The High Cost of Prescription Drugs," which describes the issue, possible policy solutions, and arguments on each side of the issue. Make a list of explanations on each side of the issue from functionalist and conflict perspectives. Which perspective and corresponding positions seems most supported by what you learned in Chapter 14?

Key Arguments:

1.

2.

3.

4.

Functionalist Explanations:

1.

2.

3.

4.

Conflict Explanations:

1.

2.

3.

4.

InfoTrac College Edition Online Exercises

For the following exercises, log on to the online library of InfoTrac College Edition at http://www.infotrac-college.com/. Make note that InfoTrac has implemented a new registration system that will allow easier access to InfoTrac through the use of a personalized username and password.

Once you've created your username and password you may proceed directly to the Log On page. To create an account, register your passcode packaged with your textbook, and create a username and password,

ef
Chapter 14
edd

Chapter 14

268

by following the online prompt. After you are logged in, click on "Infotrac College Edition." You will arrive at a screen that enables you to search topics.

Keyword: **alternative medicine**. Pick two articles of interest that discuss the problems of alternative medicine. What are the main problems that are discussed? How do these concerns compare to the criticisms of alternative medicine discussed in Chapter 14?

Keyword: **malpractice insurance**. Find three articles that discuss the malpractice insurance crisis. What are the reasons behind the increase in malpractice insurance? What solutions do they proposed to end this crisis? Do you believe that the tremendous hike in malpractice insurance is justified? Why or why not? Write a short opinion paper on the subject.

Keyword: **age appreciation**. Often the negative aspects of aging are stressed. Research the positive aspects of aging. What are the key factors that help one age in a positive way? What can our society do to show age appreciation?

Keyword: **euthanasia**. Arguments for and against euthanasia have become more vocal in our society. What are the policies in other countries about euthanasia and physician assisted suicide? How do their views compare with those in the United States?

Keyword: **health maintenance organizations (HMOs)**. HMOs focus on preventive health care for a fixed fee. Some HMOs are under the gun for not providing adequate care for their patients. What are some of the growing concerns of unhappy HMO subscribers? What solutions do they call for?

Keyword: **Medicare fraud**. Medicare pays some costs for people over age 65 in the United States. Sometimes the program is abused. Research the ways that Medicare is used in fraudulent ways. For example, is it abused more by the elderly or by health care providers?

Keyword: **Alzheimer's disease**. Look for articles that stress social support programs for Alzheimer's. What characteristics do they share in common? How do these programs relate to the sociological discipline?

Keyword: **Disability definition**. Search through these articles. How many definitions of disability can you find? What are the similarities and differences across definitions? Come up with your own definition.

Internet Exercises

Go to this newspaper article: http://www.newsday.com/news/health/ny-aids20-side052901.story.

Read about the changing face of AIDS/HIV. How has the social distribution of AIDS changed recently? Which groups are currently at "high risk?" After reading the article and answering the two questions, propose several solutions to the AIDS/HIV problem.

An Initiative of the Robert Wood Johnson Foundation sponsors the following Internet site:

http://www.statecoverage.net/who.htm.

Go to this page and read about those in the United States who are the uninsured. Compile a list of characteristics of those who don't have insurance. Why do you think so many people in the United States are not insured? Write a brief opinion paper about your point of view.

The World Health Organization web site at http://www.who.int/ is an excellent source of information on health issues

Death is not commonly discussed in American Society. Go to: http://www.hospicenet.org/html/talking.html for some suggestions about talking to children about death. Read the short article. Make a list of their suggestions for discussing death with children. How can you implement their suggestions into your life?

You can find much information about the American with Disabilities Act (1990) at: http://www.usdoj.gov/crt/ada/adahom1.htm.

Identify the current key issues with the Act. Write a short paper stating what you have learned about the American with Disabilities Act from this short exercise.

Go to http://www.msnbc.com/modules/quizzes/lifex.asp to find out your life expectancy. Answer the questions on your health risk. Write a short summary discussing your life expectancy, health risk, and if you are happy with your results.

Practice Tests

Fill-In-The-Blank

Fill in the blank with the appropriate term from the above list of "key terms."

1. The _____ is composed of a nation's clinics, hospitals, and other facilities for ensuring health and treating illness.

2. The _____ is the positive influence of a strong belief in the effectiveness of a cure on healing.

3. The _____ is the average age of death for a population under ideal conditions.

4. Playing the _____ involves the nondeliberate suspension of routine responsibilities, wanting to be well, seeking competent help, and cooperating with health-care practitioners at all times.

5. _____ is also known as mercy killing and assisted suicide.

6. _____ involves curing disabilities to the extent possible through medical and technological intervention.

7. _____ people are considered deficient in physical or mental capacity.

8. A(An) _____ is a society rule by elderly people.

9. _____ is prejudice and discrimination against disabled people.

Multiple-Choice Questions

Select the response that best answers the question or completes the statement:

1. What is life expectancy?
   a. the average age of death of the members of a population.
   b. the maximum age of death of eldest members of a population.
   c. the minimum age of death of among members of a population who are defined as elderly.
   d. All of the above.
   e. None of the above.

2. The longest an individual can live under ideal conditions is referred to as:
   a. the maximum average human life span.
   b. the maximum life expectancy.
   c. the maximum human life span.
   d. All of the above.
   e. None of the above.

3. The _____ is composed of government-run programs that ensure access to clean drinking water, basic sewage and sanitation services, and inoculation against infectious diseases.
    a. health care system
    b. public health system
    c. public works system
    d. Medicare system
    e. All of the above.

4. Which is a type of social cause of illness and death?
    a. human-environmental factors
    b. lifestyle factors
    c. factors related to public health systems.
    d. factors related to health care systems.
    e. All of the above.

5. Which is NOT an indicator of health inequality?
    a. infant mortality
    b. health expenditures
    c. access to sanitary water supply
    d. number of nurses and midwives
    e. All of the above are indicators of health inequality.

6. Which is considered a sociological reason for disparities in health inequality?
    a. The poor are more likely exposed to violence, and high-risk behavior.
    b. The poor are more likely exposed to environmental hazards.
    c. The poor cannot afford adequate health care.
    d. The poor tend to have less access to knowledge about healthy lifestyles as a result of less access to doctors and hospitals.
    e. All of the above.

7. Which is true regarding health inequality based on gender?
    a. Gender bias exists in medical research.
    b. Gender bias exists in medical treatment.
    c. Socially, more money is spent on men's health care in the United States.
    d. There are 40% more poor women than poor men in the United States, thus the impact of poverty on health disproportionately affects women.
    e. All of the above.

8. Which is NOT a strategy used by HMOs to keep shareholders happy?
    a. HMOs avoid covering sick people and people who are likely to get sick.
    b. HMOs try to minimize the cost of treating sick people.
    c. HMOs keep overhead charges high.
    d. HMOs work hand in hand with government subsidized health care agencies.
    e. All of the above are strategies used by HMOs.

9. _____ argues that good health requires maintaining a balance between mind and body, and between individual and the environment.
    a. Traditional scientific medicine
    b. The sick role
    c. Holistic medicine
    d. All of the above.
    e. None of the above.

10. What was the leading cause of death in the United States in 2001?
    a. pneumonia/influenza
    b. diabetes
    c. chronic lung disease
    d. lung inflammation
    e. heart disease

11. Which country had the highest life expectancy in 2002, among the following countries?
    a. India
    b. the United States
    c. China
    d. Japan
    e. All of the above.

12. Approximately how many people were there with HIV/AIDS in the world in 2002?
    a. 55 million
    b. 42 million
    c. 30 million
    d. 23 million
    e. 14 million

13. Which region of the world has the greatest number of people with HIV/AIDS?
    a. North America
    b. Latin America
    c. Western Europe
    d. Eastern Europe
    e. Sub-Saharan Africa

14. Which country had the greatest health expenditure per capita from 1999-2002?
    a. United States
    b. Japan
    c. Canada
    d. Mexico
    e. Zambia

15. Which country had the highest infant mortality rate per 1000 live births from 1999-to 2002?
    a. the United States
    b. Japan
    c. Canada
    d. Mexico
    e. Zambia

16. From the 1920s to the 1970s, native North American women were forcefully sterilized due to being perceived as "disabled." What was their alleged disability?
    a. mental retardation
    b. being native North American
    c. physical impairment
    d. autism
    e. ablism

17. When architecture and urban planning do not provide nonstandard modes of mobility for disabled people, this is an example of which form of ablism?
    a. neglect
    b. active prejudice
    c. individual discrimination
    d. ideological ablism
    e. stereotyping

18. Which sociological theory focuses on the meanings people attach to age-based groups and age stratification?
    a. functionalism
    b. conflict
    c. symbolic interactionism
    d. feminism
    e. None of the above.

19. Which is a viable projection about the growth of the elderly population in the United States in the future?
    a. By 2040, nearly 21% of the U.S. population will be elderly.
    b. After 2040, the proportion of elderly in the United States will start to decline.
    c. The growth of the elderly population in the future will present new and growing social problems.
    d. All of the above.
    e. None of the above.

20. Which category of elderly people is most likely to be poor?
    a. the "old old"
    b. African Americans
    c. people living alone
    d. people living in rural areas
    e. All of the above.

21. Which is NOT an example of ageism?
    a. segregation of the elderly
    b. stigmatization of the elderly
    c. meager Medicaid care provided to elderly
    d. discrimination of the elderly
    e. All of the above are examples of ageism.

22. Regarding euthanasia, public opinion polls show that:
    a. About two thirds of Americans favor physician-assisted suicide.
    b. Sixty percent of American doctors would not be willing to perform euthanasia even if it were legal.
    c. The Catholic Church supports euthanasia for extenuating medical circumstances.
    d. All of the above.
    e. None of the above.

23. Sociologists see aging as:
    a. a complex social phenomenon.
    b. a process of socialization.
    c. the learning of new roles appropriate to the latter stage of life.
    d. All of the above.
    e. None of the above.

True False

1. Over time, life expectancy has declined because of the depletion of our environment.

   TRUE or FALSE

2. AIDS is the leading cause of death in the poverty stricken part of Africa south of the Sahara desert.

   TRUE or FALSE

3. The higher the level of inequality in a country, the more unhealthy its population tends to be.

   TRUE or FALSE

4. Upward mobility in income has a greater positive health impact on above-median income earners than below-median income earners.

   TRUE or FALSE

5. Aside from the issue of access to medical resources, people of higher rank tend to live healthier lives even in comparison to people who have the same access but lower rank.

   TRUE or FALSE

6. The overwhelming majority of Americans agree that HMOs improve the quality of medical care.

   TRUE or FALSE

7. Most holistic practitioners reject scientific medicine.

   TRUE or FALSE

8. Pneumonia/Influenza was the leading cause of death in the United States in 1900.

   TRUE or FALSE

9. Ablism involves more than active prejudice and discrimination.

   TRUE or FALSE

10. The United States is a typical example of gerontocracies.

    TRUE or FALSE

11. The elderly are sometimes socially segregated.

    TRUE or FALSE

Short Answer

1. What do Brym and Lie mean by an "American anomaly" of health in the United States? (p. 396-398)

   _____

   _____

2. Explain Talcott Parson's concept the "sick role." (p. 405)

   _____

   _____

3. What is a "placebo effect"? Provide an example in terms of health care. (p. 406)

   _____

   _____

4. Explain ablism in terms of prejudice, discrimination, and neglect. Is ablism compounded by age, gender, social class, and race? If so, in what ways? If not, explain. (p. 409-412)

   _____

   _____

5. Explain how the deaf community typifies the new challenge to ablism. (p. 412)

   _____

   _____

6. Provide two sociological reasons why funerals are so expensive in the United States. (p. 420)

   _____

   _____

Essay Questions

1. Explain the social benefit and social consequences of for-profit health organizations from a functionalist and conflict perspective respectively. Which perspective makes most sense to you, and why? (p. 400-404)

2. From a feminist perspective, explain why the issues of health are gender issues? (p. 399-400)

3. Explain two ways global inequality influences the exposure of people to different health risks. (p. 395-397)

4. Explain age stratification from a functionalist, conflict, and symbolic interactionist perspective. (p. 412)

5. With the current and projected growth of the elderly population in the United States, sociologists anticipate a host of social problems of the elderly. Identify and explain three social problems. (p. 415-418)

6. Explain how social class, gender, and race are connected in the process of ablism. (p. 409)

7. Describe the arguments pro and con involving the process of euthanasia and its viability as a legal procedure. Why does this issue generate such intense dialogue? What other sociological issues intersect when discussing euthanasia? How do you see this issue being resolved in the future? (p. 419)

Solutions

Practice Tests

Fill-In-The-Blank

1. health-care system
2. placebo effect
3. maximum average human life span
4. sick role
5. Euthanasia
6. Rehabilitation
7. Impaired
8. gerontocracy
9. Ablism

Multiple-Choice Questions

1. A, (p. 394)
2. C, (p. 393)
3. B, (p. 395)
4. E, (p. 394-395)
5. E, (p. 395-400)
6. E, (p. 395-400)
7. E, (p. 399-400)
8. D, (p. 402-403)
9. C, (p. 406-407)
10. E, (p. 393)
11. D, (p. 394)
12. B, (p. 395-396)
13. E, (p. 395)
14. A, (p. 397)
15. E, (p. 396)
16. B, (p. 409)
17. A, (p. 409)
18. C, (p. 415)
19. D, (p. 416-417)
20. E, (p. 415-416)
21. C, (p. 417-418)
22. A, (p. 419)
23. D, (p. 412)

True False

1. F, (p. 394)
2. T, (p. 395)
3. T, (p. 395-397)
4. F, (p. 397-398)
5. T, (p. 397-400)
6. F, (p. 400-404)
7. F, (p. 406)
8. T, (p. 393)
9. T, (p. 409)
10. F, (p. 412)
11. T, (p. 415-418)

CHAPTER **15**

POPULATION AND URBANIZATION

Student Learning Objectives

After reading Chapter 15, you should be able to:

1. Describe historical trends and explanations of population growth.

2. Explain and critique the Malthusian perspective on the cycle of population growth.

3. Understand and apply demographic transition theory.

4. Explain the relationship between population growth and social inequality.

5. Describe the emergence of urbanization in the context of industrialization.

6. Explain the sociological contribution of the Chicago School to the understanding of urbanization and industrialization.

7. Contrast the theories of human ecology and urban sociology.

8. Discuss the urbanization of rural regions of the United States.

9. Describe, compare and contrast the corporate city and the postmodern city.

Key Terms

(defined on the indicated pages of the textbook, and in glossary)

demographers (424)	competition (437)
Malthusian trap (427)	ecological succession (437)
demographic transition theory (429)	urbanism (437)
crude death rate (429)	new urban sociology (439)
crude birth rate (429)	corporate city (440)
replacement level (430)	suburbanism (440)
immigration (430)	metropolitan (440)
in-migration (430)	gated communities (440)
emigration (430)	exurbs (440)
out-migration (430)	edge cities (440)
The Chicago School (436)	urban sprawl (441)
human ecology (436)	gentrification (441)
differentiation (437)	postmodern city (444)

Detailed Chapter Outline

I. POPULATION

    A. The City of God
        1. Rio de Janeiro, Brazil, is one of the world's most beautiful cities. The inner city of Rio is a place of great wealth and beauty, devoted to commerce and the pursuit of leisure.
        2. Rio is a large city, and is the 18th biggest metropolitan area in the world. Brazil has more inequality of wealth than any other country in the world.
        3. Some of Rio's slums began as government housing projects designed to segregate the poor from the rich.
        4. The brilliant 2002 movie, *Cidade de Deus*.
        5. Population growth and urbanization are more serious now than ever. Brazil is now more urbanized than the United States, with more than three quarters of its population living in urban areas.
        6. This chapter tackles the problems of population growth and urbanization.

    B. The Population "Explosion"
        1. In 1804 the number of humans reached 1 billion, and in 1987 5 billion. On July 1, 2001, there were an estimated 6.16 billion people in the world.
        2. Where one person stood 12,000 year ago, there are now 1,025 people, and by 2100 it is projected that there will be nearly 1,700 people.

    3. Fewer than 250 of those 1,700 will be standing in rich countries.

    4. Some population analysts contend that we're in the midst of a population "explosion," an image that connotes horrific events, and widespread, severe damage.

    5. **Demographers**, or population analysts, wish to convey this image.

    6. The concern of the population "bomb" is as old as the social sciences.

    7. In 1798 Robert Malthus proposed an influential theory of human population.

C. The Malthusian Trap

    1. Malthus's theory rests on two facts and a questionable assumption.

        a. The facts: people must eat, and are driven by a strong sexual urge.

        b. The assumption: while food supply increases slowly and arithmetically, population size grows quickly and geometrically.

    2. "The superior power of population cannot be checked without producing misery and vice."

    3. Two forces that can hold population growth in check:

        a. "Preventive" measures such as abortion, infanticide, and prostitution, which Malthus called "vices."

        b. "Positive checks" such as war, pestilence, and famine.

    4. The **Malthusian trap** is a cycle of population growth followed by an outbreak of war, pestilence, or famine that keeps population growth in check.

D. A Critique of Malthus

    1. Events that have cast doubt on several of Malthus's ideas and overstated pessimism:

        a. Technological advances allowing rapid growth in food production for each person on the planet is the opposite of the slow growth Malthus predicted.

        b. It is unclear what that natural upper limit to population growth is.

        c. Population growth does not always produce misery.

        d. Helping the poor does not generally result in the poor having more children.

        e. Although the human sexual urge is strong, people have developed contraceptive devices and techniques to control the consequences of their sexual activity. There is no necessary connection between sexual activity and childbirth.

E. Demographic Transition Theory

    1. According to **demographic transition theory**, the main factors underlying population dynamics are industrialization and the growth of modern cultural values. The theory is based on the observation that the European population developed in four distinct stages.

        a. The Preindustrial Period

            i. The **crude death rate**, which is the annual number of deaths per 1,000 people in a population, was high, due to poor nutrition, hygiene, and uncontrollable disease.

            ii. The **crude birth rate**, which is the annual number of live births per 1,000 people in a population, was high.

        b. The Early industrial Period.

            i. Increased economic growth and improved nutrition and hygiene.

            ii. The crude death rate dropped.

            iii. Life expectancy increased.

    c. The Mature industrial Period
        i.   The crude death rate continued to fall.
        ii. The crude birth rate fell more dramatically because economic growth eventually changed people's traditional beliefs about the value of having many children.
        iii. The crude birth rate took longer to decline than the crude death rate did, because people's values often change more slowly than their technologies.
        iv. Population stabilized. "Economic development is the best contraceptive."
    d. The Postindustrial Period
        i.   In the last decade of the 20th century, the total fertility rate, which is the annual number of live births per 1,000 women in a population, continued to fall.
        ii. The total fertility rate even fell below the **replacement level** of some countries—that is, the number of children each women must have on average for population size to remain stable. The replacement level is 2:1, ignoring any inflow of settlers from other countries (**immigration** or **in-migration**) and any outflow of other countries (**emigration** or **out-migration**).
  2. Due to the proliferation of low fertility of societies, some scholars suggest that we have entered a fourth, *postmodern* stage of population development, in which the number of deaths per year exceeds the number of births.

F. Population and Social Inequality
  1. Karl Marx
    a. As one of Malthus's staunchest intellectual opponents, Karl Marx argued that the problem of overpopulation is specific to capitalism—not a problem of too many people, but a problem of too much poverty. If a society is rich enough to eliminate poverty, then its population is not too large. Thus exploitation of workers needs to be done away with for poverty to disappear.
    b. Although Marx was wrong since overpopulation is not a serious problem in rich capitalist countries and more of a problem where capitalism is weakly developed, social inequality is the main cause of overpopulation.
  2. Gender Inequality and Overpopulation
    a. The case of Kerala:
        i.   A state in India with more than 30 million people.
        ii. Total fertility rate of 1.8 in 1991, half India's national rate and below the replacement level of 2:1.
        iii. Not highly industrialized, and among the poorer Indian states.
        iv. The decision to have children remains strictly a private matter, with no government intervention or prevention.
    b. How?
        i.   Their government raised the status of women over a period of decades.
        ii. The government helped create a realistic alternative to a life of continuous childbearing and childrearing.
        iii. The government organized successful campaigns and programs to educate women, increase labor force participation, and make family planning available.

          iv. Keralan women enjoy the highest literacy rate, labor force participation, and political participation in India.

          v. Keralan women want small families, so they use contraception to prevent unwanted births.

   3. Class Inequality and Overpopulation

     a. The South Korean case:

       i. South Korea had a total fertility rate of 6.0 in 1960. Yet by 1989, the total fertility rate fell to 1.6.

       ii. Why?

       iii. Land reform not industrialization: the government took land from big landowners and gave it to small farmers.

       iv. The standard of living of small farmers increased, which eliminated the major reason for high fertility—child labor and support for elderly.

     b. Increasing social inequality can lead to overpopulation, war, and famine.

       i. For example, in the 1960s the governments of El Salvador and Honduras encouraged the expansion of commercial agriculture and the acquisition of large farms by wealthy landowners.

       ii. Peasants were driven off the land and migrated to the cities, where they found squalor, unemployment, and disease.

       iii. These two countries with a combined population size of less than 5 million suddenly had a big "overpopulation" problem.

       iv. Increased competition for land contributed to rising tensions that eventually led to the war between El Salvador and Honduras in 1969.

 G. Summing Up

   1. Population growth is influenced by a variety of social causes, chiefly including social inequality, not from natural causes and industrialization and modernization alone.

   2. Well-intentioned Western analysts continue to insist that people in developing countries should be forced to stop multiplying, and some even suggest diverting scarce resources from education, health, and industrialization into forms of birth control including forced sterilization.

   3. They fail to see how measures that lower social inequality help to control overpopulation and its consequences.

II. URBANIZATION

 A. Overpopulation is largely an urban problem. Most of the fastest growing cities are in semi-industrialized countries where the factory system is not highly developed. Urbanization is also taking place in the world's rich countries, but is expected to increase faster in semi-industrialized countries.

 B. From the Preindustrial to the Industrial City

   1. To a degree, urbanization results from industrialization.

   2. However, industrialization is not the whole story.

     a. The connection between industrialization and urbanization is weak in the world's less developed countries.

b. Cities emerged in Syria, Mesopotamia, and Egypt long before the growth of the modern factory.

c. It was not industry, but trade in precious goods that stimulated the growth of cities in preindustrial Europe and the Middle East.

3. Preindustrial cities differed from industrial cities.

a. Preindustrial cities were typically smaller, less densely populated, built within protective walls, and organized around a central square and places of worship.

b. The industrial cities that emerged at the end of the 18th century were more dynamic and complex.

C. The Chicago School and the Industrial City

1. The **Chicago School** of sociology was distinguished by their vividly detailed descriptions and analyses of urban life.

2. Three of its leading members, Robert Park, Ernest Burgess, and Roderick McKenzie, proposed a theory of **human ecology** to illuminate the process of urbanization, which highlights the links between the physical and social dimensions of cities and identifies the dynamics and patterns of urban growth.

3. The theory of human ecology holds that cities grow in ever-expanding concentric circles, sometimes called the "concentric zone model." Three social processes animate this growth.

a. **Differentiation** refers to the process by which urban populations and their activities become more complex and heterogeneous over time.

b. **Competition** is an ongoing struggle by different groups to inhabit optimal locations.

c. **Ecological succession** takes place when a distinct group of people moves from one area to another, and another group moves into the old area to replace the first.

4. Zonal patterns of differentiation, competition, and ecological succession in Chicago in the 1920s:

a. Zone 1 was the central business district.

b. Zone 2, the "zone in transition," was the area of most intense competition between residential and commercial interests.

c. Zone 3 is the "zone of working-class homes."

d. Zone 4 is the "residential zone" that contains small, middle-class, detached homes.

e. Zone 5 is the "commuter zone," where middle, upper-middle, and upper-class families live in more expensive detached homes, and commute to work in the city.

5. For members of the Chicago school, the city involved a way of life, "a state of mind, a body of customs...traditions...attitudes and sentiments", called **urbanism**; Wirth's "urban way of life."

D. After Chicago: A Critique

1. Three major criticisms of the Chicago school approach to urban sociology over the years.

2. One criticism focuses on Wirth's characterization of the "urban way of life."

a. Research shows that social isolation, emotional withdrawal, stress, and other problems may be just as common in rural as in urban areas.

b. Research shows that urban life is less impersonal, anomic, and devoid of community than the Chicago sociologists made it appear.

     c. Even in the largest cities, most residents form social networks and subcultures that serve functions similar to those of the small community.

   3. A second criticism focuses on the concentric zone model.

     a. The specific patterns discovered by the Chicago school are most applicable to industrial cities in the first quarter of the 20th century.

     b. With the automobile, some cities expanded in wedge-shaped sectors along natural boundaries and transportation routes.

     c. Other cities formed around many nuclei.

     d. The human ecology approach presents urban growth as an almost natural process, slighting its historical, political, and economic foundations in capitalist industrialization.

   4. The **new urban sociology**, heavily influenced by conflict theory, attempted to correct the problems of the Chicago School, and stressed that city growth is a process rooted in power relations toward profit.

     a. Urban space is seen as a set of *commodified* social relations.

     b. Political interests and conflicts shape the growth pattern of cities.

     c. John Logan and Harvey Molotch portray cities as machines fueled by a "growth coalition," which tries to obtain government subsidies and tax breaks to attract investment dollars.

   5. Although the growth coalition present redevelopment as a public good that benefits everyone, the benefits are often unevenly distributed.

     a. Most redevelopments are "pockets of revitalization surrounded by areas of extreme poverty."

     b. Local residents rarely enjoy any direct benefits from redevelopment.

E. The Corporate City

   1. The **corporate city** refers to the growing post-World War II perception and organization of the North American city as a vehicle for capital accumulation.

   2. **Suburbanism** is a way of life organized mainly around the needs of children and involving higher levels of conformity and sociability than life in the central city.

   3. Initially restricted to the well to do, the suburban life became in reach of middle-class Americans following World War II, due to economic growth and government assistance. By 1970, more Americans lived in suburbs than in urban core areas, which is the case today.

   4. **Metropolitan areas** include downtown city cores, surrounding suburbs, **gated communities**, **exurbs** (rural residential areas within commuting distance to the city, and **edge cities** (exurban clusters of malls, offices, and entertainment complexes that arise at the convergence point of major highways).

   5. Factors that have stimulated the growth of exurban residential areas and edge cities:

     a. Costs of operating businesses in city cores;

     b. The growth of new telecommunication technologies that allow businesses to operate in the exurbs.

   6. Some sociologists, urban and regional planners, and others lump all these developments together as indicators of **urban sprawl**.

   7. City cores continued to decline as the middle class fled to suburbs and exurbs. Tax revenues fell. Despite urban renewal in the 1950s and 1960s, many cities remained in a state of decay.

8. In a spate of urban renewal in the 1950s and 1960s, many low-income and minority homes were torn down and replaced with high-rise apartment buildings and office towers in the city core. In the 1970s and 1980s, some middle-class people moved into rundown areas and restored them in a process called **gentrification**.

F.   The Urbanization of Rural America
   1.   The case of Napa Valley.
   2.   Napa Valley is an extreme case of what has happened throughout rural America since World War II. Agriculture has been industrialized and rural areas have been partly urbanized.
   3.   Many small towns, especially those within an hour's drive of big cities, have also been partly urbanized.
   4.   Newcomers to small-town America tend to be younger, more highly educated, more ethnically diverse, more urbane, and less committed to their adopted communities than old-time residents.

G.   The Postmodern City
   1.   The **postmodern city** is a new phenomenon that has emerged alongside of the legacy of old urban forms since about 1970. Three main features of the postmodern city:
      a.   *Privatized*—exclusive organization of access to space;
      b.   *Fragmented*—lacks a single way of life;
      c.   *Globalized*—centers of financial decision-making.
   2.   The global city has come to reflect the priorities of the global entertainment industry.
   3.   New high-tech, clean, controlled, predictable and safe forms of entertainment do little to:
      a.   Increase the economic well-being of the communities beyond creating some low-level, dead-end jobs.
      b.   Provide ways of meeting new people, seeing old friends and neighbors, and improving urban sociability.
      c.   Enable cities and neighborhoods to retain and enhance their distinct traditions, architectural styles, and ambiance.

Study Activity: Applying the Sociological Compass

After reading Chapter 15, review the concentric zone model and Figure 15.6. Consider your place of residence and the larger metropolitan area in which you live. Based on the descriptions of zonal patterns, what zone does your neighborhood fall in? What zones do the surrounding areas fall into? Categorize your neighborhood, the surrounding communities and businesses throughout the metropolitan area in which you live. Describe these areas, and explain why you categorized them in the way you did.

Zone 1:

Zone 2:

Zone 3:

Zone 4:

Zone 5:

InfoTrac College Edition Online Exercises

For the following exercises, log on to the online library of InfoTrac College Edition at http://www.infotrac-college.com/. Make note that InfoTrac has implemented a new registration system that will allow easier access to InfoTrac through the use of a personalized username and password.

Once you've created your username and password you may proceed directly to the Log On page. To create an account, register your passcode packaged with your textbook, and create a username and password, by following the online prompt. After you are logged in, click on "Infotrac College Edition." You will arrive at a screen that enables you to search topics.

Keyword: **urbanization**. Look for articles that deal with urbanization in low-income countries. How does urbanization in low-income countries differ from urbanization in higher-income countries? Write a short paper discussing the effect of urbanization in low-income and higher-income countries. How does your Infotrac research compare with what is said in Chapter 15?

Keyword: **zero population**. Search for four articles on zero population. Do most articles support the idea of zero population growth? In what context is zero population most likely to be discussed? What sociological theory is zero population related to?

Keyword: **edge city**. Look for the article by Brenda Case Scheer called, "Edge City, Morphology: A Comparison of Commercial Centers." How does this discussion of edge cities differ from the one presented in Chapter 15? Is there an edge city in your hometown? If yes, where is its location? If not, why not? Write a short paper with your findings.

Internet Online Exercises

Review the fertility rates of the countries listed in Table 15.1. Choose at least two countries with the lowest fertility rates, and two countries with the highest fertility rates. Conduct additional research on these countries using the Internet. Simply explore and see what general information you dig up regarding each country. Take notes on each country.

1. Notes on Countries

2. Country One:

3. Country Two:

4. Country Three:

5. Country Four:

1. Based on any descriptions or statistics on each country, which theory of population growth and global inequality makes the most sense to you, and why?

2. Theory of Population Growth:

3. Theory of Global Inequality:

Go to the following URL for international demographic data: http://www.census.gov/ftp/pub/ipc/www/ idbsum.html

Write a short paragraph and answer these questions. What was the population in 1990 for any two countries? What was the projected population for 2000 for the same countries? What factors do you think accounted for the population changes?

The World PopClock from the U.S. Bureau of the Census gives the complete and total population of the world and its projected population to the day, hour, minute and second. Go to this URL: http://www.census.gov/cgi-bin/ipc/popclockw

Indicate what time and date you looked up this URL. What is the total population of the world?

Tomorrow, or in two days, go back to the website and look again. What time and date is it?

What is the total population of the world now? Did the population increase or decrease?

Practice Tests

Fill-In-The-Blank

Fill in the blank with the appropriate term from the above list of "key terms."

1. _____ is the spread of cities into ever larger expanses of the surrounding countryside.

2. The _____ refers to a cycle of population growth followed by an outbreak of war, pestilence, or famine that keeps population growth in check.

3. _____ refers to the struggle by different groups for optimal locations in which to reside and set up their business.

4. The _____ is the annual number of live births per 1000 women in a population.

5. _____ is a way of life that involves increased tolerance but also emotional withdrawal and specialized, impersonal, and self-interested interaction.

6. The _____ is the number of children that each woman must have on average for population size to remain stable.

7. The _____ is the ratio of women to men in a geographical area.

8. The _____ refers to the growing post-World War II perception and organization of the North American city as a vehicle for capital accumulation.

9. _____ refers to the process by which urban populations and their activities become more complex and heterogeneous over time.

10. _____ is the process of middle-class people moving into rundown areas of the inner city and restoring them.

Multiple-Choice Questions

Select the response that best answers the question or completes the statement:

1. Which is a contention about Malthus's theory?
    a. People must eat.
    b. People are driven by a strong sexual urge.
    c. While food supply increases slowly and arithmetically, size grows quickly and geometrically.
    d. All of the above.
    e. None of the above.

2. The Malthusian trap refers to:
    a. a cycle of population growth followed by an outbreak of war, pestilence, or famine that keeps population growth in check.
    b. the annual number of deaths due to poor nutrition, hygiene, and uncontrollable disease.
    c. the process by which urban populations and their activities become more complex and heterogeneous over time.
    d. All of the above.
    e. None of the above.

3. Which is NOT a stage of European population development according to demographic transition theory?
    a. preindustrial stage
    b. early industrial stage
    c. mature industrial stage
    d. postindustrial stage
    e. All of the above are stages according to demographic transition theory.

4. Which stage of demographic transition theory involved a high crude death rate and a high crude birth rate?
    a. preindustrial stage
    b. early industrial stage
    c. mature industrial stage
    d. postindustrial stage
    e. All of the above.

5. "Immigration" is synonymous with _____, and "emigration" is synonymous with _____.
    a. out-migration; in-migration
    b. in-migration; lateral migration
    c. out-migration; vertical migration
    d. lateral migration; vertical migration
    e. in-migration; out-migration

6. Kerala, one of the poorer Indian states, was marked by low fertility rates in 1991, in spite of not being highly industrialized. Why does the case of Karela contradict the common assumption that impoverished regions display high fertility rates and population growth?
   a. Their government raised the status of women.
   b. Their government prevented women from having too many children.
   c. Infanticide was a widespread practice during this time period.
   d. All of the above.
   e. None of the above.

7. In comparison to rich countries, urbanization is expected to _____ in semi-industrialized countries.
   a. decrease
   b. increase faster
   c. be consistent
   d. be equal as
   e. None of the above.

8. Human ecology theory:
   a. stresses that city growth is a process rooted in power relations toward profit.
   b. holds that cities grow in ever-expanding concentric circles.
   c. economic underdevelopment results from poor countries lacking Western attributes.
   d. All of the above.
   e. None of the above.

9. The _____ city refers to the growing post-World War II perception and organization of the North American city as a vehicle for capital accumulation.
   a. postmodern
   b. urban
   c. metropolitan
   d. corporate
   e. None of the above.

10. Which is a main feature of the postmodern city?
    a. privatized
    b. fragmented
    c. globalized
    d. All of the above.
    e. None of the above.

11. According to Brym and Lie, the postmodern city:
    a. does little to increase the economic well-being of the community beyond creating some low-level, dead-end jobs.
    b. improves urban sociability.
    c. enables cities and neighborhoods to retain and enhance distinct traditions.
    d. All of the above.
    e. None of the above.

12. Which statement is true of the city Rio De Janeiro, Brazil?
    a. It is one of the world's most beautiful cities.
    b. The inner city of Rio is a place of great wealth and beauty.
    c. Rio is a larger metropolitan area than Chicago.
    d. All of the above.
    e. None of the above.

13. What is the projected world population for 2013?
    a. 10 billion
    b. 9 billion
    c. 8 billion
    d. 7 billion
    e. 6 billion

14. The main purpose of demography is to:
    a. figure out why the size, geographical distribution, and social composition of human populations change over time.
    b. figure out the social and geographical patterns of social inequality.
    c. figure out root social and economic causes of urban crime.
    d. All of the above.
    e. None of the above.

15. Among the world's 10 largest cities in 2015, only one will be in a highly industrialized country. All the others will be in developing countries. Which city will this be?
    a. Rio de Janeiro
    b. New York
    c. London
    d. Mexico City
    e. Tokyo

16. Which country has the highest fertility rate?
    a. Niger
    b. Liberia
    c. Afghanistan
    d. Taiwan
    e. Mexico

17. The sex ratio tends to be low where women have:
    a. greater access to health care than do men.
    b. about equal access to medicine men do.
    c. less adequate nutrition than men do.
    d. All of the above.
    e. None of the above.

18. What was the largest metropolitan area in 1900?
    a. London, England
    b. Chicago, United States
    c. Tokyo, Japan
    d. Beijing, China
    e. Mexico City, Mexico

19. Which city is the largest in the United States, 2002?
    a. Boston, MA
    b. Memphis, TN
    c. San Antonio, TX
    d. Philadelphia, PA
    e. New York, NY

20. Napa Valley, California is an extreme case of what has happened throughout America since World War II in:
    a. corporate cities.
    b. gated communities.
    c. rural areas.
    d. metropolitan areas.
    e. None of the above.

21. The movie *8 Mile* depicts the separation of the rich and the poor in the most racially segregated cities in the United States. Which city is portrayed?
    a. Chicago
    b. Los Angeles
    c. Portland
    d. Detroit
    e. San Diego

22. A decrease in the percentage of people living in high-poverty neighborhoods were biggest in the:
    a. Midwest and the South.
    b. Southwest.
    c. East.
    d. All of the above.
    e. None of the above.

23. Chapter 15 tackles the closely connected problems of:
    a. classism and racism.
    b. population growth and urbanization.
    c. development and underdevelopment.
    d. global inequality and poverty.
    e. crime and urban decay.

24. Which region is one of the most prosperous regions of the world, despite its rapid population growth over the past 200 years?
    a. Western Europe
    b. Latin America
    c. the Caribbean
    d. the Western Pacific
    e. South America

25. Which theory especially suggests that the main factors underlying population dynamics are industrialization and the growth of modern cultural values?
    a. human ecology theory
    b. demographic transition theory
    c. Marxist theory
    d. Malthusian theory
    e. None of the above.

True False

1. The concern of population explosion is as old as the social sciences.

    TRUE or FALSE

2. According to demographic transition theory, the crude birth rate took longer than the crude death rate did in the mature industrial period.

    TRUE or FALSE

3. Although their respective theories differ on many points, Malthus and Marx were generally in agreement about the problem of overpopulation.

    TRUE or FALSE

4. Initially restricted to the well to do, suburban life became reachable for middle-class Americans following World War II.

    TRUE or FALSE

5. The postmodern city provides ways of meeting new people, and seeing old friends and neighbors.

    TRUE or FALSE

6. Brazil is now more urbanized than the United States.

   TRUE or FALSE

7. Hong Kong is one of the most densely populated places in the world.

   TRUE or FALSE

Short Answer

1. Define the terms "crude death rate" and "crude birth rate." What is the relationship between these two rates in the preindustrial stage of European population development? (p. 429)

   _____

   _____

2. List and define the three social processes of the concentric zone model. (p. 437)

   _____

   _____

3. Briefly describe the contradictory characteristics of Rio de Janeiro, Brazil, as both a beautiful city, and at the same time a classic case of social inequality and urban decay. (p. 423)

   _____

   _____

4. Briefly explain the Malthusian trap, and provide an example. (p. 427)

   _____

   _____

Essay Questions

1. Explain the impact of inequality on overpopulation in terms of gender and social class, respectively. In doing so, describe the cases of Kerala in India and South Korea. (p. 431-434)

2. Explain the general approach of the new urban sociology, in light of the three main critiques of the Chicago School. (p. 436-439)

3. Explain Marx's critique of Malthus's approach to population growth. (p. 427-431)

Solutions

Practice Tests

Fill-In-The-Blank

1. Urban sprawl
2. Malthusian trap
3. Competition
4. crude birth rate
5. Urbanism
6. replacement level
7. sex ratio
8. corporate city
9. Differentiation
10. Gentrification

Multiple-Choice Questions

1. D, (p. 427)
2. A, (p. 427)
3. D, (p. 429)
4. A, (p. 429)
5. E, (p. 430)
6. A, (p. 431-432)
7. B, (p. 434)
8. B, (p. 436)
9. D, (p. 440)
10. D, (p. 444)
11. A, (p. 444-445)
12. D, (p. 423)
13. D, (p. 426)
14. A, (p. 424)
15. E, (p. 435)
16. A, (p. 431)
17. C, (p. 433)
18. A, (p. 435)
19. E, (p. 441)
20. C, (p. 441)
21. D, (p. 442)
22. A, (p. 443)
23. B, (p. 422)
24. A, (p. 427)
25. B, (p. 429)

True False

1. T, (p. 427)
2. T, (p. 429)
3. F, (p 427-431)
4. T, (p. 440)
5. F, (p. 444)
6. T, (p. 424)
7. T, (p. 425)

CHAPTER **16**

COLLECTIVE ACTION AND SOCIAL MOVEMENTS

Student Learning Objectives

After reading Chapter 16, you should be able to:

1. Identify the social conditions under which people act collectively to change, or resist change, to society.

2. Explain the formation of the lynch mob phenomena, historically, by applying breakdown theory. You should also be able to critique breakdown theory.

3. Compare and contrast breakdown theory, solidarity theory, and frame alignment theory as explanations of collective action and social movements.

4. Describe the historical trends of unionization and its recent decline in the United States.

5. Contrast "old social movements" and "new social movements."

6. Discuss the future of social movements and the prospects for postmodern revolutions.

Key Terms

(defined on the indicated pages of the textbook, and in glossary)

collective action (454)

social movements (455)

breakdown theory (456)

absolute deprivation (457)

relative deprivation (457)

contagion (457)

strain (457)

rumors (460)

solidarity theory (462)

resource mobilization (462)

political opportunities (463)

social control (463)

union density (466)

frame alignment (468)

new social movements (474)

Detailed Chapter Outline

I. HOW TO SPARK A RIOT

   A. Personal Anecdote
      1. Robert Brym almost sparked a riot in 1968.
      2. Historical events of 1968
         a. Student riots in France.
         b. Violent suppression of students in Mexico.
         c. Free speech and anti-war student movement at Berkeley and Michigan.
         d. Civil rights for American blacks and women.

   B. Under what social conditions do people act in unison to change, or resist change, to society?

   C. Three sections of the chapter:
      1. **Collective action** occurs when people act in unison to bring about or resist social, political, and economic change. Some collective actions are routine. Others are nonroutine. Routine collective actions are typically nonviolent and follow established patterns of behavior in existing types of social structures. Nonroutine collective actions take place when usual conventions cease to guide social actions and people transcend, by-pass, or subvert established institutional patterns and structures.
      2. **Social movements** are enduring collective attempts to change part or all of the social order by means of rioting, petitioning, striking, demonstrating, and establishing lobbies, unions, and political parties.
      3. The final section makes some observations about the changing character of social movements, in the context of historical attempts by underprivileged groups.

II. NONROUTINE COLLECTIVE ACTION: THE LYNCH MOB

   A. The Lynching of Claude Neal
      1. On October 27, 1934, a 23-year-old black man named Claude Neal was lynched near Greenwood. He was accused of raping and murdering 19-year-old Lola Cannidy, a pretty white woman, based on evidence that was not totally convincing.
      2. A lynch mob formed and brutally tortured and murdered Neal. The nude and mutilated body of Claude Neal was strung up on a tree in the lawn of the Jackson County courthouse, to symbolize justice.

   B. Breakdown Theory
      1. **Breakdown theory** suggests that social movements emerge when traditional norms and patterns of social organization are disrupted or breakdown. Breakdown theory may be seen as a functionalist theory, for it regards collective action as a form of social imbalance that results from various institutions functioning improperly.
      2. Following Charles Tilly and his associates, three factors may be grouped under breakdown theory. Most pre—1970s sociologists would have said that the lynching of Neal was caused by one or more of these factors.
         a. *A background of economic deprivation experienced by impoverished and marginal members of the community.* **Relative deprivation**, the growth of an intolerable gap

between the social rewards people expect to receive and those they actually receive, generates collective action, not **absolute deprivation** or extreme poverty.

    b. *The inherent irrationality of crowd behavior*. Gustave Le Bon's **contagion** theory of crowd behavior argues that the transformation of individuals into "barbarians" occurs because people lose their individuality and will power when they join a crowd. People in crowds are often able to perform extraordinary and outrageous acts.

    c. *The serious violation of norms*. Intimate contact between blacks and whites in the South was strictly forbidden. Therefore, black-on-white rape and murder were the deepest violations of the region's norms, and bound to evoke a strong reaction by the dominant race. Pre—1970s sociologists highlighted the breakdowns in traditional norms that preceded group interest, and referred to them as indicators of **strain**.

C. Assessing Breakdown Theory

    1. Since 1970, sociologists have uncovered flaws in all three elements of breakdown theory.

    2. Deprivation

        a. Research shows no clear association between fluctuations in economic well- being and the number of lynchings between the 1880s and the 1930s.

        b. In most cases of collective action, leaders and early joiners are well-integrated members of their communities, not deprived socially marginal individuals. This was the case involving the Neal lynching.

    3. Contagion: As the Neal lynching and research show, albeit wild, nonroutine collective action is usually structured by:

        a. Ideas and norms that emerge in the crowd itself;

        b. The predispositions that unite crowd members and predate their collective action;

        c. The degree to which different types of participants adhere to emergent preexisting norms;

        d. Preexisting social relationships among participants.

    4. Strain

        a. Although the alleged rape did violate the deepest norms of the Old South in a pattern that was often repeated, lynching had deeper roots than the mere violation of norms governing black-white relations. It was a chief means by which black farm workers were disciplined and kept tied to the southern cotton industry after the abolition of slavery threatened to disrupt the industry's traditional, captive labor supply.

    5. Lynching was a two-sided phenomenon.

        a. Breakdown theory explains one side—that lynching was partly a reaction to the violation of norms that threatened to *disorganize* traditional social life in the South.

        b. Lynching also grew out of, and was intended to maintain, the traditional *organization* of the South's cotton industry.

D. Rumors and Riots

    1. The study of rumor reinforces the idea that social organization underlies all collective action. **Rumors** are claims about the world that are not supported by authenticated information.

    2. While rumor transmission is a form of collective action in its own right, it intensifies just before and during riots.

3. In *Henry IV* Shakespeare wrote: "Rumor is a pipe blown by surmises, jealousies, conjectures." More recent analyses link rumors to the primary emotions of hope, fear and anger.
4. Rumors are often false and unverifiable. They seem credible to insiders but preposterous to outsiders.
5. Sociological understanding of rumors reveal the distribution of hope, fear, and anger in society and the structural flaws that lie beneath these emotions.
6. Brym and Lie's discussion of lynching leads to the conclusion that collection action is rarely a short-term reaction to disorganization and deprivation. It is usually part of a long-term attempt to correct perceived injustice that requires a sound social-organizational basis.

III. SOCIAL MOVEMENTS

A. Solidarity Theory
   1. Social movements emerge from collective action only when the discontented succeed in building up an organizational base.
   2. **Solidarity theory** is a variant of conflict theory, and suggests that social movements are social organizations that emerge when potential members can mobilize resources, take advantage of new political opportunities, and avoid high levels of social control by authorities.
      a. Most collective action is part of a power struggle. The struggle intensifies as disadvantaged groups become more powerful as a result of **resource mobilization**, or the process by which groups engage in more collective action as their power increases due to their growing size and increasing organizational, material, and other resources.
      b. Solidarity theory links the timing of collective action and social movement formation to the emergence of new **political opportunities**, which occurs when influential allies offer insurgents support, when ruling political alignments become unstable, and when elite groups become divided and weaker. Collective action takes place and social movements crystallize under these conditions.
      c. Government reactions to protest influence subsequent protest. Attempts by governments to diffuse a protest through **social control** measures, such as concessions and co-opting protest leaders, may encourage protesters to press further, in response to beliefs that the government is weak and indecisive.

B. Strikes and the Union Movement in America
   1. Workers have engaged in collective action in three ways: unionization, creation of labor parties, and striking.
   2. The example of 1934, as one of the bloodiest year of collective violence in American history.
   3. In 1945, unionization reached its historical peak in the United States. **Union density** (union members as a percentage of non-farm workers) remained above 30% until the early 1960s.
   4. The United States has the lowest union density for any rich industrialized country today. What accounts for the post—1945 drop?
   5. Resource mobilization.
      a. The industrial working class has shrunk and become weaker, yet is the precise source of strength of unionism.

b. The industrial working class has been weakened by globalization and employer hostility to unions. For example, employers could now close American factories and relocate them in other countries like Mexico and China.

6. Political opportunities.
    a. Government action has limited opportunities for union growth since the end of World War II.
    b. In 1947, Congress passed the Taft-Hartley Act in reaction to a massive post-World War II strike wave.
        i.   Unions could no longer force employees to become members or require union membership as a condition of being hired.
        ii. The act allowed employers to replace striking workers.
    c. Based on resource mobilization theory, less social organization means little protest.
    d. Comparing historical periods, we see low union density has helped to virtually extinguish the strike as a form of collective action.
    e. Over the short term, strikes tend to be more frequent during economic "booms" and less frequent during economic "busts."
    f. Since the mid-1990s, the American Federation of Labor-Congress of Industrial Organizations (AFL-CIO), the largest union umbrella organization in the United States, has sought to reverse the trends in the decline of unionization, by organizing immigrants, introducing feminist issues, and developing new forms of employee organization and representation more appropriate to a postindustrial society.

C. Framing Discontent
    1. **Frame alignment** is the process by which individual interests, beliefs, and values either become congruent with the activities, ideas, and goals of the movement or fail to do so. Frame alignment has recently become the subject of sustained sociological investigation by scholars in the symbolic interactionist tradition.
    2. Frame alignment can be encouraged in several ways. Social movement leaders can reach out to other organizations that contain people who may be sympathetic to their movement's cause.
    3. Movement activists can stress popular values that have so far not featured prominently in the thinking of potential recruits. They can also elevate the importance of positive beliefs and values about the movement.
    4. Social movements can stretch their objectives and activities to win recruits who are not initially sympathetic to the movement's original aims, which may water down the movement ideals. Alternatively, movement leaders may decide to take calculated action to appeal to nonsympathizers on grounds that have little or nothing to do with the movement's purpose. For example, when rock, punk, or reggae bands play at nuclear disarmament rallies.

D. Refrain: Back to 1968
    1. Frame alignment theory stresses face-to-face interaction strategies employed to recruit nonmembers.
    2. Resource mobilization theory focuses on the broad social-structural conditions that facilitate the emergence of social movements.
    3. The two theories help clarify Robert Brym's experience in 1968.

    a. He lived in a poor and relatively unindustrialized region of Canada where people had few resources to mobilize.

    b. Many of Robert's classmates did not share his sense of injustice, and thus received an unsympathetic hearing.

IV. SOCIAL MOVEMENTS FROM THE 18TH CENTURY TO THE 21ST CENTURY

A. Determinants of Collective Action and Social Movement Formation

1. Altogether, breakdown theory, solidarity theory, and frame alignment theory provide a comprehensive picture of the why, how, when, and who of collective action and social movements.

2. Breakdown theory partly answers the question of *why* discontent is sometimes expressed collectively and in nonroutine ways.

3. Solidarity theory focuses on *how* these social changes may eventually facilitate the emergence of social movements—and speaks to the question of *when* collective action erupts and social movements emerge.

4. Frame alignment theory directs our attention to the question of *who* is recruited to social movements.

B. The Future of Social Movements

1. Inspired by the civil rights movements of the 1960s, so-called **new social movements** emerged in the 1970s, and are distinguishable for their breadth of goals, the kinds of people they attract, and their potential for globalization.

2. Goals

    a. Some new social movements promote the rights of humanity as a whole to peace, security, and a clean environment, such as the peace movement, environmental movement, and the human rights movement.

    b. Other new social movements promote the rights of particular groups excluded from full social participation, such as the women's movement and the gay rights movement.

    c. The emergence of the peace, environmental, human rights, gay rights, and women's movements.

3. Membership

    a. New social movements attract a disproportionately large number of highly educated, relatively well-to-do people from the social, educational, and cultural fields, such as teachers, college professors, journalists, social workers, artists, actors, writers, and students.

    b. Their higher education exposes them to appealing radical ideas.

    c. They tend to possess jobs outside of the business community, which often opposes their values.

    d. They often get personally involved in the problems of their clients and audiences, and sometime become advocates.

4. Globalization Potential

    a. New social movements have more potential for globalization than did old social movements.

    b. Social movements were typically *national* in scope up until the 1960s. Many new social movements since the 1970s increased the scope of protest beyond the national level.

        i.   Members of peace and environmental movements pressed for *international* agreements binding all countries to protect the environment and stop the spread of nuclear weapons.

   c.   Inexpensive international travel and communication facilitated the globalization of social movements.

        i.   The case of Greenpeace.

        ii.   In 1953, 110 international social movement organizations spanned the globe. By 1993, there were 631.

Study Activity: Where Do You Fit In?

After reading Chapter 16, re-read the set of questions posed by Brym and Lie on page 472. In addition to engaging the exercise described in the text, carry out the activity from a slightly different angle. As Brym and Lie suggest, "try applying solidarity and frame alignment theory." Being a student on a college campus, you may have been part of an audience of a political rally, presentation, or discussion. If not, seek out an opportunity on your campus or community to participate in such an event that deals with some political issue, such as a faculty rally, student protest of tuition, an anti-war rally, a meeting of minority advocates, an AFL-CIO sponsored event, and so forth. Make a list of the issues discussed. Make note of personal and emotional response to the event. Did you find yourself to be emotionally charged or bored with the activity? Why? Describe what you did or did not do about it. Explain your response or lack thereof, in terms of solidarity theory and frame alignment theory.

List of Issues:

Your Personal and Emotional Responses:

Explanations of Your Personal Responses and Action or Inaction:

Solidarity theory:

Frame alignment theory:

InfoTrac College Edition Online Exercises

For the following exercises, log on to the online library of InfoTrac College Edition at http://www.infotrac-college.com/. Make note that InfoTrac has implemented a new registration system that will allow easier access to InfoTrac through the use of a personalized username and password.

Once you've created your username and password you may proceed directly to the Log On page. To create an account, register your passcode packaged with your textbook, and create a username and password, by following the online prompt. After you are logged in, click on "Infotrac College Edition." You will arrive at a screen that enables you to search topics.

Keyword: **Land mines**. Those who advocate the elimination of land mines may be considered part of a new global social movement. Look for articles that deal with the elimination of land mines. How widespread is this social movement? Do you think there is a new global social movement in this area?

Keyword: **Human cloning**. Look for articles that deal with human cloning and collective action. What specific aspects of collective action are portrayed in the articles? Do you think that there will be a human cloning social movement in the future?

Keyword: **bioterrorism.** Bioterrorism is a type of terrorism that strikes fear in people's hearts. Look for articles that discuss how a society can prepare for this type of terrorism. What type of bioterrorism is discussed most frequently?

Keyword: **Million Mom March**. This social movement supports gun control. What type of social movement is this?

Keyword: **Promise Keepers**. Research this social movement and classify it according to the characteristics of a social movement in Chapter 16.

Internet Exercises

For this exercise, go to http://www.aflcio.org/, the Web site of the AFL-CIO. Navigate through the Web site to learn as much as possible about their organizational goals, activities, scope, resources, and so forth. Based on the information you acquire, identify the characteristics of the AFL-CIO that coincide with solidarity theory and frame alignment theory. Make a list of organizational goals, activities, scope, resources, and so forth. Categorize the organizational characteristics of the AFL-CIO in terms of solidarity theory and frame alignment theory. Do you have any suggestions on strategies for the AFL-CIO to consider in light of what you learned in Chapter 16?

September 11, 2001 is a tragic day to remember in American history. International terrorist groups changed American's lives forever. To learn about international terrorist groups go to this site: http://www.specialoperations.com/

Research two different groups. How do these two groups differ from the Ku Klux Klan in the U.S.?

Write a short paper noting your comparisons.

The Hate Directory lists hate groups and has many links to websites. It is located at: http://www.bcpl.net/~rfrankli/hatedir.pdf.

This is a helpful site for research and discussion purposes. Research two groups on this list. Does your research support the idea that your two groups could be classified as social movements or collective action? Compare the ideas of social movements and collective action in Chapter 16 with your two groups in a short paper.

Recent media attention has been given to the gay and lesbian movement. The homepage of The Gay and Lesbian Activists Alliance is located at: http://www.glaa.org/

This organization is the oldest continuously active gay and lesbian civil rights organization.

It was founded in 1971 to advance the equal rights of gay men and lesbians in Washington, DC. Look at the main issues of the alliance and discuss how they fit in with the progressive steps of collective behavior discussed in the text.

Practice Tests

Fill-In-The-Blank

Fill in the blank with the appropriate term from the above list of "key terms."

1. _____ is the number of union members in a given location and time as a percentage of nonfarm workers.

2. _____ occurs when people act in unison to bring about or resist social, political, and economic change.

3. _____ is a condition of extreme poverty.

4. _____ is the process by which exteme passions supposedly spread rapidly through a crowd like a contagious disease.

5. _____ is the process by which individual interests, beliefs, and values become congruent and complementary with the activities, goals, and ideology of a social movement.

6. _____ are claims about the world that are not supported by authenticated information.

7. _____ refers to the process by which social movements crystallize due to increasing organizational, material, and other resources of movement members.

8. _____ refers to the means by which authorities seek to contain collective action, including co-optation, concessions, and coercion.

Multiple-Choice Questions

Select the response that best answers the question or completes the statement:

1. _____ are enduring collective attempts to change part or all of the social order.
   a. Routine collective actions
   b. Nonroutine collective actions
   c. Race riots
   d. Social movements
   e. None of the above

2. Which theory of social movements is most consistent with functionalism?
   a. breakdown theory
   b. solidarity theory
   c. frame alignment theory
   d. resource mobilization theory
   e. None of the above.

3. _____ is an intolerable gap between social rewards people expect and those they actually receive.
   a. Contagious deprivation
   b. Absolute deprivation
   c. Relative deprivation
   d. Deprivation density
   e. None of the above.

4. Which is a factor that caused the lynching of Claude Neal in 1934 according to breakdown theory?
   a. A background of economic deprivation experienced by impoverished and marginal members of the community.
   b. The inherent irrationality of crowd behavior.
   c. The serious violation of norms.
   d. All of the above.
   e. None of the above.

5. Which theory is most closely a variant of conflict theory?
   a. breakdown theory
   b. solidarity theory
   c. frame alignment theory
   d. All of the above.
   e. None of the above.

6. _____ is a process by which groups engage in more collective action as their power increases due to their growing size and increasing organizational, material, and other resources.
   a. Resource mobilization
   b. Political opportunities
   c. Social control
   d. All of the above.
   e. None of the above.

7. Which is NOT a way workers have engaged in collective action?
   a. unionization
   b. creation of labor parties
   c. striking
   d. social control
   e. All of the above are ways workers have engaged in collective action.

8. Union density refers to:
    a. the success rate of labor unions since the 1980s.
    b. union members as a percentage of non-farm workers.
    c. the level of resource mobilization of unions.
    d. All of the above.
    e. None of the above.

9. Based on resource mobilization theory, less social organization means:
    a. more protest.
    b. violent protest.
    c. little protest.
    d. All of the above.
    e. None of the above.

10. Frame alignment can be encouraged when:
    a. social movement leaders limit recruitment only to people with the same social class position.
    b. social movements constrain their activities strictly to the relevance of the mission and goals.
    c. movement activists stress popular values that have so far not featured prominently in the thinking of potential recruits.
    d. All of the above.
    e. None of the above.

11. Which theory focuses on *why* discontent is sometimes expressed collectively and in nonroutine ways?
    a. breakdown theory
    b. solidarity theory
    c. frame alignment theory
    d. All of the above.
    e. None of the above.

12. _____ theory directs our attention to the question of *who* is recruited to social movements.
    a. Breakdown
    b. Solidarity
    c. Frame alignment
    d. All of the above.
    e. None of the above.

13. Which theory focuses on *how* social changes may facilitate social movements?
    a. breakdown theory
    b. solidarity theory
    c. frame alignment theory
    d. All of the above.
    e. None of the above.

14. Which is NOT a characteristic of new social movements that distinguish them from old social movements?
    a. goals
    b. membership
    c. globalization
    d. organization
    e. All of the above are characteristics of new social movements that distinguish them from old social movements.

15. Which of the following is an indicator of the organizational power of unions?
    a. resource mobilization
    b. union density
    c. organizational inertia
    d. collective action
    e. None of the above.

16. Research on riots, crowds and demonstrations shows that:
    a. Although nonroutine collective action may be wild, it is usually socially structured.
    b. when nonroutine collective action is wild, there is no social structure to it, but rather social chaos.
    c. when nonroutine collective action is socially structured, it is never wild.
    d. All of the above.
    e. None of the above.

17. Which state had the highest frequency of lynchings of black victims from 1882 to 1964?
    a. Mississippi
    b. Louisiana
    c. Alabama
    d. Florida
    e. Tennessee

18. Around what year did the frequency of lynching of blacks peak between 1882 and 1932?
    a. 1932
    b. 1922
    c. 1912
    d. 1907
    e. 1892

19. Which is(are) among the statements made in Chapter 16 of the textbook regarding social movements, in the wake of the destruction of the twin towers of the World Trade Center on September 11, 2001?
    a. Increased government surveillance of social movements is entirely unnecessary.
    b. Giving the government a free hand to increase surveillance of social movements could endanger democracy.
    c. Americans have very clear and easy choices to make about which movements are dangerous since September 11, 2001.
    d. All of the above.
    e. None of the above.

20. Between 1925 and 2002, union density peaked around:
    a. 2000
    b. 1985
    c. 1965
    d. 1945
    e. 1935

True False

1. In support of breakdown theory, research shows a clear association between fluctuations in economic well-being and the number of lynchings between the 1880s and the 1930s.

   TRUE or FALSE

2. Although lynching was barbaric and wild, nonroutine collective action such as lynching is usually structured.

   TRUE or FALSE

3. The United States has the lowest union density for any rich industrialized country.

   TRUE or FALSE

4. The Taft-Hartley Act sparked the proliferation of contemporary labor unions.

   TRUE or FALSE

5. The environmental movement is considered a "new social movement."

   TRUE or FALSE

6. New social movements tend to attract a disproportionately large number of the underclass.

   TRUE or FALSE

7. International travel and communication facilitated the globalization of social movements, since these resources remain inaccessible to most members of social movements due to their continued social disadvantage and lack of education.

   TRUE or FALSE

Short Answer

1. Explain how lynching is a two-sided phenomenon in terms of "disorganization" and "organization." (p. 456-460)

_____

_____

2. Explain how government's attempts to diffuse a protest by offering concessions can backfire and further encourage protesters to press further. (p. 462-463)

_____

_____

3. Explain the impact of the Taft-Hartley Act on unionization. (p. 467)

_____

_____

Essay Questions

1. Draw Figure 16.5, which illustrates the determinants of collective action and social movement formation by integrating breakdown theory, solidarity theory, and frame alignment theory. Explain the figure. (p. 473)

2. Compare and contrast breakdown theory and solidarity theory. (p. 456-460, 462-463)

3. Explain the major differences between new social movements and old social movements. (p. 472-476)

Solutions

Practice Tests

Fill-In-The-Blank

1. Union density
2. Collective action
3. Absolute deprivation
4. Contagion
5. Frame alignment
6. Rumors
7. Resource mobilization
8. Social control

Multiple-Choice Questions

1. D, (p. 455)
2. A, (p. 456)
3. C, (p. 457)
4. D, (p. 456)
5. B, (p. 462)
6. A, (p. 462)
7. D, (p. 463)
8. B, (p. 466)
9. C, (p. 462-466)
10. C, (p. 468-472)
11. A, (p. 456)
12. C, (p. 468)
13. B, (p. 462)
14. D, (p. 474)
15. B, (p. 466)
16. A, (p. 455)
17. A, (p. 459)
18. E, (p. 459)
19. B, (p. 464)
20. D, (p. 466)

True False

1. F, (p. 456-460)
2. T, (p. 455-456)
3. T, (p. 466)
4. F, (p. 467)
5. T, (p. 472-476)
6. F, (p. 472-476)
7. F, (p. 474-476)